APPARITIONS
OF THE MADONNA
AT OLIVETO CITRA

APPARITIONS
OF THE MADONNA
AT OLIVETO CITRA

Local Visions and Cosmic Drama

Paolo Apolito

Translated by
William A. Christian Jr.

The Pennsylvania State University Press
University Park, Pennsylvania

Library of Congress Cataloging-in-Publication Data

Apolito, Paolo.
    [Il Cielo in terra.   English]
    Apparitions of the Madonna at Oliveto Citra : local visions and
cosmic drama / Paolo Apolito ; translated by William A. Christian Jr.
        p.   cm.
    Includes bibliographical references and index.
    ISBN 0–271–01795–3 (cloth : alk. paper)
    1. Mary, Blessed Virgin, Saint—Apparitions and miracles—Italy—
Oliveto Citra.   2. Oliveto Citra (Italy)—Church history—20th
century.   I. Title.
BT660.O44P6613   1998
232.91′7′094574—dc21   98–20833
                                                                 CIP

Copyright © 1998 The Pennsylvania State University
All rights reserved
Printed in the United States of America
Published by The Pennsylvania State University Press,
University Park, PA 16802-1003

For Giuseppe and Rosa

Contents

Translator's Note with Supplemental Bibliography

Societies in Western Europe seem to undergo both periods of spiritual excitement in which people are more open to signs from heaven or elsewhere, and lulls during which those who claim direct messages from the divine are ignored, ridiculed, or persecuted. Since the late 1960s, Catholic Europe has been in the throes of a kind of reenchantment, with its immediate model the visions at Medjugorje and its background the intensive promotion of the visions of La Salette, Lourdes, and Fatima. Paolo Apolito had the good fortune to be present virtually at the start of public visions not far from his home in Salerno, the preparation to observe how the visions gained credence as apparitions, and the persistence to follow how the town and its church sorted out the many apparition messages and dealt with the pilgrims who arrived from throughout southern Italy. His two books on the subject are rare, firsthand studies of apparitions in progress.

Il Cielo in Terra is the second of these books, but the first to be translated into English. It describes the cult that developed at Oliveto Citra around the ongoing visions, the seers and messages that became dominant, and the interpreters who connected the visions to a cosmic struggle of good and evil and the events at the end of time.

The avid contemporary demand for divine revelation means that much of the apologetic literature about contemporary apparitions is quickly published in translation. When possible I have used published English-language originals or translations for citations in the text and I have replaced non-English sources in Apolito's bibliography. Occasionally I have been able to find some, but not other, citations in an English-language version, and in these cases I include both English- and non-English-language editions in the bibliography.

I am grateful for the generous assistance of Justin Vitiello, and to James Scott, Kay Mansfield, Rebecca Aviel, and the Program for Agrarian Studies at Yale University. I thank Patricia Mitchell for her thoughtful copyediting.

Since Apolito wrote this book, apparitions have continued to gain followers among Catholics, and scholars have paid more attention to the phenomenon, present and past. I list some of their work, along with a few older references, below.

I have included a few explanatory footnotes, which are numbered. The author's footnotes are indicated by asterisks.

Bax, Mart. 1995. *Medjugorje: Religion, Politics, and Violence in Rural Bosnia.* Amsterdam: VU Uitgeverij.

―――. 1985. "Popular Devotions, Power, and Religious Regimes in Catholic Dutch Brabant." *Ethnology* 24, no. 2: 215–20.

Berryman, Edward. 1994. "The Social Construction of the Divine: A Study of Religious Apparition Stories." Ph.D. diss., Boston University, Boston.

Blackbourn, David. 1993. *Marpingen: Apparitions of the Virgin Mary in Bismarkian Germany.* New York: Knopf.

Carroll, Michael P. 1992. *Madonnas That Maim: Popular Catholicism in Italy since the Fifteenth Century.* Baltimore: Johns Hopkins University Press.

―――. 1986. *The Cult of the Virgin Mary: Psychological Origins.* Princeton: Princeton University Press.

Christian, William A., Jr. 1998. "L'oeil de l'esprit: Les visionnaires basques en transe, 1931." *Terrain* 30: 5–22.

―――. 1996. *Visionaries: The Spanish Republic and the Reign of Christ.* Berkeley and Los Angeles: University of California Press.

―――. 1992. *Moving Crucifixes in Modern Spain.* Princeton: Princeton University Press.

Claverie, Elizabeth. 1994. "Racconti biografici e apparizioni: I pellegrinaggi di San Damiano e di Medjugorje." *La Ricerca Folklorica* 29: 95–100.

―――. 1991. "Voir apparaître: Les apparitions de la Vierge à Medjugorje." *Raisons Pratiques* 2: 1–19.

―――. 1990. "La Vierge, le désordre, la critique." *Terrain* 14: 60–75.

Edelman, Nicole. 1995. *Voyantes, guérisseuses et visionnaires en France, 1785–1914.* Paris: Albin Michel.

Fattorini, Emma. 1994. "In viaggio dalla Madonna." In *Donne e fede: Santità e vita religiosa in Italia,* ed. L. Scaraffia and G. Zarri. Rome-Bari: Laterza.

Gallini, Clara. 1998. *Il miracolo i la sua prova: un etnologo a Lourdes.* Naples: Liguori.

―――. 1994. "Lourdes e la medicalizzazione del miracolo." *La Ricerca Folklorica* 29: 83–94.

―――. 1993. "La soglia del dolore dai racconti di guarigione di Lourdes." *Etnoantropologia* 2: 8–31.

Kselman, Thomas A. 1983. *Miracles and Prophecies in Nineteenth-Century France.* New Brunswick, N.J.: Rutgers University Press.

Lewis, I. M. 1989. *Ecstatic Religion: A Study of Shamanism and Spirit Possession.* 2d ed. London: Routledge.

Margnelli, Marco. 1996. *L'estasi.* Rome: Sensibili alle foglie.

McKevitt, Christopher. 1991. "San Giovanni Rotondo and the Shrine of Padre Pio." In *Contesting the Sacred: The Anthropology of Christian Pilgrimage,* ed. J. Eade and M. J. Sallnow. London: Routledge.

Niccoli, Ottavia. 1990. *Prophecy and People in Renaissance Italy (Profeti e popolo nell'Italia del rinascimento* [Rome: Laterza, 1987]), trans. Lydia G. Cochrane. Princeton: Princeton University Press.

Nolan, Mary Lee, and Sydney Nolan. 1989. *Christian Pilgrimage in Modern Western Europe.* Chapel Hill: University of North Carolina Press.

Romano, F. 1997. *Madonne che piagono: Visioni e miracoli di fine millennio.* Rome: Meltemi.

———. 1996. "La Madonna pellegrina: Apparizioni della Madonna della Pace a Carpi." *La Ricerca Folklorica* 33: 123–49.

Smith, Valene J., ed. 1992. *Pilgrimage and Tourism: The Quest in Guest.* Annals of Tourism Research, vol. 19, no. 1. New York: Pergamon Press.

Staehlin, Carlos Maria. 1954. *Apariciones: Ensayo Critico.* Madrid: Razón y Fe.

Stirrat, R. L. 1992. *Power and Religiosity in a Post-Colonial Setting: Sinhala Catholics in Contemporary Sri Lanka.* Cambridge: Cambridge University Press.

Taylor, Lawrence J. 1995. *Occasions of Faith: An Anthropology of Irish Catholics.* Philadelphia: University of Pennsylvania Press.

Wojcik, Daniel. 1996. "'Polaroids from Heaven': Photography, Folk Religion, and the Miraculous Image Tradition at a Marian Apparition Site." *Journal of American Folklore* 109, no. 432: 129–48.

Zimdars-Swartz, Sandra L. 1991. *Encountering Mary: From La Salette to Medjugorje.* Princeton: Princeton University Press.

IL CIELO IN TERRA

*Costruzioni Simboliche di
un'Apparizione Mariana*

PROLOGUE

ON THE EVENING OF MAY 24, 1985, in Oliveto Citra, a small town two hours south of Naples in the region of Campania, a few boys reported that they saw the Madonna. Thus began an extraordinary phenomenon of collective visions that at the time of this writing continues still. I was able to be in the town for the five days following the first declaration of visions, when the phenomenon was in the formative stage and had not yet gathered the strength and conviction of a "real event," which, in the eyes of the thousands of pilgrims who visited there in the coming months, it would acquire.

My experience of work in the field is reflected in part in a previous book, *"It Is Said They Have Seen the Madonna": A Case of Apparitions in Campania* (*"Dice che hanno visto la Madonna": Un caso di apparizione in Campania*), published in 1990. In that book I considered the interactions among the different social actors at the origin of the supernatural "event." I paid special attention to what they said, following an insight of ethnomethodology that what people were saying was not separate from the event-in-the-world but a part of it. "The accounts (justifications, explanations, discourses) of the social actors are constituent elements of what they are recounting, of that reality about which they are speaking, furnishing descriptions, explanations, connections, judgments, etc." (M. Wolf 1979, 129). The particular approach of my research was derived from a fundamental question that occurred to me little by little over the first weeks: How did an *account* of children, based on their *subjective* experience, become a real-world *event* with an *objectivity* that remains evident for the majority of those who go to Oliveto?

This question derives from an anthropological perspective (it is not the only one, obviously, for phenomena like these), and, hence,

> it is not for the anthropologist to answer the question whether the Madonna appeared or not. But let us say that she did appear. Her dramatic entrance into the world of persons would make no sense if they had not attributed a sense to her appearance, if they had not recognized as valid certain signs and testimony, if they had not produced information and news about the event—in short, if they had not produced the context of her apparition. What renders the Madonna visible is the context. It is this work of persons as they define the apparitions that the anthropologist examines. (Apolito 1990, 33)

The anthropologist works among people. And people are organized in communities with leaders, conflicts, objectives, and interests that differ for individuals, groups, and classes. Furthermore, a community *communicates* things by means of a common language. The community with its conflicts, its leaders, and its codes for communication all became the "places" of my study. Through a complex and detailed process I identified in such places a series of small, successive shifts that, in a form and way unintentional for the people involved, have transformed what was *word* into a *this-world reality*. By means of symbolic codes learned in the first years of life, what is *narrated* tends to assimilate and monopolize what has *happened*. As a consequence, the account-of-events appears to be the events-being-recounted, thus concealing the processes of symbolic construction that translate what happened into its narration.

The account of the events then seems to be not the result of the use of culturally significant models of relevance—of making coherence, plausibility, and verisimilitude in which the continuum of experience finds scansion, diachronic order, and sense—but rather the photographic reproduction of things as they happened, almost as if these things had in themselves the meaning that the symbolic work attributes to them. Observation of everyday life soon makes it clear that the account *constitutes* facts rather than *reproduces* in words their factualness. Hence, in my study of Oliveto Citra, the first approach could not be the reconstruction of "the events as they happened" but rather an understanding of how the canon of the account of the apparitions as it became accepted was constructed. I had to avoid *considering the events as givens*; that is, I had to avoid conceiving the events as if they were *for* humans (and not *of* humans), self-produced (and not produced by people), and self-defined (and not defined and adjusted by people in a continuum of acts).

> A *world* has been created and now everyone depends on it. No longer can anyone deduce that it is the result of intersecting moves, because the strategic weight of these moves in the construction of the whole is gone from the plane of consciousness, relegated in the narrative reconstruction as a group of curious, colorful details, atoms of narrative rhetoric, and referred to as such. Certainly one cannot pretend that for us "readers" today these are proofs of how things really occurred; they are merely indications of how from the intersections of experiences, actions, and symbols the world of apparitions came to be produced. (Apolito 1990, 170)

I then tried to break up the events and reduce them to the "moves" of the actors who had constituted them before they became events *to be recounted*, without the meanings that the actors would attribute to them and that would have rendered them stages of the "marvelous" story. The linearity, the clarity, and the concatenation of the final, official story of the events—the version local authorities subsequently published—were retroactively broken down into casua! words and small acts in search of their hidden implications of sense and sedimentation in the final structure of meaning. To the actors the events appeared as an extrahuman reality, a celestial presence. To me as a researcher they appeared as the unintentional result of human interactions, the structuring of significant knots in the grain of human activities.

In my first book on Oliveto Citra, an extensive initial segment had to do with the actions regarding the critical choice of the category *seeing* as appropriate for explaining the "events." When, in the very first phases of the apparitions of Oliveto Citra, some boys declared, "We saw the Madonna," the adults who heard them had two options. They could *refute* the declarations saying, "No, you did not see, either because you are deluded, you dreamed, you were pretending, or whatever," or they could take them seriously, asking, "What did you see?," showing surprise, amazement, or distress, thus implicitly accepting the declarations, as if replying, "Yes, you did see." That is what happened.

It did not matter whether the adults could agree about *what it was* the children saw. What mattered was that they accepted the declarations of the boys (which was merely a "proposition" of having seen something), and it was this acceptance that *constituted* the children as seers. (It would have been quite different if the adults had in fact replied, "No, you did not see, either because you are deluded, you dreamed, you were pretending, or whatever"; then the children would have been not seers but rather dreamers, pretenders.) In this space between the person who *sees* (says so) and the person who *sees the seeing* (decides to), the *word* (of the children, of the adults) was transformed into an *event* (someone "saw" something), and produced that event. Across this divide, the children went from *saying* they were seers to *being* seers, which means, in essence, that *the others* accepted the declarations of the children (clinical psychiatric files are replete with persons who *said* "I see the Madonna," etc., without being believed). The acceptance of the proposition-declaration, "We see," occurs if, in verbal reactions, we unintentionally move from the subjectivity of perceptual experience ("I see") to the objectivity of the thing seen (something is seen).

Once the semantic category of *seeing* was agreed upon to describe "what is happening here," the successive phases fell into place almost naturally. Seeing implies an object in the world that is *seen*; that is, the property of describability is transferred from a group of subjective perceptions to an object in the world.

> By the mere fact that I choose a noun to describe information from the senses, for example the word *book* to describe my present perceptions, I gather a multitude of impressions in a mass independent of me, endowed with its own unity, maintained through space and time. From the moment I say, "I see a book," I stop describing my perception and substitute for it, without realizing it, that which I perceive.
>
> "I see" constitutes that which is seen inasmuch as it makes a choice among descriptive possibilities, decides that "what is happening here" is a perceptual reaction of a subject faced with an object. (Ibid., 211)

From the moment it is accepted that the experience of the proposer "I see" is defined as an experience *of vision* (and not of dream, of deceit, etc.)—with the obvious but unrecognized implication that there is something there to see—the joint world of the social actors is reformulated on the basis of the *fact* that there is someone who sees something (or better yet, something seen by someone). Collective discourses will be built up from this acquired *fact* and all the emphasis will shift from "*Is there* something?" to "*What is it?*," that is, to the identification and hermeneutic of the object implicitly acquired. The "words" used will be based on the "given" that there is *something* that is seen. This does not mean, of course, that the Madonna is the object in question, but the effort to demonstrate that it really is her is made much easier. At Oliveto Citra it became a question of considering whether it was the Madonna, the Devil, a ghost, a UFO, and so on, but thereafter there was an external objective entity that had been crystallized from what were, at first, only subjective experiences. But that is not all. The subjective experiences were limited to *proposing* an external object, but accepting the proposition led to *imposing* on the subjective experiences the external object by *necessity*: The seers had been affected by something external to them.

A second important segment of my argument in *"It Is Said They Have Seen the Madonna"* had to do with the *word*.

Before what happened came to be called "apparition," before it acquired this identity, there was an intense collective process that came to light. Above all it was the product of conversation, of gossip, of storytelling, of myth, all together produced *ad hoc* from the context. Between the first events, the first accounts, and the apparition as an established fact there was an infinite, detailed, intense activity of sustained linguistic interaction of the context.

It is hard to overemphasize the fundamental role of language in the broad sense on the construction of the apparitions. Undoubtedly there were at work general cultural factors, traditions, the effects of a particular historical, social, and economic moment, and of a particular cultural strategy of the Catholic Church aimed at recovering a religiosity of experience and emotion. And local leaders more or less disposed to guide a religious movement on the rise played an important part. But these general and particular factors, external and internal, would not, in the specific details of the events, have allowed the apparitions to obtain the remarkable collective consensus that they did without the help of a powerful mediator—language—which worked to catalyze all those forces that were constructive and exclude the others. (Ibid., 53)

The apparition, described by protagonists, witnesses, curious bystanders, and even critics as a visual event, was revealed in the analysis as predominantly an event of words. The visions were surrounded by a symbolic world that words had built around them. Without this symbolic support the visions would have been something else: folly, deceit, undeciphered experience.

But the word soon came up against three limitations: (1) its own power to configure symbolic worlds, since once it constructed a world, it became dependent upon it and could not go beyond it because that world appeared to be a reality independent of words; (2) the influence of the Church, which, once it intervened to accept the "events," could not tolerate the word being questioned; (3) above all, the "ritual" bonds of the forms given to the collective word, the kinds of discourse, the emotional styles of communication, and the modalities of expression of conversational appearances and conflicts. "At Oliveto the ongoing social relations, provisional situations, casual interactions, and the relevant spectrum of possible kinds of discourse were more decisive than individual speakers" (Ibid., 75).

A third important segment in the analysis concerned the control of asymmetries among the protagonists.

For a few weeks the Madonna was a metaphor for conflicts between people and between roles; people used this new, improvised resource in their ongoing conflicts, hoping to derive from it all advantages possible given its novelty. . . . [T]he story of the "events" of the apparition was in reality an elaboration of personal, social, and political relations, expressed in conflicting reconstructions of what happened. (Ibid.)

In particular, the role of the leaders—the traditional ones and those proposed in the community of the apparitions—immediately became determinant for the success of the events. Early doubts about a mistake or a deception were resolved, often unintentionally, by their intervention.

The phenomenon would not have taken hold if all had depended on the credibility of the children. Even when the children were, at first, taken seriously, few people believed in the apparition of the Madonna. In *"It Is Said They Have Seen the Madonna,"* I tried to demonstrate that, in spite of their claim to have withheld judgment, the main community leaders contributed decisively to the transformation of the visions from a subjective experience to objective events. In the first place, simply by talking about it, they inevitably endowed the varied and uncertain reconstructions of events that they considered with coherence, even when they addressed them critically. The testimony of the witnesses was almost always fragmentary and often contradictory and incoherent. Drawing them together into the same narrative scheme itself gave the happenings a storylike structure that endowed them with coherence and plausibility. This narrative, imbued with a structural logic, constituted the events all the more since the events themselves were not yet established by the fragmentary testimony of the first protagonists.

The implicit acceptance by the leaders was a decisive act from which, in fact, the phenomena were constituted, while in appearance the phenomena simply gained credibility. The role of the seers was surely important but that of the leaders was much more so. The seers limited themselves to (or were limited by) recounting "things as I lived them." The leader, on the other hand, recounted "the things that occurred." As a result, the normative power of the leaders was far greater. By situating themselves as the center of meaning and the controllers of the events, the leaders were able to delineate the arena in which people were permitted to have experiences of visions; that is, they decided what was external to visionary experience—spurious, implausible—what simply did not exist. The leaders' control of the word gave them control of the events.

Furthermore, the leaders, especially the parish priest, sought to reduce the importance of the seers as a whole by making a distinction between seers and visions. Given the hazards of personal subjectivity, the seers might wander into unorthodox terrain at any moment. But the visions could be configured into a coherent, orthodox scheme by the leadership. By distinguishing the human subjects from their experience, the leaders could control the very experience of the seers; that is, the words that defined it and, through the words, the production of the apparitions.

The leaders controlled the production of the events in yet another way. Their prudent "attention" generated positive expectations among the curious spectators. Given the leaders' lack of hostility toward the events, the spectators adopted attitudes of piety, which the leaders themselves then interpreted as a general faith in the events. In this way, the leaders were affirmed in their attitude of *attention* and, little by little, opened themselves to *acceptance*, however prudent. In a circular process, the increase in their support generated stronger support in the devout, which in turn affected the leaders, increasing their own belief. Hence, in a cyclical feedback, each leader contributed to the growth of the events without realizing that they were seeing in the mirror of others their own growing conviction, yet assuming, to the contrary, that it was the events that were imposing their own evidence.

Finally, my fourth segment of analysis was centered on the formation of a structure of definite, stable actions, of a *context*.

> The "context" created at Oliveto can be defined as a systematic and organized configuration of actions that by structuring rules and procedures creates and produces the apparition and makes it an earthly event, orients linguistic and non-linguistic acts, filters and selects the events that can be recounted, both the subject matter and the interpretive possibilities, makes behavioral, expressive, conceptual, rhetorical, and semantic structures available, and, in short, produces reality. The distinguishing aspect of context is precisely that it provides tools useful for the production of reality. (Ibid., 176–77)

The context was defined at the culmination of the long intense activity of collective interaction during the first weeks of the events at Oliveto Citra. From that period on, *the interplay of the words and the actions* of the actors lost salience and visibility and was replaced in collective attention by the *extralinguistic reality* of the "presence [*presenza*]" produced, regulated, and circumscribed by words, but which the actors perceived as external, underlying, and stimulating the organized world of the apparitions. The mythopoetic power of the word might have constructed other symbolic worlds in an infinitely productive interplay. But once the words issued from the play of forces in the field, they followed the course of the particular symbolic world that they themselves had created and became possible only within its limits. The actors no longer had theoretically infinite possibilities for defining the events. A syntax, so to speak, was born, and the constituted (created) symbolic world imposed its own codes.

The word of everyone, horizontal,[1] that had decisive importance as a

---

1. For the author, "horizontal" speech is that which takes place in a context where one person's speech is as good as another's. It contrasts with speech that is hierarchically valued, within contexts where some people's speech has more weight than others.

forum for judging the authenticity of the apparitions in the first weeks now was considered marginal, secondary, and useless compared to the cogency of the "events." What counted was that it was *Her* and that now *Her* word had intervened. Her speech authorized only one human speech—that of the hierarchy of leaders—which had to lead the faithful, aroused by the "objectivity of the Marian presence," along the path of orthodoxy. It was not that the uncontrolled speech of people disappeared—on the contrary, it proliferated—but it lost its role and was seen as a sign of human weakness in the face of the transcendence that had invaded the world.

{1}

Professore—here there is no room for chit-chat + the Madonna is here {March 15, 1986}*

*The graphical conventions for my transcriptions are as follows:

+	pause within an intervention
—	brief pause within an intervention
[PAUSE]	pause between one intervention and another
. . .	suspended speech
[. . .]	part of text left out
vowel repeated	vowel sound drawn out
//	point at which one speaker begins intervention during the intervention of another, leading to an overlap
#	intervention entirely within the turn of another speaker
(n)	sign for the numbering of the participants in the conversations
{n}	sign for the number of order of the fragment transcribed; placed at the beginning
{date}	date on which quote was recorded; placed at the end (used, even when the text is not reported, to indicate the date of recording)
[ ]	notes in the transcription
italics	terms used in my analyses
dG	don Giovanni (the parish priest)

res	researcher
mv	male voice
fv	female voice
cv	child voice

I prefer the word "intervention" to the technical term "speaking turn," because it is more general. The transcriptions have used all the kinds of conversational presence useful for the analysis. Consequently the number of order (n) does not always coincide with speaking turns, since I often report overlapping speech that does not interrupt the turn of the speaker (with the sign #) and "back channels" or "complementary channels" (Goffman 1981).

Abbreviations

AC Archivio Comitato (Archive of the Committee)
B *Oliveto Citra terra di Maria*. Bollettino a cura del Comitato "Regina di Castello" (numbered from 1 to 16 and undated, then 1/1990, 2/1990, 3/1990)
r reprint 1–6
rel. relazione (report)

This instruction echoes a message that the seer Bernadette reported from the Madonna herself:

> Dear children,
> I invite you speak little and pray a lot. With words you will obtain nothing; only with prayer can you better understand everything and receive more. (B, r, 56)

The marginalization of conversation led to another decisive consequence for the definition of the story of the events. In the very first days, the need for formulating the perceptual experience of the seers in ways that could be shared and recognized imposed a dependence of what was seen on what was spoken. The children, constrained by the adults, tended to cut back progressively on the creative excitement of their visions in order to match *what was seen* to a norm recognized by everyone, one particularly desired by the leaders and derived from the institutional canon of sacred images. These constraints impeded the elaboration of visions that were complex or fantastic. (The seer Aurelia, whose visions were particularly rich and fanciful, was quickly excluded, and the boys kept quiet about their fantastic visions, although they told them to each other.) In the first phase, then, horizontal speech reigned supreme. But when the authenticity of the apparitions was affirmed and agreed upon, horizontal speech was no longer necessary, and in its place the vision came to acquire all the legitimacy that, if not totally denied, was certainly limited at first. It was then that conflicts among (and between) leaders, seers, spectators, and devotees moved on to the *management and control of visual codes* and the possibility of reinvention or, on the contrary, blind repetition.

A decisive moment was the publication of a written version of the events. At first, it was an anonymous, faint, dittoed sheet. Then it was signed by the parish priest. And finally it was included several times in the bulletin published by the "Queen of the Castle" Committee (Comitato "Regina del Castelo"), which had been set up to assist the priest. The publication emerged at the end of the long intense activity that identified what was *possible* and *plausible*. In the first months, this work was entrusted entirely to the oral accounts of witnesses, seers, and leaders in conversations and arguments at the site of the events.

The written text reduced, simplified, and standardized the entire process of oral excitement, which also had been decisive for the outcome of the phenomenon. Its addition to the collective activity defined what was the legitimate version of the events or, rather, what really happened at Oliveto. The rest—everything that was present as oral material—was more or less set aside, came to be forgotten, and then was treated as if it never had occurred. It is not surprising that the parish priest was the author, for he by then controlled the train of events. From then on, the curious and the devout coming to Oliveto knew that the events of the apparition had been exactly those described in the written version.

Before this written account, the devotees who went out to Oliveto could find many people from whom they could get information and, hence, could obtain varying accounts, which might have led to doubts about the authenticity of the phenomena. Such people might even draw their own conclusions about the credibility of their informants and might refuse to believe the "events" due to a bad impression of the informants themselves rather than what the informants said. (Many persons, for instance, became skeptical after talking to the children—whose interactive dimension adults could not stand, given the children's inability to adapt to conversational rituals.) If, therefore, the devout first had difficulty in finding out through conversation what were the "true events," later, with the written text, "the events" became clear and the subjective positions of the protagonists, seers, and leaders disappeared. If previously the devout were forced to compare, interpret, and combine the various versions that the actors gave out, subsequently they had the "text" that seemed to be a faithful account of the events. With this base the devotees could listen to the different oral propositions of the protagonists if they wanted, but were in no danger of disappointment, since the devotees already had the canon in hand, the photograph of the reality. The written word, then, came to cancel out all the intersubjective activity that was at the origin of the "events."

Below is the written version of the phenomena:

REPORT OF THE APPARITIONS OF THE MADONNA NEAR THE
CASTLE OF OLIVETO CITRA (PROVINCE OF SALERNO)

Prologue

1) This account of the events that have taken place in Oliveto Citra from May 24, 1985, on, has only the character of human testimony, and has been composed only for the love of truth and the duty to inform and does

not intend in any way to impede or anticipate the judgment of the competent ecclesiastical authority.

2) Hence, everything in this report, whether in regard to names, or in regard to messages, is always understood as the meaning and the thinking believed by the seers.

The Events

On the evening of May 24, the feast of Saint Macarius the Abbot, Patron of Oliveto Citra, toward 10 o'clock, a group of boys, between eight and twelve years old, were playing in front of the little plaza of the Rufolo pharmacy, at the foot of the medieval castle, while in the nearby Garibaldi plaza the civic festival was going on, enlivened by musicians and the sounds of a concertina.

From the little plaza an alley goes up toward the castle at a very steep angle and, passing under an arch with an iron gate, leads to the entrance to the castle about eighty meters away. The castle is largely in ruins from the wear and tear of the weather (it dates from 1145) and above all from the devastating impact of the earthquake of November 23, 1980.

At a certain point, the children see a luminous trail streak across the sky toward the castle—a falling star—and they shout that it is Martians. During a pause in the little plaza they note the crying of a baby coming from inside the gate.

Four times they shuttle running back and forth from the little plaza to the Garibaldi Plaza. Finally, one of the more enterprising boys throws a stone at the gate, and after a few seconds they see a very beautiful woman with a babe in arms, smiling.

This vision leaves them as if in shock, and one of them is even unable to speak. A youth who by chance was passing by, takes the boy by the hand and accompanies him to the Iannece bar for a cordial to bring him out of his prostration.

The others gather there as well, and cry out, "We saw the Madonna." Mrs. [Sandra] C., who runs the bar receives the news positively and turns to her assistant R. [Ada] saying, "They have seen the Madonna!" and [Ada] with a skeptical tone replies, "Come on! Especially these ones saw the Madonna!"

The boys, with wounded pride, say, "It's true, come and see," and run out to the little plaza of the castle.

[Ada], out of curiosity or perhaps from an interior impulse, follows behind the group. She has hardly reached the boys when she sees outside the gate of the castle the image of a young lady with a face of indescribable beauty, dressed in white with a blue mantle embroidered with gold, a crown of stars around her head with a band in which, in the front, was inserted a plaque of gold with silver filigree, and who held with her right arm her child against her breast, from whose little hands hung a rosary. This vision frightens both the boys and [Ada] and they begin to back up, when the vision, with her right arm, asked them not to flee, and addressing [Ada] with a very tender voice says, "You will always see me at night." The girl too entered a state of shock and was taken to the nearby Civil hospital, where the doctor on duty, Giuseppe Santinelli, when he heard the cause for her crisis, asked her a series of questions to determine the psycho-pathological condition of the patient. The diagnosis of the doctor was that "the girl is healthy in body and mind, and her condition is as if she has had a big fright."

The next night [Ada] had the vision of the Madonna in her house, and with great simplicity asked, "Why did you choose me?" The vision replied, "I have not chosen you alone, because many will see Me, but only those who have the courage to believe will remain."

From that point on [Ada] has had the vision about thirty times in the same form and has received messages of prayer, penance, and also of fasting. (B 1, 1–2)

Up to this point, then, I have considered *how* a "world" was constructed, and this process was the subject of *"It Is Said They Have Seen the Madonna."* But after accounting for the *how*, there still remains the *what* that was then constructed: the symbolic dimensions, the relations between this new symbolic field and the ones around it, those that preceded it and those that existed at the same time. Once the fertile power of the word had been reconstructed and the assumption that the world created was the assumed one was avoided, it was time to analyze that symbolic reality. Different issues in the two phases of the research determined the use of different methods.

The starting point in the second phase was the interconnection of the symbolic production based on traditional local cultural levels with an international symbolic dimension that I call "Catholic visionary culture." The symbolic context the analysis required went beyond the immediate region; it could be understood only in the perspective of well-known modern apparitions: Lourdes, Fatima, and, above all, Medjugorje in the former Yugoslavia, the most famous of present-day Marian visions. Comparison with these influential cases may help in understanding the particular kind of symbolic production that characterized the apparitions at Oliveto. This book is the result of that enterprise.

In addition to the obvious continuity in subject matter, this book has something else in common with *"It Is Said They Have Seen the Madonna"*: a kind of conscious emotional subversion that occurred in the process of its writing.

It cannot be thought of as self-justifying that one considers the psychological burden of a research project of this kind, above all in the period in which frequently hundreds of pilgrims cried out "There She is!" and wept and became agitated and fell on their knees, sweeping everybody along in the emotional throng. It does not seem useful for me to skip over the sensitivity, more human than professional, which in those moments rendered me present for the others, even though I was the only outsider completely incapable of seeing what for the rest, including other nonseers, was possible if not evident. At that moment one could measure all the *distance* between the researcher and the people of the research, that is, when the experience of the world diverged, leaving the researcher in the loneliness of his proud conceptual categories, his conceptual compactness, while the others participated in the magmatic and choral perceptive experience.

Next there was a *closeness* for two reasons: the use of the "word" as an instrument for the organized reformulation of ecstatic experience on the part of the pilgrims; and the reflective wonder on the part of the researcher for the kind of *schizoid vertigo* he felt when trying to keep his intellectual balance while his body was sending visible signals of experiential solidarity to the ecstatic pilgrims around him, through muscle tension, his closeness to other bodies, the warmth of his eyes, the *pathos* of his being. I do not think it possible to express this kind of field experience in my anthropological writings without the risk of sensationalism. But it is not right to omit entirely this part of my experience when I was developing the concepts in this book. (Apolito 1990, 37–38)

In the field there was not only a reassuring *distance*—classic, obvious, and necessary—between the researcher and the people of his research. There was also a *closeness*, troubling because it was produced in a "schizoid vertigo," which is to say that I entered a "new" distance, this time between different parts of myself as I felt this emotion. When it is time *to write*, the distance takes on its full function—classic, obvious, and necessary—but this distance almost entirely erases that nexus of closeness (*to them*) combined with distance (*within me*) experienced in the field.

Hence, this distancing in the *writing up* of the piece of biographical experience shut off in the field, even though it led to the development of concepts in *"It Is Said They Have Seen the Madonna,"* is also to be found in this book. Here, too, after more months, more distance from the field, I have written by the rules of anthropological literature and have chosen as my audience the scientific community and whoever else, students or readers of another kind, chooses to refer to this community. The subjects of my research are much less the interlocutors of my writing now than they were in the field experience. But even less present as an interlocutor, perhaps, is the Me of that piece of biographical field experience; or rather, he is here, but recognized as the *other*, the-one-in-the field, not the-one-who-writes.

> Not without a certain initial annoyance, I understood later that even field diaries, interviews, and conversations I had many months earlier were documents useful to understand the phenomena and my different approaches to them, but also to identify the ways in which an observer who is critical but open can get involved in the relatively rapid process of the construction of the "events," within which, even as a researcher (but not only one), he is implicated.
>
> I admit it made me a little dizzy when I realized that I too was a subject of analysis; but it had to be faced were I to address the embarrassing, but urgent, question of the place of the researcher in a special study like this on visions and relative words, that is, on the weight of words and the lightness of the senses, on the distance between the *experience* of the body and the *sense* of the experience. (Ibid., 41)

This is not simply a trivial matter of the *pathos* of the internal conflicts of a troubled individual. It is one of epistemology, not psychology. Anthropological writing, in at least this case, is unusual in that it comes out of a fieldwork experience that, crudely speaking, does not occur on the same levels on which one later "writes it up." In contrast to other students of society, but also to students of the humanities, the anthropologist defines his cognitive dimension on planes of psycho-physical experience (the *field*) different from those on which he takes up the transcription (the blank page). This dimension takes shape in the course of a life that involves planes of feeling that do not allow the detachment, analytic construction, and intellectual exercises involved in academic anthropological writing.

With this book, in the meantime, I conclude—though not because there is nothing left to understand—the phase of biographical experience and research connected to the apparitions of Oliveto.

At the end of the writing, I think back to all the people I have known as a result of the apparitions. The feeling of a common humanity is, as I have said in *"It Is Said They Have Seen the Madonna,"* what makes those people and the experiences I shared with them important to me.

This feeling is also present in, but not sufficient to, remembering with gratitude the reactions, observations, and new stimuli that Clara Gallini, Tullio Tentori, Pietro Clemente, Francesco Faeta, Annibale Elia, Rino Mele offered me in regard to my first book on the subject. To them I owe thanks for additional insights in the present work but not, obviously, for any new failings, which are all my own.

Paolo Apolito
University of Salerno, December 1991

INTRODUCTION

IN RECENT YEARS, SOCIAL SCIENTISTS who have studied visions and related phenomena in the Roman Catholic world have remarked on the neglect of these matters, given their evident importance for Catholicism. For example, a sociologist of religion, Michael P. Carroll, observes that

> despite the importance of Marian apparitions to so many Catholics, these apparitions have not attracted much attention from sociologists of religion. This neglect is mildly puzzling. It certainly cannot be attributed to the fact that visionary experiences in general hold little interest for sociologists of religion. On the contrary, one of the dominant concerns to have emerged in the sociology of religion over the past ten to fifteen years is a concern with mystical experiences, and scales designed to measured such experiences almost inevitably inquire about religious visions. Nevertheless, despite this recent concern with mysticism, and despite the visibility of Marian apparitions and their impor-

tance within the Roman Catholic tradition, the literature on these apparitions is, as I have said, sparse. (Carroll 1985, 57)

The situation is no better in anthropology, even though anthropologists from Tylor on have recognized the importance of visions in human culture. In Italy, in spite of an extraordinary flowering of phenomena of this nature, anthropologists have been little attracted to them (so little that recent studies, if I am not mistaken, can be counted on the fingers of one hand).

According to Carroll, research on visions, in particular Marian ones, falls into three categories. First, some Catholic authors seek to distinguish "true" apparitions from "false" ones. In addition to Thurston (1927 and 1933), Billet and Laurentin et al. (1973), authors cited by Carroll (1985), there are articles in *Civiltà Cattolica* by Galot (1985) and Mucci (1989) on the theological foundations of apparitions in Italy. In his imposing works, René Laurentin assembles and interprets the documents of Lourdes (Laurentin 1957–61; Laurentin 1961–64). (It is strange that Carroll, who writes about Lourdes [1985], does not cite them.)

In recent years, Laurentin has abandoned the prudent wisdom of his earlier work to promote with enthusiasm the kind of visionary Catholicism that has proliferated in the aftermath of the apparitions of Medjugorje, in the former Yugoslavia. In this vein, he has written an impressive number of books, booklets, pamphlets, and articles—printed in an extraordinary variety of places and tongues—that demonstrate the authenticity of a number of the more recent apparitions, most particularly those at Medjugorje. The bishop of Mostar, responsible for Medjugorje and critical of the apparitions there, has insinuated that the French Mariologist has profited financially from the books. Laurentin indignantly rejects the accusation, but has himself pointed out that his articles have improved the circulation of *Glas Končila*, the newspaper of the diocese of Mostar (Laurentin 1986a, 165). Perhaps Laurentin's most singular work is *The Apparitions of the Blessed Virgin Mary Today*. Here, the theologian examines several dozen apparitions, identifying some positive element, major or minor, even in those officially rejected by ecclesiastical authorities. The sources he uses in this enterprise are not up to the strict canons of scholarship that he himself applies to Lourdes—at least not those sources he cites for Oliveto Citra.

A second category of studies on visions includes

studies that take the fact of a particular Marian apparition as given, and which then try to explain the popularity of the cult which develops around this apparition as a response to prevailing social concerns. Examples of this sort of study would include the attempt by Turner and Turner (1982) to link the popularity of the Lourdes cult to the concerns of a postindustrial society, the various attempts (E. Wolf 1958; Lafaye 1976; Kurtz 1982) to relate the Guadalupe cult to the social dilemmas created in Mexico by the Spanish Conquest, and Christian's (1981) study of apparitions in Renaissance Spain. (Carroll 1985, 57)

To this list one should add Bax (1990), who studies the apparitions of Medjugorje and explains them as the result of conflicts among religious elites, but especially those between the bishop and his diocesan clergy, and the Franciscan order, who were directly involved through the friars in the parish.

Finally, a third category, in which Carroll places his own study, consists of attempts to identify psychological processes at the origin of the visions. I will dwell more on Carroll's studies because, in a way, they are direct "competitors" to the perspective I employ in *"It Is Said They Have Seen the Madonna"* (1990) in that both he and I try to reconstruct the genesis of an apparition. But Carroll looks psychoanalytically *in interiore homine*, while I look to the "town plaza" (Geertz 1973), that is, the social and public forum in which ideas take shape.

In an article published in 1983, Carroll examines fifty Marian apparitions that occurred between 1100 and 1896 (dates he takes from a work by Walsh of 1906) in order to understand how they originate. In summary, Carroll observes that

Marian apparitions derive from an especially strong sexual desire for the opposite-sex parent formed during the Oedipal period, and that such apparitions are most likely to occur when sexual outlets are blocked in later life. This would explain why such apparitions occur with equal frequency to males and females, and why most seers are sexually mature individuals who lack obvious sexual partners. (Carroll 1983, 216)

The willy-nilly application of the Oedipal model to quite diverse historical, social, and cultural situations provokes a certain perplexity. But, above all, there is an excessive documentary reductionism that attributes a narrative coherence to lives of seers based on incomplete information and inevitably produces highly simplified, if not simplistic, explanations. Carroll's entire argument depends on the fact that, for forty-five of the fifty seers in the sample, he is able to establish that

> 40 percent were clerics of one sort or another (e.g., priests, nuns, brothers), 20 percent were unmarried adolescents and 18 percent were unmarried adults. I am well-aware that being a cleric or an unmarried adolescent is not a sure guarantee of celibacy in this or any other society. Still, the fact that nearly 80 percent of our seers were sexually mature individuals who lacked any *obvious* sexual partners, and the fact that only a very small percentage (4 percent) of these seers were married at the time of their apparitions, are facts that at the very least are consistent with the "sexual sublimation" hypothesis and must be accounted for by any "good" explanation of these Marian apparitions. (Ibid., 210–11)

The lack of detailed references to sources makes it particularly difficult to judge the appropriateness of his diagnosis of "sexual sublimation" for each case. One is left with little more than a working hypothesis. But Carroll's analysis leads him into another kind of reductionism. Observing that most of the apparitions in the period he examines take place in Italy, Carroll finds an explanation for them in the fact that since "the nature of the Italian family intensifies, in both males and females, sexual desire for the opposite-sex parent, this argument can also account for Italy's predominance with respect to Marian apparitions" (Ibid., 216).

Where does Carroll get his conviction that Italian families have such precise psychoanalytic and social traits, and, furthermore, that these traits are stable enough to explain a sample of seers that stretches over nine centuries? He gets it from an article by Anne Parsons in 1969, in which Parsons uses data drawn from her own quite limited fieldwork in the Neapolitan area.

A second study by Carroll (1985) seeks to explain two classic nineteenth-century apparitions, La Salette and Lourdes, with a psychodynamic approach. Carroll bases his discussion of La Salette on information that contains few details on the lives of the two principal seers. He interprets the main "hallucination" of La Salette—the Virgin who holds back the arm of her son who wished to punish sinners—in a way similar to the explanation initially given at La Salette by Maximin (one of the two seers), that is, a mother hit by her son. Since Maximin was frequently beaten by his stepmother, Carroll concludes that the hallucination of the seer "is an attempt to gratify an unconscious wish to harm his stepmother, which derives from the intense hostility that was engendered in Maximin by the abuse that he had suffered at her hands" (Carroll 1985, 63).

In regard to Lourdes, Carroll recalls the female figures on whom Bernadette was psychologically dependent: her mother, with whom it seems she was not on good terms; a woman from the nearby village of Bartres, with whom the girl had spent long but not particularly happy periods; and her aunt and godmother, Bernarde, with whom Bernadette was very affectionate and in whose house she had spent happy times. Carroll contends that the "hallucination" of Bernadette was the result of her attraction to her aunt Bernarde, with whom she theoretically wanted to live. And then

> what would have provoked such a hallucination? Consider that in January 1858, Bernadette had just returned from Bartres, where by her own testimony she had felt unloved and rejected. She found herself living in a lice-infested household, where the window in her room overlooked that dung heap. She knew from past experience that good meals in the Soubirous household would be hard to come by. In this situation, it is not unreasonable to suggest that young Bernadette might have longed for those 1–2 years when she had lived in relative comfort with her godmother, a woman with whom she had an especially warm relationship. The hallucination of Aquero, modeled as she was on Bernarde, can therefore be seen as an attempt to gratify Bernadette's desire to be living once more in comfort with her loving godmother, rather than in poverty with her natural parents. (Ibid., 69)

Furthermore, Carroll assumes he can explain the famous phrase of the apparition, "I am the Immaculate Conception," as Bernadette's unconscious reference to her aunt. He starts from the assumption that, for Bernadette (as for many Catholics not well schooled in doctrine), the Immaculate Conception refer not to the conception of Mary without stain by her mother, Anne, but to the virginal conception of Jesus by Mary herself. The author further points out that before becoming dogma in 1854 the idea of the Immaculate Conception was widespread in Catholicism, with the feast day on December 8 already observed at least 150 years before the apparitions of Lourdes. Here is Carroll's explanation:

Given that Bernadette was generally ill-educated, and given what her biographers consistently describe as her "excessive modesty" [. . .], it is highly likely that she was not particularly enlightened about sexual matters. In the mind of such a person "a woman who gives birth to a child without the aid of a natural *father*" could easily be taken as more or less synonymous with "a woman who gives birth to a child without aid of a *husband*. This means, then, that Bernadette could easily have associated the phrase "immaculate conception" with an unmarried woman who gives birth to a child. As the reader will have guessed, Bernadette's Aunt Bernarde was just such a woman. Bernarde in fact gave birth to *two* illegitimate children. (Ibid., 71)

The difficulty in accepting Carroll's analyses arises from the relentless psychological reductionism that pervades them, and which are based only on meager documentation. What written sources exist (including even those he does not use fully) are the product of the filters of the people around the seer. Given the distance in time, we have no oral sources.

Even if more detailed and trustworthy sources were available, there is a fundamental limitation to Carroll's psychoanalytic and psychodynamic approach. At a certain point, Carroll remarks in a note that Bernadette heard words from the Virgin only during the third apparition.

The third apparition, when Bernadette both saw *and* heard Aquero for the first time, was also the first time that she had been accompanied to the grotto by adults who accepted the authenticity of her visions; previously she had been accompanied to the grotto only by other children. This seems consistent with the findings [. . .] that childhood hallucinations are intensified whenever an adult does anything to suggest to the child that the hallucination is real, even if this means only that the adult pretends to "chase away" whatever it is that the child sees. (Ibid., 68 n. 6)

This is an important point because Carroll admits, if only in passing, that the "hallucination" of the seer is insufficient for an apparition to develop; others around the seer must validate and elaborate on what the seer has said. In other words, a *context* of apparitions must be created. It is this context that distinguishes an apparition from a hallucination as a scientific problem; otherwise, there would be no difference between Bernadette's account and a psychiatric account of personal hallucinations.* In short, a psychological approach of this kind is insufficient to understand a social phenomenon of such dimensions. Such an approach may help to understand the personality of the seer, but the seer is not the exclusive, or even the decisive, element in the genesis of the social phenomenon, which is organized on a quite different level.

So, to the three categories that Carroll proposes, I would add a fourth (in which I would place my work), comprising studies of the context of social interaction in which the apparitions unfold and the processes by which they are shaped. At the conclusion of his work on the first month of 1931 apparitions in a town in the Basque country, Ezkioga, William Christian states:

> This examination of the first month of the Ezkioga visions may suggest the importance of the context in which "prophets" and charismatic leaders formulate and gradually fix their messages. In the Basque visions and movements, general anxieties and hopes are answered by individuals with instructions said to come from God, but it seems clear that the cultural content enunciated is as much a consensual product of followers and the wider society as of the leaders, the prophets, or the Saints. The audience, the Greek chorus, the hagiographer, the message takers and the message transmitters should be as much the focus of our attention as the charismatic figures on whom *they* are concentrating. (Christian 1987, 163)

Christian, who uses ideas from Ottavia Niccoli's studies of apparitions in the sixteenth century (1982, 1985), works with newspaper and oral sources to describe "how visionary experience was selectively molded to articulate people's concerns at a complex turning point in Basque history" (Christian 1987, 140).

In a Spain that had just emerged from the dictatorship of Primo de Rivera as a republic, but was headed for civil war and Franco's dictatorship, the apparitions of Ezkioga played a significant role, especially in the Basque

---

*In this book I use the term "apparition" rather than "vision" precisely in order to emphasize the aspect of collective formalization of the event, since, as I maintained in *"It Is Said They Have Seen the Madonna"* (part 4 of chapter 5), even were the original impulse to come from conscious deception, in given circumstances the events might play out in the same way.

country, where the effects of conflicting ideologies could be felt in daily life, dividing families and disturbing the kind of collective security that rural social life had long enjoyed. From sources such as newspapers of differing stripes, direct oral testimony, and contemporary accounts, Christian composed a description of the complex interplay of needs, demands, and motivations that guided the principal actors in the events—seers, leaders, and observers, all more or less directly involved in the defense or the attack of one or another ideological position. In this way, they formed a new power, which they then tried to use to their best advantage.

1

MANAGING THE
APPARITIONS

The Pilgrimage to Oliveto Citra

WITHIN DAYS, NEWS OF THE APPARITIONS spread throughout Campania. In the
first weeks after May 24, pilgrims from Campania began to arrive, first in
small, then in larger, groups and then, though less frequently and in smaller
numbers, from elsewhere in southern Italy: Basilicata, Puglia, Abruzzi,
Lazio, Calabria, and even Sicily. In a matter of months, Oliveto became an
impressive pilgrimage center, the most important among recent apparitions
in the south of Italy, and one of the more important in the entire country.
Emigrants journeyed from Canada, the United States, and Australia. A
group of nuns arrived from Sri Lanka, one of them witnessing an apparition.
High-level clergy were noted there from the first days. Jesuits from Naples,
among them Father Rastrelli, the author of a book on Medjugorje (Rastrelli
1987), were present at the end of May. Robert Faricy, Jesuit and professor of
spiritual ecclesiology and the contemporary theology of prayer at the

Pontifical Gregorian University in Rome, went often and subsequently published a book on Oliveto, *Mary Among Us* (*Maria in mezzo a noi*) in two editions, in 1986 and 1987. Faricy informed the French Mariologist René Laurentin, who first spoke with some of the Oliveto seers in Rome, went to Oliveto in May 1988, and referred to the phenomenon in his book *The Apparitions of the Blessed Virgin Mary Today* (*Le apparizioni della Vergine si moltiplicano*).

Some parish groups organized regular visits to Oliveto. The Annunciation of Our Lord parish of Palermo had among its members habitual seers at Oliveto. The parish of Saint Peter Capofiume of Bologna in 1986 published and distributed an elegant newsletter, *Oliveto Citra, Land of Mary*. To Oliveto then flocked various church and prayer groups, often those considered on the fringes of their community or known to be exponents of a particularly reactionary Catholicism. Pilgrims were given anonymously written handouts on the anticipated end of the world and leaflets of small religious groups like the Opera di Maria Vergine e Madre (Work of Mary Virgin and Mother) of Gioia del Colle (Bari), and the Dives in Misericordia movement of Centurano (Caserta), as well as of better-known groups like the Gioventù Ardente Mariana (Impassioned Marian Youth), the Marian Eucharistic Centers, and other charismatic renewal groups. Luigi Gaspari, who had been a favorite disciple of Padre Pio,[1] came often from Bologna to Oliveto. There he distributed his opus *Quaderno dell'amore* (Notebook of love) and gained considerable influence over some members of the Queen of the Castle Committee. Relatives, friends, and supporters of the seers at Medjugorje turned up from time to time. The Medjugorje messages circulated through organized groups with exceptional rapidity—one or two days after their release by the seers in Yugoslavia. In short, Oliveto became a great laboratory for religious excitement, an obligatory reference point for those in Italy, especially in the South, who cultivated an emotional religiosity open to visions. According to Faricy, two hundred prayer groups formed in Italy and abroad that "recited every day at the same time the Holy Rosary and the same prayers from Oliveto Citra" (Faricy and Pecoraio 1987, 111). There was a shower of "confirmations" of the Oliveto apparitions.

---

1. Padre Pio da Pietrelcina (Italian Capuchin, 1887–1968) was born 120 kilometers north of Oliveto, and lived most of his life at San Giovanni Rotondo, in Puglia, 250 kilometers to the west. He was said to receive stigmata in 1918, and for much of his life was a focus of spiritual attention and pilgrimage, in his last years especially by traditional Catholics at odds with the ideas of the Second Vatican Council.

Many claimed that at Medjugorje the Madonna had said that she would appear at Oliveto as well (for example, Giulio, one of the Committee leaders {March 8, 1986}), even though it contradicted the Medjugorje seers who said that their apparitions of the Madonna would be the last ones in the whole world (Bianchi and Dogo 1985, 49). In the same vein, a seer-priest from Argentina "felt" the Madonna at Oliveto, and well-known seers such as Natuzza Evolo from Paravati and lesser-known ones such as Armida Passaro from Agropoli were involved in confirmations.

The sacred center at Oliveto stimulated other subsidiary apparition sites that claimed a connection to the Oliveto events. The Madonna told pilgrims that she had appeared in other villages of Campania, including Bellizzi, Casavatore, Cardito, and Agropoli, and in other places in Italy, including Maropati and Rome. Other seers let it be known that the Madonna was still present in her places of former apparitions, such as Lourdes. To one seer she said, "I know you, I saw you at Lourdes and I knew you would go back" (AC, January 2, 1986). The transcendent came closer in these places where the Virgin had been and was now present—bright rents in the heavy curtain that separates this world from the world beyond—places, the Madonna makes known, "where I and the Holy Spirit work great miracles of spiritual and material grace" (B 13, 24).

A note on the Oliveto events from the Vatican press agency at the beginning of November 1985 made the rounds in the Italian press, and major newspapers (*Il Giorno*, *La Stampa*, *Il Giornale*, *Il Corriere della Sera*, *Il Messaggero*, *La Repubblica*) sent reporters. *Il Mattino* of Naples had already reported the matter in June. The popular magazine *Gente* mentioned the events several times starting in November, but its competitor *Cronaca Vera* had already covered the story in July; *Panorama* covered it in February 1986. Lidia Ravera wrote about Oliveto in her article "Yearning for Religion" in *Cosmopolitan* in July 1986. The newsweekly *L'Espresso* sent Cristina Mariotti, whose piece led to controversy and threats of a lawsuit in Oliveto. Almost all of the articles on Oliveto had an ironic tone and were heavy on local color, but nonetheless they helped spread news of the events. Italy's public television network included the events in news broadcasts on all three of its channels. The journalist Enzo Biagi referred to Oliveto in a special broadcast of his highly regarded television news program *Spot*, directly from Medjugorje. Channel 5 devoted a fifteen-minute segment to Oliveto, and a videotape of this broadcast was shown to pilgrims in the town upon request.

Marco Margnelli and Giorgio Gagliardi, directors of the Center for Study and Research on Psychophysiology of States of Consciousness and authors of studies on the ecstatic states of the youths of Medjugorje (Frigerio, Bianchi, and Mattalia 1986), administered tests on the state of consciousness of the Oliveto seers on three occasions (in October 1985 and March and May 1986) at the request of the ARPA (Queen of Peace Association). The results (Margnelli and Gagliardi 1987a) were not particularly encouraging for the Oliveto seers, in contrast to those for the Yugoslav seers (certified as in altered states of consciousness). The National Center on Unidentified Flying Objects also took notice, sending two members from Salerno to investigate (Carione and Serrone 1986).

Beginning in November 1985, the Committee maintained a register of pilgrims, though the number of visitors is approximate, as generally only those pilgrims who came on organized bus trips signed, and not even all of these, as some groups did not stop at the Committee office to announce their arrival. Other pilgrims came as individuals or in small groups in automobiles, and few of these registered. Nevertheless, the number of pilgrims who did sign the register was substantial, as these are winter months.

November (last 10 days)	1,715
December	2,112
January	3,336
February	1,499
March (first 15 days)	1,587
Total (4 1/2 months)	10,249

Most of the pilgrims who registered, of course, came from Campania, but there were also organized pilgrimages from Palermo and Messina in Sicily, Giarre, Pescara, and Le Marche. A number of pilgrims came from the cities of Naples (830), Salerno (303), and Benevento (154). But towns in the wider metropolitan areas of Campania sent the highest number of pilgrims, proportionate to their population: Pagani ([Province of] Salerno), 594; Nocera Inferiore (Salerno), 372; S. Egidio Montalbino (Salerno), 244; Scafati (Salerno), 409; Pompeii (Naples), 214; Marcianise (Caserta), 276; Sant'Antonio Abate (Naples), 400; Cardito (Naples), 563; Grumo Nevano (Naples), 504; and particularly Frattamaggiore (Naples), 2,334. This last number is remarkable, particularly since the town is adjacent to and practically indistinguishable from Grumo Nevano. When one adds the two figures from Frattamaggiore and Grumo Nevano (2,838), it turns out that 27 percent of the 10,249 pilgrims who registered came from these two townships. At one point, the two towns had four important seers, one of whom remained a seer over all the years of my study. Perhaps these figures can also be explained by an especially efficient pilgrim tour bus service in these two towns.

As a rule, the towns with the most pilgrims were centered in an area that in recent years has undergone a brutal socioeconomic transformation, with sharp discrepancies in wealth, a notorious deterioration in the tone of civil society, collusion between organized crime and politicians, and a general anxiety about personal security. These are not marginal towns; on the contrary, they are focal points of economic development in Campania, even though this development is untrammeled and leads to little improvement in collective well-being.

In terms of religion, the areas that sent the most pilgrims stand out for the extroverted nature of their collective piety. With the arrival of large numbers of pilgrims from the plains of Campania between Caserta and Naples, the Nocera area, and the towns around Vesuvius, the cult of the Madonna of the Castle of Oliveto underwent a radical transformation from the relatively contained, subdued tone of the first weeks, when only people from Oliveto and the surrounding villages were present. The theatrical religiosity of northern Campania—best expressed in the pilgrimage to the Madonna dell'Arco[2] (see Rossi and De Simone 1974; Tentori 1979)—made itself right at home among the houses and the somewhat surprised residents of Oliveto Citra. Laments, cries, physical and emotional excitement, group devotion, and rhythmic choral prayer descended on the peaceful highland village and rendered more evident—almost indisputable—that the events were prodigious. The apparitions were reproduced in other places in the town—streets, corners, ravines. They were replicated in other towns in Campania—Casavatore, Cardito, Frattamaggiore, Grumo Nevano, Boscotrecase, Sant'Antonio Abate, Pagani, Battipaglia, Agropoli; and were predicted in still others—Brusciano and Camposano. The Committee members, unprepared for the unusual manner of support for their apparitions, were overwhelmed by this wave of corporeal piety in which fainting spells,

2. The feast of the Madonna dell'Arco is perhaps the most important and emotional in Southern Italy. Considerable numbers of pilgrims enter the church, about ten kilometers from Naples, in a kind of altered state, in hope of a miracle or in thanks for a previous cure.

collective fits, and demonic possessions occurred every evening, imposing a mood of collective drama. At first the people of Oliveto shared the positive opinion that the "Neapolitans" (as the local people called them)[3] themselves had of these phenomena. For many of the "Neapolitans," spectacular devotional piety like that at the feast of the Madonna dell'Arco, to which they frequently referred, was conclusive proof of the authenticity of the visions at Oliveto. Over time, however, skeptical positions and negative judgments emerged. Pilgrims who had been to Yugoslavia, for example, remarked on the difference between the measured and restrained piety at Medjugorje and the overheated and immoderate piety at Oliveto. At that point a policy was adopted, at first timidly, then with increasing firmness, to discourage the "Neapolitan" manner. The idea spread that some people were faking theatrical visions of the Madonna because they were paid by the travel agencies that brought thousands of pilgrims. The parish priest himself made this claim in an interview (Mantero and Chersola 1989, 15). In any case, it took about two years to bring the devotion under control. One result of this policy was a drastic reduction in pilgrims from northern Campania, replaced only in part by those from the rest of Campania and other regions.

Doubtless, the theatrical and physical religiosity of the "Neapolitans" disturbed the restrained manner of the people of Oliveto; though much of the success of the apparitions was due to these pilgrims, who constituted the great majority (88 percent of those who registered). They came from very large towns in which the media played up the events at Oliveto and had a critical role in the spread of the news. The television stations, newspapers, parishes, and prayer groups that were principal agents in the spread of the news were, for the most part, located in the well-developed Campania plain, the source of the emotionally expressive pilgrims and seers.

The social-anthropological aspect of the pilgrimage—social class, social sectors, cultural levels—did not have the salience it had in the classic studies of peasant or folk religion of past decades. It would not be appropriate in the case of Oliveto to speak of subordinate classes, not even substituting for class the notion of social sector. Consider, for example, the make-up of the Queen of the Castle Committee. It included young students, male and female, in professional schools and universities, and its leaders

---

3. Neapolitans would, strictly speaking, be people from Naples or its province. The villagers of Oliveto Citra applied the term to pilgrims from a wider area, including northern Campania, and then to persons with a theatrical piety, hence the author places their special usage in quotation marks.

were liberal professionals: Fulvio, Michele, the doctor who examined the seer Ada in the hospital, and the wife of a prominent dentist, who was also the mother of two seers. Among the seers—aside from Ada, who was referred to in one book as "the holy shepherdess" (Bonin and Renzetti 1979)—the following were typical: Nello, an important seer from a family of shoemaker artisans in Grumo Nevano; Giorgio, a student; Benedetta, a respectable "bourgeois" housewife; Remo, a white-collar employee of the electric company; and Umberto, a mechanic.

It is not possible, either, to characterize as subaltern, in sociological terms, the ways that the news of the apparitions spread and gathered force. It was the social and cultural organizations and prayer groups of the Neapolitan parishes (whether or not the parish priests were in favor) that nurtured the apparitions. Priests from outside the area were critically important for the spread of news of the apparitions. Two kinds of priests were involved: authorities on visions who wrote books about the Oliveto phenomena; and others, less charismatic but even more influential because of their position in the structures that could more or less institutionally build a consensus (parishes, prayer groups and centers, lay associations, etc.). The role of the clergy demonstrates that in a phenomenon like this we do not find a sociological tendency toward "lower" social or cultural sectors, in contrast to the phenomena studied in the 1950s and the 1960s.[4] It seems that a vaguely defined middle sector acts as a factor of cohesion and blurs social distinctions, in spite of the clearly hierarchical aspect of symbolic production.

In this respect, there has formed in recent years what could be called an international Catholic visionary culture, whose productive dimension, clearly hierarchical, can be identified in the following various *places*.

1. Places where apparitions have taken place that have attracted a mass following. Christian (1987), Bax (1990), Apolito (1990) show clearly how in these places dynamic hierarchies of power evolve, certainly not hard and fast, but substantially identifiable in given situations. The apparition is used as a new resource in the struggle to redefine the structure of local power, whether to change the internal dynamics of leadership, to co-opt new social subjects into it, or to

4. The author refers to studies like those of De Martino on folk religion or Lanternari on the religions of the oppressed (see Bibliography).

defend against external or extralocal attack, without, in any case, relinquishing established spheres of internal influence or self-confirmed domains.

2. An entire sector of local industry sustained by local culture that supports the visionary culture with ever more abundant, well-distributed, and attractive products. This sector uses the latest technology—videotapes, local radio stations, fax transmission of the latest Marian messages—in addition to the traditional publishers. But it also spreads its message by "archaic" media like broadsides, devotional leaflets, and, above all, word-of-mouth, both outside and inside churches through religious enthusiasts, prayer groups, "inspired" priests, and plain folk.

3. A network of Church leaders, composed of prominent theologians, entire sectors of religious orders, factions in conferences of bishops and in the Vatican Curia. It was the Vatican press agency that first spread the news of Oliveto in November 1985, and it was Vatican policy to foment mass piety by encouraging a certain idea of "hot" Catholicism of full stadiums and cheering throngs, of group emotions.

The Institutions of the Apparitions

The collective practices that developed around the nucleus of the apparitions constituted the self-evident, implicit, and unarguable rationality of the events, which never became an issue, as it appeared obvious and formed the basis for the *normal* course of the *things*. In fact, it was itself based on a *guided* course of *actions*. A complex of acts, habits, practices, and repetitions occurred and reoccurred, forming sedimentary and automatic reactions. This slowly institutionalized the events, rendering them stable and durable, part of the everyday panorama of things that existed as a given, as the world. The parish priest, the Committee, the seers, the devout, and the curious interacted in a new world they themselves had created, which was held together not by a common truth—there were various, multiform, local levels of truth even for the same person*—but by the common practices of the context. Some constellations of collective action worked in a particular way as stable institutions to prop up the apparition as a *made* event.

---

*On this, see *"It Is Said They Have Seen the Madonna,"* chapter 5, part 4.

The Practice of a New Cult in Space and Time

Every evening at a given hour—about 9 o'clock in the summer, 7 o'clock in the winter—the devout and the curious gathered with the seers in the little plaza of the events; group prayers, Rosaries, readings, and hymns were soon organized. The first messages of the Madonna were pressing requests for group prayer, and the Committee quickly made this appeal known. Later, messages institutionalized the Marian wish for the Rosary at 8:30 every evening.

The steps leading to the ruined castle became a central place for the town; previously, this place was peripheral. Ada, the main seer, confessed to me in an interview that she hardly knew the spatial layout of the environs of the castle where the events took place, the gate on the path to the castle and the steps. The children who went to play there knew they were at a boundary to a forbidden territory, a scary place—and in fact, scared they were. It was not a well-known, recognized place like the plaza where the fiesta took place and where the children came from.

The rediscovered centrality of the Oliveto castle is a good example of the construction of new meaning. The new became embraced and incorporated by the ancient. For many people of Oliveto, according to the Committee member Fulvio Piranese, the castle was already a place of apparitions: fifty years previously a lady in black; fifteen years previously another lady, the very one, some said, in the apparitions of 1985. Then there was a drunk, a "Communist," who had seen an image on the wall. Local tradition also held that it was a place where there were nocturnal processions of the dead. It was also a place, as Michele, one of the leaders, remembers, of unspeakable "disgusting deeds" of grim medieval lords: outrages, brutality, torture, inhuman imprisonment. Based on this tradition, there grew up the legend of apparitions of spirits in distress.

Two seers who had visions on the second day of the 1985 apparitions, but who later disassociated themselves from the phenomena in disagreement with the Committee, suggested to me the possibility that the "lady in black" had returned, disturbed by efforts to repair the castle after the earthquake of 1980 {March 22, 1986}. Other townspeople maintained that in the course of the repairs, "jack-hammers were always breaking, until the contractor had to give up on it" (Margnelli and Gagliardi 1987b, 51). For this set of reasons, the castle became a symbolic place in the town, for some people a disturbing one that stood for "the strangeness within us." It also became their deep space, the cornerstone of their history, the symbol, among others, of the wound of the earthquake of 1980, itself part of a deep symbolic history. Finally, it became the boundary, one might say, between a space that was permeated with culture and one that was strange and Other.

Indeed, the newfound centrality of the castle was a result of the construction of new meaning. Because of the visions, the disturbing connotations of the castle were replaced by the reassuring quality of a place of the Divine Mother. "Let's go to the castle / to see Mary" are the first lines of a poem written by Fulvio Piranese that became the official hymn of Oliveto after the Madonna asked the seer Benedetta to learn the melody sung by an invisible choir on October 29, 1985.

The Madonna herself insistently invited the pilgrims to return to the site of the apparitions and expressed her pleasure when they did so. Her insistence reveals an implicit identification of a *sacred center*, which spreads out in concentric circles, gradually losing power and significance. For the devout of Oliveto, not going to the apparition gate, even if one prays somewhere else, is a behavior qualitatively inferior to going to it, for the Madonna coincides with the physical site of her appearance. Likewise for out-of-towners, praying away from Oliveto does not have the same importance as praying at Oliveto. And once they reach the apparition town, going to the gate is essential, even if it means a long wait in line. People attribute to the Madonna herself a predilection for this practice, since she expressly asked the seers to do so, and through the seers, the sick and other devotees who paused out in the plaza, to go up to the gate. The trip to Oliveto is experienced as an entry to and an exit from an imaginary sacred area, across liminal or "liminoid" thresholds (Turner and Turner 1978, 35) that lead in to the center. The pilgrims are accompanied from the time of their departure by the phenomena that show that Mary is pleased. The sun works prodigies of light and movement in the towns from which the pilgrims come at the beginning of the trip, or during the bus ride, or at the arrival at Oliveto, or when leaving the apparition town. Other pilgrims comment with pleasure on the improvement of the weather on the day of departure after a previous spell of bad weather. The egocentricity of the devotional act—*one's own* act— activates a selection of temporal and serial referents by which one notices good weather during *one's own* pilgrimage but not bad weather during the pilgrimages of others.

The Formation of a New Sphere of Narrativity Prolonged in Time and Widespread in Space

After circulation of the written text, verbal activity concerning the events neither ceased nor diminished. On the contrary, word-of-mouth remained an important element in further developments, a cultural catalyst that made possible the transition from the experiences of individuals to the identification of "what really happened," as well as what significance to attribute to these experiences. All this, it is true, carried the risk of contradiction, redundancy, hyperbole, and minimization that narration entails and which the leaders tried to attenuate and control. Despite the efforts of the Committee to limit the prestige of the events, the numerous pilgrims who streamed into Oliveto—and even more so, the numerous persons who closely monitered the phenomena—maintained a permanent presence of narrative and informative speech about the apparitions that obviously encouraged new production, interpretation, and molding of the events. But through bulletins and other sources of information the leaders and the Committee played much more active roles than the mere assemblage of individual accounts, roles that *constituted* one truth of the apparitions: the apparitions' very existence. They set up a permanent office for the supervision of the events that, if it could not stabilize the truth, at least made it possible to dominate the amorphous and unorganized magma of horizontal speech that, in the first days of the apparitions of Oliveto, swept across Campania and elsewhere.

A sample of narrative excitement, here of the boys who were the first protagonists, makes clear the risk of proliferation of symbolic worlds that uncontrolled speech can provoke. The example has to do with an unusual vision of a horse and a horseman, not present in the official accounts or the written text—not even in my first interview with the boys on May 30, 1985. In fact, in that prior interview, the boys told me *not* to believe in the apparition of a horse.

{2}

(1) Gerardo: Don't believe the flying horse business.
(2) Dario: Some said there was a flying horse with sword in hand.
(3) Gerardo: And that he was waving it around.
(4) res: Who said it?

(5) Gerardo: Ubaldo.
(6) Dario: No, Alfredo.
(7) Claudio: No, Mimmo. {March 30, 1985}

One year later, on May 17, 1986, when I was standing with two Oliveto youths, Am. and G., one of the boys, Claudio, told me first about a horse and horseman, and then about two horses.

{3}

[. . .]
(1) Claudio: [The horse] was on the rock—above Civita—and
              then—emerged—I don't know—how—moved quickly
              up our street—behind a truck—which was stopped.
(2) res: Just the horse or the horseman too?[5]
(3) Claudio: Both + the horseman every time I saw him was laughing.
(4) res: He laughed?
(5) Claudio: A smile that frightened me + like those movies.
(6) res: Westerns?
(7) Claudio: No.
(8) Am.:   *Horror movies?*
(9) Claudio: *Uh—the guys that when they are going to kill
              somebody sometimes smile*—this way ++ later I saw
              with Aurelia—the girl from Contursi + we were up
              there—we saw + I don't know how to explain it + a
              horseman—and another time the horseman was on the
              wall I think and that's all.
[. . .]
(10) res: That horseman, who was he? + did you find out?
(11) Claudio: Gerardo and me and the guys from the first evening +
              we said it might be a saint—Saint Macarius—but they
              said it could not be Saint Macarius—I think it
              couldn't be Saint Anthony—because + I don't
              remember, it's been a year—we had said it might be a
              saint, that's all—I don't know which one.

---

5. In this conversation, the key term *cavaliere*, used throughout, is rendered "horseman" until it takes on the specific connotation of "knight."

(12) res: And why then did it make the smile that was a little
                nasty?
(13) Claudio: It wasn't a smile—he made +++ his face scared me.
(14) res: If it was a saint it shouldn't have frightened you.
(15) Claudio: No, his face made me laugh the way it was—but the
                smile + how + he made noise—scared me.
(16) G.:   Then you actually heard him laugh?
(17) Claudio: Yes, but on the first evening + that's why we went—we
                saw something or other +++ something like a horseman.
(18) Am.:   So, the first evening you saw the rider as well?
(19) Claudio: Yes.
(20) Am.:   *Whom did you see first, the Madonna or the horseman?*
(21) Claudio: *First we saw the horseman I think*—we said who could
                it be? they had said it was the light—up there that
                came—from the bandstand and we wanted to have an
                adventure—you know?
(22) Am.:   [*Laughing*] As an adventure?
(23) G.:   They wanted to go and look.
(24) Claudio: Yes, like when you go into the jungle + like that + to
                look.
[. . .]
(25) Am.:   [The horseman] made faces?
(26) Claudio: Yes, he laughed and moved . . . he made faces—I
                think he had the sword next to him—*he was like a
                knight of the old days—of castles with a coat of iron* +
                and he didn't have the armor—just the sword.
[. . .]
(27) Am.:   And did Ada too see the horse?
(28) Claudio: I do not know I never asked her + I think so—once Ada
                and I together + we saw an angel I think—something
                like that—then the knight—but I don't remember—the
                knight had something funny—*the horse had wings*—a
                horse that flew had wings—another + the one
                that . . . —there were *two horses*—knights—one was
                different—one had the horse . . . and the one I saw
                was white—the man was white—he was dressed in
                white and the horse had wings + the other one I think
                was + the horse black—something like that—the

knight was dressed in white or + red I think—or the
horse as well—I should get the others to remind
me—because if I am going to tell about it it's better.
{May 17, 1986}

In this reconstruction, the flying horse with its knight became a central
element of the apparition and, at a certain point, halved off to form an
additional horse and rider (28). In another reconstruction, offered to the
correspondents of the National Center on Unidentified Flying Objects
(NCUFO) by two boys, Claudio and Dario, in the presence of the boys'
mother, there was another halving off, not of horse and rider, but of color.

NCUFO:	A normal man?
Claudio:	Dressed in white . . . in black and white.
Mother:	What you mean by "black and white?"
Dario:	It looked like this. His eyes were black or white. One time I ~~saw~~ them white, another time I saw them black. The color . . . every time I saw him changed.
	(Carione and Serrone 1986, 42)

In my interview, the horse was the first figure to appear (21), preceding even
the Madonna. It was a magically-winged horse (28) with a knight who
seemed to have stepped out of a medieval illustration, a sword at his side
(26). We were, of course, in front of a medieval castle. But the image is
complex. There is a medieval element, "a knight of the old days," who then
slips ambiguously from the symbolic terrain of the saints (is he Saint
Macarius? Saint Anthony?) to that of horror movies like *The Shining* (8–9).
In more recent interviews (Marotta 1990, 208, 220), the boys again spoke of
the horse and horseman, seen this time from the window of the school a few
days after the apparitions began on May 24, 1985.

There is another interesting theme in this interview that modifies these
boys' accounts of the year before. At that time, Gerardo said that behind
their backs appeared "a thing that was tiny, fat, red and a little black."
Claudio added that it was "chubby and had little blisters all over its face,"
while Gerardo concluded, "that it stood for all our sins + and had the tail of
the Devil behind it, complete with the pointed tip." To my incomplete
question, "How did you know that the blisters . . . ," Gerardo answered,
"The Madonna told Tommaso." Hence, it was the Devil.

A year later, it was described to me:

{4}

(1) Claudio: Then my brother saw in the oasis [a grassy angle near
                the castle] two men—one small and another like
                Jesus—and the little monster was ugly + and after I
                saw it I looked—I said to my mother—when they
                came + and I heard some sounds—I don't know—I
                looked toward the . . . —other friends did,
                too . . . [a boy arrives] he saw it. too.
[. . .]
(2) res: You were saying that your brother saw Jesus with the
                little monster.
(3) Claudio: Not just me and my brother, also other people—the
                man was standing still—the little monster walked
                back and forth fast—it was scary—behind the
                Madonna was the horned one—a little monster so
                tall—fat—like this + feet and arms could bend over
                and stretch this far—here it was very still and with a
                bone that moved—around like this—like—and it
                scared us—it had, like, red ears and eyes.
(4) res: Was it with the Madonna or with Jesus?
(5) Claudio: The first little monster was behind the Madonna—*the
                second we were not sure if it was Jesus*—it seemed to
                be because it had a white beard ++ the second was
                not like the first—it was taller and had + *a lot of little
                blisters*
(6) res: Why?
(7) Claudio: I don't know—Tommaso saw the same little
                monster—and asked him "what are those little
                blisters" on his face + and he told him "they are all
                the sins of this town." {May 15, 1986}

Another figure has emerged (1) in addition to the diabolic monster of the
first vision, a figure that seems to be Jesus himself.

With the appearance of the two "monsters" it is possible to construct
another precise symbolic world, an alternative to that of the Marian
apparitions. Here is how their appearance is reconstructed in a recent book
that seeks to interpret Marian apparitions as UFO sightings:

The boys furthermore saw two moving figures going out of a little garden (called "oasis"). One was very tall, about 1 meter 95, and dressed in white, with a long beard and short hair. Around his waist like a belt he wore a sash that hung down to his knees. In contrast the other was very short, no higher that 1 meter. But he was monstrous, horrible. He did not seem to be wearing any clothes, and his skin was completely green. He had red eyes with a black point, pointed ears, and two fangs sticking out of his mouth. His face was covered with little blisters. (Malanga and Pinotti 1990, 41–42)

In the report of the Salerno correspondents of the NCUFO, which formed the basis for the account of Malanga and Pinotti, the parallel with creatures from outer space is even more explicit.

When the boys described the little "green being," they gave details and descriptions that fit almost exactly, as if it were the same thing, a humanoid that appeared on August 22 1955, in Kelly, a place near Hopkinsonville, in Kentucky (USA). This creature, which had nickel-colored skin, had the same appearance (including unusually big eyes) as the one seen at Oliveto Citra. (Carione and Serrone 1986, 79)

The two correspondents included sketches by the boys and a composite drawing by an architecture student, which they considered similar to drawings of the UFO creature from Kentucky.

Obviously, this narrative freedom in conversation was extremely danger-ous from the point of view of the constitution of the apparitions, making it necessary for the leadership to centralize the truth through political and religious management by means of the Queen of the Castle Committee. The leaders' decision to reduce the role of semantics and, for all intents and purposes, exclude the boys, proved far-sighted and critical to the success of the apparitions. A reconstruction based on the boys' oral testimony would never have led to the formation of an event-in-the-world, and the same danger existed with the other protagonists and with the general propagation by word-of-mouth of unsupervised messages.

But the simplification and drastic reduction of oral stories prompted by the parish priest Don Giovanni did not entirely preempt "narrative contami-nation" in the following months, for a charismatic phenomenon cannot remain active without a broad word-of-mouth network, however controlled.

That is the reason for Don Giovanni's attempt, in the following years, to institutionalize the cult, to render human speech less legitimate than that of the Madonna, and, finally, to regulate (and, for some seers, terminate) the visionary experience.

The Activation and Utilization of a Channel for Celestial Messages

The leaders homed in on the Madonna's messages, which, over time, became the Committee's almost exclusive concern. Moreover, the number of seers swelled enormously from the initial handful of boys that Ada had joined. Each seer had her or his Marian message to report and the Committee often had to sit through excited accounts of visionary experience in order to arrive at the *core* of the Marian message. For the edification of pilgrims, the Committee's bulletins dedicated more and more space to these messages. Here, too, we see the guiding hand of the leadership. As the message took precedence over the experience of vision, the *word* (of the Virgin, of the hierarchy) prevailed over the *vision*. The *apparition* could not be justified merely as a marvelous *vision*. If God "gives permission" to appear, to use the expression of Don Giovanni, of necessity it must be to edify mankind with something to be transmitted, some message. This message cannot be revelation, which, strictly speaking, ended with the coming of Christ, but rather a divine exhortation in order to convert people. A few days after the first event, Don Giovanni thought it was of fundamental importance that the apparition repeated "pray" three times to Ada. He considered this instruction a "proof." Mere seeing was not enough—it would be difficult to account for in orthodox terms. Rather, it was these words, however commonplace in church discourse, that served to justify a supernatural intervention.

The *word of the Madonna* could be used as a kind of throttle by those who administered official religious language. On the one hand, the Madonna's word could limit the word among seers and believers, dangerous in its potential for excited narrative. On the other hand, displacement of attention to the "message" undermined the power of *collective seeing*, which the official canon of sacred images alone had great difficulty in controlling.

The attention devoted to the messages assumed that a certifiable channel of communication had been opened with the supernatural and, in particular, with the Madonna. Once the channel was activated, any pronouncement by a seer could be a message from the Madonna. This assumption played a significant role in the institutionalization of the apparition. What needed to be figured out was no longer *if she spoke*, but *what she spoke* and *to whom she spoke*; that the Madonna was indeed speaking was no longer in doubt. Who might be sending the message was no longer the issue. The message itself was the issue, and onto this matter were grafted branches of conflictive interaction. No longer did people argue over who spoke it, but rather what was being spoken to people about conversion, prayer, and so on. "Persuasion, appeal, rhetoric, and direction," aspects of communication focused on the recipient (Hymes 1974, 22), became the focus of linguistic activity about the apparitions of the Madonna.

The Queen of the Castle Committee

The installation of the Queen of the Castle Committee is perhaps the most decisive of the acts that constituted the apparitions. From the very first days, the parish priest and Fulvio Piranese gathered evidence in the form of interviews and conversations with the seers, including tape-recorded descriptions of the visions with corresponding questions. This entailed considerable work, and because a number of persons, especially youths, were willing to help, the parish priest formed a Committee for this purpose. Its headquarters was a room on the second floor of a building in the little plaza that faces the steps to the castle, ten meters away. From this vantage point, it was possible to keep track of the events as they occurred, organize and regulate the prayers, and keep people aware of the constant, vigilant presence of the leaders. The Committee center became a second point of reference, in addition to the apparition site, for those who went to the plaza. The pilgrims, as they faced and watched the apparition site, were constantly aware of the power and authority behind them.

Over time, a written collection of testimony from the seers became the main business of the Committee. Some seers were barely literate and, hence, merely dictated their testimony, which was "edited" in transcription. Even the seers who had no trouble writing often found themselves in a weakened psychophysical state after their visions or, in any case, preferred to speak while someone from the Committee wrote what they said. Much of the testimony in the Committee archive is in the original handwriting. The unwritten protocol of questions that the Committee members followed when putting questions to the seers and transcribing the replies tended unintentionally to eliminate vision content that did not coincide with the objective of the leaders, which was to consolidate a base of proofs of the apparitions, make clear their religious meaning, and circulate the messages of the Madonna that were "true." Visionary effervescence, folkloric superfluities, and idiosyncrasies were trimmed away. The seers were asked not to dwell on "useless" details, but instead to concentrate on the visual aspects of the apparition and, above all, its message.

The Committee's control of the overall direction of the events became decisive for the very existence of the apparitions and, later, for the particular direction given to their organization. Without the Committee, and in particular without the parish priest Don Giovanni, it is possible that the apparitions would not have existed, and it is certain that they would quickly have faded away.

The Committee's control extended fundamentally to three aspects of the collective production of apparitions: messages, seers, and cult.

Messages

In the very first issue of the *Bollettino* there appeared the first messages of the Madonna, and from the second issue on, almost all of the space in the bulletins was allocated to messages. Even more than the Madonna of Medjugorje, the Madonna of Oliveto spoke a great deal and entrusted the seers with hundreds and hundreds of messages, only a small proportion of which were published.

In regard to the Madonna's messages there developed a thinly disguised struggle between the Committee and the seers, for the former took upon itself the job of deciding which messages were valid. "The Celestial Mamma has given out hundreds of messages, but only about 250 have been published, for they are carefully evaluated and only those in accord with the Gospels, with Catholic morality, and the teaching of the Church are published" (B 11, 8).

In this somewhat inexact and contradictory formulation, the Committee asserted its authority to select authentic messages from those it judged otherwise. For this purpose, it frequently referred to a message from the Madonna that expressly asked the Committee to serve as a filter (message to Giovanni, February 16, 1986). But among the seers there were those who complained about other selections as well, particularly by the parish priest, of wording within messages otherwise held to be valid. One such episode led to a considerable amount of argument. The message for "all humankind" that Benedetta declared that she wrote down under dictation by the Madonna on January 10, 1986, was published by the Committee as a handout but with the qualifying phrase "which is claimed to have been dictated by the Madonna," which disappointed the seer. A few days later, it reissued the message omitting the qualifying words "which is claimed to have been." But the changes Benedetta especially complained about were in the message itself. In fact, they were rather minor: "all people" became "all men"; "he is not joking and he has no fear of men" became "he has no fear of the arrogant and the indifferent"; "men should not bow down to God alone" became "men should not love God alone"; and there were a few others. These changes were sufficient to cause a dispute that, although neither explicit nor public, was nevertheless sharp and noticeable. The parish priest Don Giovanni responded, "I'll take it up with the Madonna." But doubts about whether any man, even the religious leader of the community, could and should change the words of the Madonna were stubbornly maintained, though discretely in order not to undermine the organizational work of the Committee. With an implicit reproach, Faricy includes the original text of the message in his book and mentions that it was printed by the Committee "with some corrections" (Faricy 1986, 55–56).

René Laurentin, the most famous and authoritative supporter of a number of Marian apparitions, has had direct experience with unacceptable messages from prominent seers. He has addressed the difficulty of maintaining an equilibrium between the charisma of the seers and the institutions of the Church.

> We should not forget the relative nature of spiritual communications, marked by the particular character of different seers, according to the adage of Thomas Aquinas: "All that is received, is done so by means of the receiver (*Ad modum recipientis*)." Every seer adds something of his or her own. So it is unnecessary to conclude hastily that everything said is the word of God. (Laurentin 1986b, 25)

The need to filter messages in order to locate authentic celestial communications puts the Church back in the center of the apparitions and subordinates the charismatic possibilities of the seers. This is a decisive, not incidental, aspect of the practical construction of apparitions. Apparitions are supposedly transcendent breakthroughs in human history. In practice, they often turn out to be a new ecclesiastical resource either for use in conflicts in which the Church (or a part of the Church) is involved or to revive tired pastoral routines with a kind of theatrical evangelization. Elsewhere, I have addressed the political-ideological use of Lourdes and Fatima in the struggle between the Church and modern "errors" (Apolito 1990, 17ff.). Bax (1990) underlines for Medjugorje the strategic role of the apparitions in the conflict between Franciscans and the bishop of Mostar. For Oliveto, there was a stimulus in the religious enthusiasm and fervor produced by the apparitions in the town and in the wider area of the pilgrimages. Christian (1987) has maintained that, for Ezkioga, emphasis on certain messages bolstered the ideological defenses of religious conservatives who were headed for what looked to be violent conflict with anticlericals. In all these cases, the attentiveness, interpretation, and control of the messages become critical in the management of the new resource.

Perhaps the best example for the importance of the control of the messages is that of Medjugorje. After an initial period of benevolent attention, the bishop of Mostar, the local ordinary and, hence, the legitimate authority for ruling on the validity of the events, took a rather early position against the phenomena. The main reason was that one seer, Vicka, transmitted a message in which the Madonna supported two friars that the bishop had suspended *a divinis*; in effect saying that the bishop was in the wrong. The bishop knew the Madonna could not be the source of the messages because the Mother of the Church, as the Second Vatican Council proclaimed her, would never call into question the hierarchical authority of the institution founded by Jesus Christ. But then consider how the bishop of Split, strongly in favor of the apparitions, explains Vicka's message: "But we do not think that the Madonna said this; rather we hold this to be Vicka's interpretation. Here a human element intervenes; perhaps Vicka under the strong suggestion of a friar replaced the Madonna's words with her own thoughts" (Bertani 1986, 23).

From an ethnomethodological perspective, this opinion is very useful for revealing mechanisms that produce the meaning and the "truth" in apparitions. From the bishop of Split's interpretation, one might suppose that what this message shows would be the rule, not the exception. If this message could have been suggested to Vicka, then so could every message, including the ones accepted, published, and held to be authentic. Is the girl unable to distinguish in this instance between the voice of the Madonna and those of friars who support the two brothers punished by the bishop? Then potentially she will never be able to distinguish between voices. Who then will make these distinctions for the seer? The appointed authority that adopts the messages that are valid and rejects those that are not? And how? By what criteria will it distinguish the "human" components from the "divine" ones? Not on the basis of *external* and *objective* criteria, independent of human volition, worked out as a function of the new connection between heaven and earth. By all evidence there is a *decision* at the base of the reception of the messages. Implicitly, it is decided that authentic messages are those that reaffirm the general pastoral policy of the Church, particularly as held by religious leaders. Here one can clearly identify how the institution, in the instance of Marian apparitions, does not submit to charisma, as one might suppose, but on the contrary takes control of it in order to strengthen itself.

At Oliveto, when the parish priest could not overcome the opposition of those who were shocked by his changes in the messages, he simply dismissed it and continued his task of eliminating invalid messages and changing valid ones. There are numerous instances of this practice. As Michele once told me, the changes often served the need to standardize the literary style of the messages {June 16, 1986}. Sometimes they served to clarify a message that was hard to understand or summarize it; at other times, they served to attenuate a message's apocalyptic severity. Tommaso said, "The time available before the catastrophe is very short" (AC); here the word "catastrophe" was replaced by "chastisements" (B, r, 11), with an evident change in meaning.

The close attention that the Committee and, in particular, Don Giovanni paid to the messages doubtless derived from the institutional cultural logic that assigned to *seeing* a role of mere support for the *word*. But this attention was also due to an awareness that the messages could back up the overall strategy for directing the cult and the behavior of the pilgrims. The messages of the seers most attuned to the intentions of the Committee were often useful for the Committee's purposes. In the case of other messages, less appropriate from the Committee's point of view, its pedagogical role could justify some of the terminological changes it made. For example, the general opinion was that Don Giovanni substituted his own "he has no fear of the arrogant and the indifferent" for the phrase in Benedetta's message, "he . . . has no fear of men," in order to neutralize local opponents and agnostics by placing them directly in the divine line of fire.

Although the modification of messages was a matter for debate, their origin was never an issue. If a message passed the Committee's muster, it was certain that it came from the Madonna. The parish priest himself paid attention exclusively to the instructive possibilities of the message and cared little about other aspects. A philological study of the messages would help to understand their cultural, linguistic, and ideological sources. Some messages clearly derived from other apparitions. For example, a message of Benedetta repeated virtually word for word one from Medjugorje:

[The Devil] has become aggressive because he realizes that little by little he is losing his power and he does all he can to destroy marriages, he stirs up trouble among the Ministers of the Church, and he terrorizes and haunts people who are weak. (Benedetta in B, r, 62)

Satan has become aggressive because he is losing his power. He is destroying marriages, he is making trouble between priests and religious, and he haunts people. (*La Madonna a Medjugorje* [Cittadella: Bertoncello Artigrafiche, 1985], 94)

The replication of messages did not raise doubts as to their authenticity; at times, on the contrary, the connections were pointed to with pride. Umberto, one of the seers recognized by the parish priest Don Giovanni, emphasized to Alberto Comuzzi, the editor of the magazine *Jesus*, that the messages he received were the same as those of Vicka, the Yugoslav seer (Comuzzi 1989b, 52). In the circularity of the "matters that were incorrigible" in the context (Apolito 1990, 178)—that is, propositions that tell us not how the world is, but rather how it is described—the fact that the messages of Oliveto repeated those of Yugoslavia became a proof that they came from the Madonna. Such a proof would have a certain plausibility in a society without mass communications over long distance, supposing that the Madonna wanted to say the same thing in places widely distant and cut off from each other. But in this society, in which the Medjugorje messages arrived at Oliveto with only one or two days delay, such a notion was the result of a matter that was "incorrigible," that is to say, indisputable. In any case, in the internal dynamics of the apparition community, dispute over the manipulation of the words of the Madonna was much more useful.

In fact, the manipulation of messages was only one salient aspect of the more general manipulation of visionary experiences that systematically occurred when seers gave their testimony to the Committee, which nobody involved found disturbing. In addition to the implicit unwritten questionnaire I referred to above, the control of the vision experience was the result of the system of testifying. The interview of a seer by the Committee member on duty, which could be quite lengthy, was quickly reduced to a few lines that summarized the vision and the message. This summary would even be put in quotes, as if it were the Madonna's direct words rather than a synthesis of a seer's recollections.

Seers

The Committee considered this judicial mode of testifying essential in order to avoid its own entrapment in the fantasies delivered by dozens of seers at Oliveto. Fulvio observed sardonically that 75 percent of the "crazy" people in the area had been attracted to Oliveto and, in a more serious vein, reminded me that, a year after the first apparition, between seven hundred and one thousand persons had seen the Madonna and about fifty had spoken with her. The extraordinary accumulation of visions entailed two threats to the Committee's control: an unstoppable production of symbolic models of a visionary kind and the construction of a network of personal relations among seers and devotees that would cut out the Committee.

The first threat was dealt with through the process of official certification of testimony; the second, through a series of measures essentially aimed at preventing the development of individual charisma that might challenge the Committee's authority.

The parish priest laid down quite precise rules of behavior for seers: do not alert others to your visions with shouts or hullabaloo; do not interrupt the choral prayer; do not stop for long at the gate even when having a vision. Above all, two rules were repeated emphatically: go only to the parish priest in case of vision, without telling messages to nearby pilgrims and do not set up privileged channels of relations with believers. The latter rule was clinched by a message from the Madonna to which Don Giovanni referred when he greeted a group of pilgrims:

{5}

Do not ask the seers to ask me for favors—come to the gate and pray to me yourselves. {April 26, 1986}

The vast number of seers was a consequence of this policy of intervention. In the period of greatest enthusiasm, since no particular charismatic person served as a central point of reference who could personalize and "make physical" a mediation with the Madonna, every pilgrim was impelled to experience, in ways more or less sharp and evident, this connection for him or herself; hence, the mass visions. Clearly, this situation served the purposes of the Committee leaders better than the articulation of a charisma that would provide a seer direct and stable control of relations with pilgrims and believers.

The seers that the Committee tolerated were those who accepted its authority. Some followed the priest's instructions and refused to give the believers around them the messages that they had just received in a vision, instead referring them to the Committee office, where they would make their declarations. But some did maintain a certain influence over groups of believers, always careful not to cross the Committee. Finally, there were others, more ambitious and more disposed to become central charismatic figures, who entered into conflict with the Committee. But, little by little, these "pretenders" were shunted aside and neutralized. The replication of apparitions that, at a certain point, occurred in other towns of Campania were, among other things, an attempt on the part of some seers to escape the control of the Oliveto Committee leaders.

During the struggle between the Committee and the "trouble-making" seers, there was an increase in two kinds of communiqués from the Madonna: ambiguous messages that disapproved of the Committee's actions and messages that warned believers against "false prophets" or praised the Committee's work—for example, "the supporters [of the Committee] are doing the right thing" (message to Serena, January 26, 1986, AC).

There was one touchy period when Remo, an exuberant seer from Frattamaggiore, "invaded" Oliveto and the Committee office. Remo, an employee of the national electric company, reported that Jesus had given him the gift of automatic writing through which the Madonna, Jesus, God, Saint Paul, and other saints would routinely send messages for him and his group of followers. Especially when the priest was away from the Committee office attending to parish duties, Remo would take over as the leader of the phenomena. He passed on the credibility of visions and messages, gave advice, explained discrepancies, commented on the events, and foresaw outcomes for individuals and collective events. He even predicted the end of some seers' visions and the beginning of the visions of others whose names he alone knew and who considered him their primary point of reference. Fulvio himself came under Remo's influence, above all because a substantial number of celestial messages transmitted by the automatic writing were directed personally to him.

Don Giovanni had great difficulty in tolerating all this, but was not able to get rid of Remo completely. At the beginning of 1986, two unconfirmed prophecies of Remo led to his undoing. Through the automatic writing he foretold that Fulvio would receive the stigmata by Easter and confirmed a prophecy then circulating among many seers that by the month of March there would be three days of total darkness as a sign of God's wrath for the sins of mankind. He was wrong in both cases and lost much of his credibility. But these errors by themselves would not have been enough to cause his downfall if his opponents had not seized on them and played them up. Indeed, the prophecy of three days of darkness was published regularly in the *Bollettino* and maintained by many other seers who, nonetheless, kept their credibility. Not even the critical mistake of the prophecy about an important leader like Fulvio dealt the final blow, for other unfulfilled prophecies circulated about Fulvio from seers who did not suffer for it. The ultimate cause for Remo's demotion was his claim of preeminent leadership, and these pretexts were used to cut his charisma down to size.

It would be incorrect to assume that the parish priest and the Committee were faced with a situation that they did not know how to stop or avoid, and of which they did not approve. No, the Committee's support of the phenomena was total. My field diary for February 1, 1996, written in the thick of things, may shed light on the complicity of the Committee in the experience of mass visions.

In the Committee office is being questioned a twenty-year-old youth from Angri, Giuseppe, who evidently undergoing a "presence crisis." He contracts his facial muscles as if he has something in his throat that bothers him and he wants to vomit it out. Around him, silent, are members of the Committee and other curious onlookers. Giuseppe speaks in a very low voice and has trouble doing so. He is drenched, especially his legs, as if he had been kneeling on the wet ground. When he speaks he seems inspired, but what he says is totally banal. The Committee does not think of evaluating the psychological side of Giuseppe's experience, but focuses on a single precise objective: to obtain the message of the Madonna. In order to do so it must separate those phrases in which Giuseppe expresses his own opinion from those dictated by the Madonna. They constantly ask him whether he or the Madonna is the source of what he is saying. He always answers that what he is saying does not come from him, but does not say where it comes from. Giuseppe wants to go back to the castle and goes off with two friends.

Then a female seer is questioned, a weeping teenager, also soaked, who says she saw, beyond the gate, the Madonna who wore a white or a blue dress—she cannot recall which—with gold bands that adorned her dress, with gloves or black hands; the Madonna was weeping. But, she specifies, she did not see the details clearly, just a "all pink." How she could see the tears if she could not see the details, no one asks. The girl is sent off after she signs her declaration, and Giuseppe returns. He seems to have gotten over his crisis and speaks more easily and willingly. He picks up a Bible on the table and flips through it until he gets to a passage in Matthew about the end of the world. Then he mutters that God comes first and that many neglect him because they think too much about the Madonna.

At this point, Don Giovanni reacts, says he does not agree, that love for the Madonna draws people closer to God. From then on Don Giovanni becomes very suspicious of the youth. [. . .] Giuseppe continues to talk and maintains that often at apparition sites people are making money. This assertion sets off a hermeneutic argument, which the lad swiftly resolves by declaring that this does not occur at Oliveto. [. . .] He claims his experience was not "technically" a vision, although, with his eyes closed, he did experience in his stomach a sensation of clarification, a kind of interior illumination. And he can elaborate that when he says he sees colors, it was not with his eyes, but in his stomach. The fact is that he does not say right off that he has seen or heard the Madonna—indeed he made that distinction about the love of God—but rather his experience consists in having heard with clarity and strength things that he knew already, but which he believed little or not at all. This goes for the gospel verses about the end of the world, for the generic charges he levels at the world and at mankind—hypocritical, mean-spirited, etc. But the desire for messages from the Madonna is so strong that the Committee in the end will have him sign a message from the Madonna. [. . .]

When a member of the Committee, a doctor, asks a critical question, "But how do you know it was the Madonna who spoke to you," Don

Giovanni intervenes, "Oh no, stop right there; I could just as well ask, how can you be sure it was *not* the Madonna." [. . . When he leaves] someone in the Committee says that he wanted to "look good" in front of his friends in Catholic Action, of which he is a leader, and another says that this time he wanted to pull rank over Don Giovanni, since he is normally under the authority of the clergy. But, nevertheless, his declarations are considered valid. Giulia, responding to the general skepticism that arose after the doctor expressed serious doubts about the youth, says that in any case there must be something to it. Then Don Giovanni concludes that the doctor is the typical skeptic, and she is the typical credulous female. (Field diary, February 1, 1986)

The alternation and the overlapping of doubt and trust did not hinder the constructive enterprise of visions in which seers, Committee, believers, and parish priest all played their part.

Cult

The third sphere of the Committee's intervention, also fundamental, involves the control of the cult of the Madonna of the apparitions. Here, too, the main obstacle came from the "Neapolitan" seers. Whenever one of them had a perceptual experience of any kind—and this happened a lot—she or he would shout or vigorously get the attention of those nearby and sometimes of the entire plaza. A *strong* experience of vision, then, often would lead to fainting and a state of *trance*. Apart from other adverse effects on the non-"Neapolitan" pilgrims, these extroverted practices made it impossible to continue the collective prayer, Rosary, or hymn in progress. For this situation as well, Don Giovanni laid down strict rules for behavior: do not indulge in excessive gestures, do not weep or scream, and avoid excess of any kind. A sign was then placed at the top of the steps: "Seers given to fainting cannot go up to the gate." Seers knew that when the priest was around they could not let themselves go. After a while, those delegated to maintain order were instructed to repress quickly and without hesitation any episodes of agitated visions; especially at first, this resulted in sharp friction with some believers.

When he addressed groups of pilgrims, Don Giovanni often dwelled on this point. On one such occasion he said:

{6}

I would like to ask those of you who are privileged to see the Madonna
+ not to disturb the prayers because—the Madonna has asked for
prayer—prayer—prayer + if you see the Madonna—see her on your
own—thank her + and if there are any messages tell us afterward—you
should tell them to us—and do so before going off and speaking to this
person—or that one—you should speak with the priest + he is the one
in charge of . . . + so when you see the Madonna—don't go attracting
attention in the middle of the plaza—because if you do this you will not
please the Madonna. {January 18, 1986}

Soon a large number of messages from the Madonna came to support the
Committee's position. In a message of Ubaldo, the Madonna entertained the
Committee's desire for a line of pilgrims that moved smoothly past the gate:
"The last thing the Madonna told me to do was to let the priest know that the
people who were at the gate should stay there for a short time only so others
can have the chance to see her" (AC, December 27, 1985).

Other messages published in the *Bollettino* sought to eliminate the
extroverted piety of the "Neapolitans." One message attributed to the
Madonna the request for "a silent and heartfelt prayer" (B, r, 44); another
instructed, "When you come to this holy place do not cry out; pray in
silence" (B, r, 55). A month later, a new message reiterated, "You should
remain in silence and pray" (B, r, 66).

One episode typifies the acceptance of the request for discipline by the
Committee and the Madonna. A female seer told of hearing "a very sweet
voice that asked me to go up toward the gate." But she did not move: "In
order not to disturb the prayer, I did not go up at once, but only after I
finished praying." Obviously, the seer was bearing in mind the instructions
of either the Committee or the Madonna not to disturb the prayer. Indeed,
when the woman reached the gate she feared she "would not hear Her any
more," and when instead she realized that the Madonna was still there, she
hastened to say, "I ask your pardon for not coming out at once, but I did it
in order not to disturb the prayer." The Madonna showed that she was
pleased: "Thank you, daughter, you did the right thing" (B, r, 57).

The pious extroverts responded to these restrictions by having vision
experiences, especially of a *weak* kind (vague, indefinite sightings), in the
side streets of the neighborhood, away from the plaza, the Committee office,

the Committee loudspeaker, and the group prayers. To counter their response, Don Giovanni reported in his talk, cited above, of January 18, 1986,
a message from the Madonna that "she is to be found in the place where she
normally appears." A woman seer told me later that the Madonna was upset
because of the "error" of the pilgrims who were moving out away from the
plaza.

In order to discourage the uncontrollable experiences of collective visions, the Committee imposed a rhythm of continuous prayer that rendered
difficult the collectivization of the vision because of the attention that the
prayer demanded. Evening after evening the pauses between the fifteen
mysteries of the Rosary and its hymn were shortened. For indeed, it was in
these pauses that the collective phenomena unfailingly occurred, facilitated
by cries and shouts in the absence of prayers.

The Committee fulfilled its objectives with the *ritualization* of the presence in the plaza, which eliminated any room for religious and visionary
creativity. Every pilgrimage that turned up at Oliveto thus encountered a
fixed organization and itinerary. Upon arrival in the plaza, a prayer was
always in progress that was necessary to join. Pilgrims would line up to file
past the apparition gate, where those in charge of order gruffly prevented a
prolonged stop even of those having visions. I tape-recorded an exchange
between one of the guards, implacable in the line of duty, and a male seer.

{7}

(1) mv guard: You see the Madonna?
(2) seer: Yes.
(3) mv guard: Then come back around and see her again.
(4) mv 1:   [who did not catch the brusque tone of mv] He sees
               her? He sees her?
(5) mv guard: Yeah, and if he sees her—he comes back around and
               sees the Madonna again. {March 15, 1986}

Finally, the group of pilgrims stopped at the Committee office to give
testimony and pick up copies of the bulletin. Only on the rare occasions
when no member of the Committee was present could there be episodes of
untrammeled religious excitement.

Within two years of the beginning of the apparitions, Oliveto had become
a discrete and subdued place of pilgrimage, little different from any other

Church-approved pilgrimage site in Campania, such as the shrines of the Madonna of Pompeii or San Gerardo di Materdomini. No longer was there collective religious enthusiasm. Only individual visionaries remained, those who adopted the requisite manners, places, and times for telling what they saw. Even if what they reported was quite interesting in its religious creativity, it had to be discreet and in accord with the Committee's objectives of ritual discipline.

Once the resistance of the extroverted pilgrims was overcome, the messages did not return to themes related to the control of the cult but rather dwelt on the kind of spiritual attitude one should have when approaching the gate, again following the new, more properly spiritual, preoccupations of the Committee. A message on January 17, 1988:

> Do not hurry through prayer after prayer [. . .]. It would be very nice if down below, before going up to the gate, you purified your soul with a good examination of conscience so that you left there all the dross that renders your soul impure; pray down there and then come up to me with a little more silence even in your prayers. (B 12, 17)

Immersed in the everyday details of the administration of the apparitions, the Committee was of necessity involved in the conflicts that the apparitions produced. For a considerable period it had ten to fifteen members, most of them young. But then some began to drop out. Although the parish priest was always the undisputed leader, given his role as the spiritual head of the town, there were internal disputes within the Committee in which he, too, participated. Members had difficulty reconciling their views on the direction to give the events: some felt a more organic connection to the unpredictable visionary world of the seers, while others were above all disturbed by its heterodox potential. Some wanted to allow the seers more leeway, while others, in agreement with the priest, worked to establish a ceremony that would thwart the seers' uncontrolled enthusiasm. At one point there was a spate of gossip between some Committee members and outsiders that led to friction within the Committee, and some members withdrew for varying lengths of time. The arrival in Oliveto of Luigi Gaspari, a disciple of Padre Pio, encouraged in some youths on the Committee a kind of mysticism at odds with the pragmatism of Don Giovanni. Two of those close to Gaspari resigned because, they wrote in a letter, "We consider that [the Committee's] exclusively administrative function is, at this point, absolutely limiting."

They felt the Committee should be working to convert the pilgrims. Finally, there arose disagreements over what to do with the money that pilgrims contributed for the construction of the chapel requested by the apparition. Some influential members of the Committee dropped out for good.

In spite of the attempts to keep secret the more or less irremediable differences that emerged within the Committee, some things leaked out, and seers began to bring in messages that commented on the Committee's internal affairs. Giovanni reported that the Madonna foresaw "a period of great suffering and that afterwards calm would return" (AC, February 16, 1986); on the same occasion, he said she ordered him "to tell the Committee that what should stand out was not EGO but GOD." On May 15, Tommaso reported a more alarming message: "From now on Satan will persecute you every moment of your lives. So when you feel that there are disagreements among you, pray with all your heart; only then will I be able to come and help you" (AC). Another undated handwritten sheet by Tommaso was even more dramatic:

> In front of the gate, the figure of the Madonna appeared to me and told me that if what happened this afternoon in the Committee was supposed to have anything to do with her, it would be better in the future that no photographs be taken that involved her (?). Then she told me that Mrs. . . . was weeping and that she did not want the woman to weep because every person is her child and not to worry because it is the Devil who typically meddles in things.

PROTAGONISTS AND INSTRUMENTS
IN THE CREATION OF THE
WORLD OF THE APPARITIONS

Sources of the Sacred

AS WE HAVE SEEN, the process of symbolic production in Oliveto was not neutral. It involved social forces and preexisting spheres of conflict and established or contested domains of power. The cultural "work" that began in the summer of 1985 in Oliveto had to do, above all, with the hermeneutics of both the presence and the language of the Madonna, based on what Umberto Eco defines as the "symbolic mode," that is, a "semantic-pragmatic attitude" (Eco 1981, 881).

> [It is] a procedure not necessarily of production and always using a text, which can be applied to every text and every kind of sign, by means of a pragmatic decision ("I wish to interpret symbolically") that produces

on the semantic level a new function of signs, associating with expressions already endowed with codified content new amounts of content, as much as possible indeterminate and decided by the recipient. (Ibid., 911)

One particular aspect of the symbolic mode is most germane to the Oliveto situation.

In mystical experience the material to be assigned a symbolic expression is to a certain extent suggested by tradition and by some *auctoritas*, and the interpreter is persuaded (*should* be persuaded) that these are not cultural matters, but *referents*, aspects of an extrasubjective and extracultural verity. (Ibid., 911–12)

Tradition and *auctoritas*[1] are two concepts central to interpretive conflict and its analysis. Clusters of *auctoritas*, however unstable and provisional, make possible the production of meanings and the crystallization of the *history* of the apparitions. The meaning or facts produced by the Committee did not always win out. While the *auctoritas* of the Committee was crucial, it was not exclusive. Other *auctoritates* regarding the form of the Madonna and what she said rose and fell in the course of the collective visions. While the vision content approved by the Committee was central, other possible content took shape nearby that contributed in a disorderly and haphazard manner to the production of a general sense of mobility, to the perception that the content was not definitive because the apparitions were not yet over. This alternative content rendered it impossible for the Committee to transform completely the spontaneous enthusiasm of the visions into a fixed ritual and cultural tradition.

The Committee, which focused on the collective process, tried to fix and delimit the hermeneutic procedure of discerning signs in order to determine a profile of the apparition that was *definite*, as well as an identity for it that was fixed and circumscribed. The fluctuating collective hermeneutic work, in contrast, was based on assertions such as "I think," "I heard," "It is as if,"

---

1. The author uses *auctoritas* (pl. *auctoritates*) to mean authority recognized for delimiting, defining, verifying, and legitimating perceptions and interpretations. *Auctoritas*, in his sense, may be well established, like that of the Catholic Church for its followers, or be ad hoc and temporary, like that briefly established in a casual conversation.

"I saw it this way—how about you?" It enormously enriched a profile of the Madonna that was *possible*, but which risked heterodoxy.

The Committee was the center that *decided* the correct aspect and proper signs of the Madonna, delineating the official profile of the apparition. It approved and reduced, objectivized in legitimate terms, the collective work. When the *Bollettino* reported the signs of the apparition, it often distinguished between the "language of images" and "messages." It seemed to be working on one level to pin down the physical-corporeal aspects of the Madonna, and on another to pin down her use of language in order to arrive at a precise and expert evaluation of the Marian presence. The goal was to be able to say *this* is the way the Madonna appears; and *that* is the way she speaks and what she says. As a rule, the leaders tended to modify substantially the Madonna's physical appearance in order to fit traditional and generic stereotypes and give exclusive priority to messages that fit the ongoing story of the events.

But the procedures for a collective definition of the apparitions were more complex than the members of the Committee imagined. These procedures emerged, with varying degrees of efficacy, from three different sources: (1) the examination and filter of the Committee; (2) basic symbolic material drawn from the descriptions of complex visions given by the *strong* seers— the seers most important and "prolific"; and, (3) collective visions that were *weak*—those that were unclear, simple, worked out in the crowds near the castle, and often not specified in precise testimony but that constituted the interpretive humus for the signs ratified by the Committee.

All the constitutive procedures, whether those of the Committee or others, gradually took as a common point of reference not the traditional religious culture of *normal* times but rather the version of official Catholicism constructed through worldwide visionary phenomena. Lourdes, Fatima, and Medjugorje became the paradigms of reference for all the participants in the Oliveto apparitions. As in other famous and not-so-famous apparitions, what happened in the places where the Madonna had appeared inevitably became the most legitimate, available, and germane source of the sacred and thereby the measure of the truth of what was happening at Oliveto Citra.

The constitutive procedures that were unofficial—basically those not supervised by the Committee or, in particular, the parish priest—had another effective reference point in the practices of popular Catholicism that were once valid and legitimate from the official perspective but which the Church now actively opposed. Above all, at the beginning, when it was unclear what was happening, there was immediate recourse to traditional symbolic explanations. The Committee itself was not entirely immune to these explanations.

At Lourdes, after an initial skepticism due to a fear that her daughter was fibbing and would make the family a laughing-stock (Carroll 1985, 67), Bernadette's mother began to think that the apparition was a soul in Purgatory (Estrade 1934, 66). A neighbor, who from the start took seriously Bernadette's description of her vision, noticed that what Bernadette said she saw corresponded exactly to that of Elisa Latapie, head of the Daughters of Mary, who had died a few months before, at the age of twenty-eight (Ibid., 68). Hence, the first explanations proposed for the perceptual experience of Bernadette were drawn from the traditional and contemporary symbolism of the souls in Purgatory. On the heels of Bernadette's visions there were other visions by other seers, many of which were folkloric representations of the Devil (Ibid., 190–202).

Similarly, at Ezkioga, where there was a powerful tradition of apparitions of the dead, one of the first seers thought she saw a soul in Purgatory (Christian 1987, 154). At Banneux, in Belgium in 1933, the mother of a seer thought what appeared was a witch (Mantero 1987, 19).

In keeping with the oral traditions of all of southern Italy, the people at Oliveto told about processions of the dead in the very place where the apparitions occurred. Furthermore, there had previously appeared a woman dressed in black, who was considered an ancient inhabitant of the Oliveto castle. At first, some considered the apparitions of 1985 as the return of the woman in black.

At Kibeho in Rwanda, the schoolmates of one of the seer girls thought that the visions were the result of "sorcery worked by spirits," an idea that took hold because the seer came "from a region famous for the belief in spirits and their powers for evil" (Maindron 1984, 39). I could add many other examples to confirm that, at the beginning of an apparition, the "Greek chorus" (to use Christian's metaphor) turns to the symbolic repertory most close at hand to explain the unusual events that have interrupted everyday life. Even in the period in which the events were being structured, reference to this repertory continued. At Medjugorje, for example, an entire preexisting tradition of popular medicine connected to poultices of plants and flowers mixed with earth was revived and found new efficacy through the phenomena of the apparitions.

For eleven years, Cvija Kuzman had suffered from polyarthritis.

On the eve of feast of the Assumption, August 15, 1981, she climbed the hill of the apparitions, She carried with her a little soil. With that soil, mixed with water, her daughter massaged her three or four times, reciting seven Our Fathers, Hail Marys, and Gloria Patris, and a Credo. And she was completely cured. (Juarez 1987, 164)

And:

Bozica Susac, from Liubuski, long had an open wound on her chest. The doctors had been unable to heal it. She took a little grass from the apparition hill and, with the water in which she had ground the grass, she washed the wound. Two or three days later the wound healed, and it has not returned. (Ibid., 165–66)

And:

Anda Maric, from Sinj, had an accident. Cutting corn tassels, she hurt an eye, and with that eye she could see no more. What is more, it hurt a great deal. She did not want to go to the doctor. Her husband went to Medjugorje. He brought some grass from the apparition hill. Anda washed her eye with the water in which the grass had been ground, and prayed. She quickly regained her sight, so she says, and the pain disappeared. (Ibid., 168)

It would be a mistake, however, to think that these symbolic levels provided a structure for the events as they evolved. Their use at the outset enabled people to fill the void of meaning that inevitably occurs when someone says they have had celestial visions. In this way, at least the person is not labeled as crazy or accused of fraud. But later, when the phenomenon is legitimated by institutional levels of society, folkloric symbolism is no longer taken seriously and is pushed to the margins of accounts and their interpretation. Their potential as sources for the sacred is reduced; if they remain "in the air," they are transformed, neutralized, and rendered opaque, their identity denied.

The episodes of healing at Medjugorje are cited by most authors with no acknowledgment of their folkloric level, but simply as evidence of the prodigious quality of the apparitions. Indeed, when a hagiographer suspects an "other" cultural level, he or she immediately expunges this aspect and translates it into safer terms. For example, Mantero describes a healing practice based on a washing of an ailing part of the body with water mixed with earth and flowers from the apparition hill at Medjugorje and comments: "When she did this it was not superstition or magic, but all the simple faith that a mother could manifest for the love of a son struck by a tragic misfortune whose life is in danger" (Mantero 1987, 136).

Yet the symbolic folkloric levels do not disappear altogether; they merely lose visibility and transparency, even when they participate in the constitution of the symbolic adhesive that constitutes the *context* of the phenomena. This is proven indirectly: when an apparition is condemned by a Church authority, these aspects come to the fore again. Christian shows how the ideology of relations with the dead was very strong between the seers and their supporters at Ezkioga, but there was little trace of this in the Catholic press because the press and the clergy who favored the apparitions did not consider this aspect positive. But as soon as the apparitions were rejected by Church authorities, visions of the dead "bloomed forth in print," for at that point the press began to attack what up until then it had been supporting (Christian 1987, 155), rendering visible unacceptable aspects that until then had remained hidden.

The Supernatural Experiment

Once the terms of the intersubjective construction of an objective situation—how the *events* were *produced* by persons—have been clarified, we may proceed to analyze these events, thus avoiding at least two kinds of misapprehension.

One has to do with the confusion of the "object" of research with its "resources," something ethnomethodologists criticized in the "contemporary sociology" of the 1960s. I have examined this aspect in detail in *"It Is Said They Have Seen the Madonna."* In that study I did not use reconstructions of the apparition "event" furnished by the protagonists as the "object of the research," but rather I used them as "resources for the research" in order to identify the processes and practices by which a consensus was constructed that permitted a sense of certainty as to the "events" of the apparitions.

A second misapprehension is evident in what I call "the supernatural experiment." A good portion of believers as well as skeptics generally try to find an *experimental* verification of a *physical* basis for the phenomena. Indeed, if the "events" are produced by persons, in terms of the conferring of meaning, and people thereby enter the arena of the production of symbols, "the objective situation" is not independent of experimental evaluation. On the contrary, it is constituted by this kind of evaluation. The phenomena are not *external* to the persons involved. In this context, Ernesto De Martino pointed the way when he commented on attempts by parapsychologists to measure the objectivity of magical powers. In the process, they ignored the historicity of the magical phenomena—their human and cultural component, their subjectivist specificity—and attributed a *givenness* to something that in fact was a symbolic construction.

> In order to prove them one would have to take the phenomena as givens, whereas their nature is precisely that they are still in the realm of human decision and therefore are "a-legal" or "multi-legal," given the free-floating mixture of representations, affects, and human intentions. (De Martino 1973, 69)

Clara Gallini has pointed to an analogous situation in the attempt by nineteenth-century positivists to reduce the symbolic domain of "magnetism" to naturalistic fact, an attempt that produced as a byproduct other, newer, symbolic forms. "But the 'mysticism of the fact'—the absolutization of the image of science—could only lead to involution: to the return of otherworldly phantoms, to the evocation of the souls of the dead called to appear with the consent of the scientists" (Gallini 1983a, 215).

At Medjugorje, and to a lesser extent at Oliveto, there were a number of experiments on the psychic states of the seers and on their *trances*. These tests, involving as they did psychic "data," did not completely eliminate the subjectivity that, in some ways, is inherent in this kind of testing procedure. Subsequent experiments sought to evaluate other kinds of "givenness" in the kinds of phenomena associated with the Medjugorje apparitions. I refer in particular to efforts to verify the presence of and measure the amount of "spiritual energy" in the apparition chamber. A Polish-American doctor named Lipinski brought to Medjugorje an apparatus he called "Spiritual Energy," with which he recorded the presence of radioactivity at levels much greater than normal, 100,000 millirads. From this he deduced the presence of a powerful spiritual energy (Sala and Mantero 1986, 71–73).

Lipinski was effectively, if unintentionally, proposing a naturalistic reduction of the "spiritual" to physical data.

These experiments were challenged by the Genovese scientist Emanuele Mor, "doctor in physics, director of the Institute for the Study of Marine Corrosion of Metals, of the National Research Center (the only institute of its kind in Italy and among the most important in Europe)" (Ibid., 95). According to Mor, write Sala and Mantero, "Lipinski's research, although it is very interesting, is superficial to the extent that it does not define all the relations between positive and negative ions. The Genovese physicist, thanks to new intuitions, is endeavoring to improve this kind of scientific approach" (Ibid., 71).

Indeed, Mor performed tests after Lipinski's that led him to assert that there was no spiritual radioactivity. Based on Mor's tests, the theologian René Laurentin asserted that Lipinski's hypothesis of measurable spiritual energy appeared to be "illusory and unscientific." In fact, Mor subsequently measured an ionization of the air ten times greater than normal. The Italian physicist did not challenge testing of the supernatural but simply suggested it be done with better instruments that would open "new areas for scientific investigation into the mysteries of the supernatural" (Laurentin 1986a, 179).

At Oliveto, we do not find a debate of this kind. But we do find the idea, common in the visionary culture, of scientific testing of the supernatural. In issue 14 of the *Bollettino*, an anonymous article questioned the assertions by scientists, based on Carbon 14 testing, that the Holy Shroud of Turin is a forgery no older than the thirteenth century. The author pointed out that Carbon 14 dating is based on the measurement of radioactivity. But,

> we all know from gospel accounts that Jesus' resurrection was flashing and dazzling etc. . . . Hence, rich in (radioactive?) energy. [. . .] Can one be certain that the resurrective event did not add to the Holy Shroud a measure of radioactivity that would distort the result of the test? (B 14, 24–25)

Hence, the Resurrection is viewed as a kind of nuclear explosion that gave off enough radioactivity, which throws off the analysis.

The "oddness" of this propensity to test the supernatural is significant. (Here I use "oddness" in the same way that ethnomethodologists refer to reality that is an effect of common sense as "anthropologically odd.") In all the locations of contemporary apparitions there is an abundance of tests, empirical proofs, "objective" demonstrations, and medical-scientific investigations, ranging from those using machines and gauges, on the order of Lipinski and Mor, to others that are more improvised. In a way, the "weak" perceptions of devout spectators also serve as tests—the perfumes, rays of light, currents of air, and so on, that they notice when a seer is having an encounter with the Madonna. These spectators have in common with those more "scientifically" prepared the desire for objective "data." The "positive" results of these experiments are offered by supporters as some of the most important reasons for holding the phenomena to be true.

One is taken back to the sessions of spiritism in the nineteenth century, which "pretended to demonstrate positively, with data, the existence of the afterlife" (Gallini 1983a, 59). In reality, the neopositivistic attempt to prove scientifically the truth of apparitions demonstrates the weakness of the ideology that produced them, and leads unwittingly to the same dead end as nineteenth-century magnetism. Clara Gallini shows how magnetism demonstrated its weakness in its confrontation with the scientific culture of the time by adopting its methods and instruments.

> The magnetist seeks to borrow from physical and natural sciences the experimental method for the verification of facts, which makes their replicability the basis for the discovery of the laws that underlie them [. . .] the terms of the context for the conferral of a meaning can only be those dictated by the more powerful kind of knowledge: truth or falsehood, the sole discriminatory criteria. (Ibid., 57–58)

In contemporary visionary culture, there is a widespread dependency on the scientific cultural code, which people consider quite powerful and to which they look for legitimation of the vision events. Such an attitude is quite distant from the often antiscientific climate of nineteenth-century apparitions, which, in contrast to magnetism, did not try to find an external legitimation. In 1872, the anonymous author of "The Miracle and Our Lady of Lourdes," which appeared in *La Civiltà Cattolica*, reacted to a provocative invitation of Ernest Renan. Renan suggested a commission of physiologists, physicists, chemists, and historians be named to examine the proper conditions for a miracle in which a dead person would be resuscitated, in order to arrive at a correct scientific opinion. The anonymous author commented: "Does human pride so rebel against the Omnipotent? And does he pretend to call Him down to his court, to pass judgment on his work, to test marvels according to his own whim?" ("Il miracolo e nostra Signora di Lourdes," *La Civiltà Cattolica* 23, no. 7 [1872]: 641–57).

Typical of this attitude is the diocesan policy in regard to miracles at Lourdes. It first became known that miracles were happening at Lourdes in 1862, four years after the apparitions there. Bishop Laurence of Tarbes, the ordinary, authenticated the apparitions and approved the findings of his commission, which had proven, in addition to the heroic testimony expressed in Bernardette's life and the conversion of masses of pilgrims, the miraculous nature of seven cures. It is significant that "the hearings on the cures were run by a subcommission headed by Canon Baradère. The clergy who comprised it took on the task of deciding on the historical truth and discerning supernatural origins, with tasks that were not only theological, but also properly scientific" (Locatelli 1979, 13 n. 3). Hence, the truth of the miracle was, at the dawn of the Lourdes phenomenon, entirely in the hands of Church authorities, who had undertaken "tasks that were not only theological, but also properly scientific."

This first judgment was not to be the only one. Indeed, Bishop Laurence, "who in his youth was interested in medicine, took the opportunity to obtain a qualified scientific opinion and personally invited Dr. Vergez, a professor on the faculty of Medicine of Montpellier, to give his judgment" (Ibid.). The report of the doctor agreed only partially with that of the diocesan commission. What is especially noteworthy, however, is that Dr. Vergez divided the cases into three categories, the first of which he called "cases that possess fully and in an evident manner a supernatural character" (Ibid.). Locatelli, a professor of theology in Milan, commented:

> Today a man of science would limit himself to declaring simply whether a cure is explicable or not from a clinical point of view. Then, as we see, the line of demarcation between the business of the clergy and that of scientists was certainly less clear than it is today. In any case, in spite of this uncertainty, the episcopal commission considered, finally, the verdict of scientific knowledge of the time, and reached the conclusion it did. (Ibid.)

In fact, things happened differently. The ecclesiastical authority decided a cure was miraculous or less so, referring to its own system of knowledge, theological categories, and categories from the religious world. Medical knowledge, when it was used, was co-opted into the religious jurisdiction and kept in that realm. In the case of Dr. Vergez's intervention in the field of unusual cures, medical knowledge moved into the discourse of theology, nullifying the autonomy of its own conceptual categories and taking the religious jurisdiction as the model for its own interpretation; hence, a *medical* conclusion that was an abdication of medicine as to the *supernaturalness* of the cure. The ideological religious context, in the wake of the apparitions of Lourdes, was oriented by the First Vatican Council, according to which "humanarum artium et disciplinarum cultura" should lead to God "scientiarum Domino" ("Esame critico dell storia del conflitto fra la religione et la scienza di Guglielmo Draper," *La Civiltà Cattolica* 28, no. 2 [1877]: 298–313).

It is noteworthy, finally, that the Bureau des Constatations Médicales, the medical board dedicated to the scientific evaluation of the miraculous cures at Lourdes, was not established until the twenty-fifth anniversary of the apparitions, and only then because "of the need to refute the apriorist criticisms and malevolent insinuations of antireligious and anticlerical circles" (Locatelli 1979, 18). It was established, that is to say, in 1883, in a climate of increasing defensiveness regarding scientistic ideology. But even then the Church did not relinquish its preeminence but rather bent medicine, at least devout medicine, to its ideological frame of reference. *Lourdes, Histoire médicale*, by Gustave Boissarie, the director of the Bureau, was published in 1891. If, until then, publications on the miracles of Lourdes had all been

> edifying stories that might make references to medicine but did not make these references their central point [. . .], with the *Histoire médicale*, the medical discourse becomes central and leads the reader into a world in which malady and healing are drastically broken down and reduced to mere physical signs that only a clinical observation has the right to decipher in order, subsequently, *to admit its own impotence and trust to the final reasoning of religion and miracle*. (Gallini 1990a, 113, my italics)

Given this background, one might be surprised at the increasingly common testing of the supernatural at apparition sites, for it seems to propose a new kind of dependence on science for wonders; in fact, things are more complex. In any case, believers take a variety of postures: from a certain skepticism toward scientism (in the case of Laurentin) to more optimism about the possibilities for scientific evaluation (from experimenters in the field like Lipinski, Mor, and many others) to those who truly expect that science will demonstrate the supernatural. But all these positions—and this distinguishes the visionary culture from magnetism—reject the principle of replicability for extraordinary phenomena (for a miracle is by definition a gratuitous act of the divine that cannot be predicted), yet at the same time they accept experimental verification. Consequently, there emerges a third protagonist, not clearly perceived, that we may term the "technological."

There are those in the visionary culture who, on principle, propose a return to the preeminence of religious authority, thereby recovering the character of *signs* that turn-of-the-century positivists overlooked with their objectivist analysis of data. The signs in question were obviously not the cultural ones that Gallini criticizes the magnetists for ignoring but rather signs from heaven. René Laurentin writes:

> The polarization of the official reports of the *wonders* is so strong that it [. . .] has diverted attention from the *signs*, centering exclusively on the *wondrous* aspect that, if misunderstood, becomes detached from the *sign* aspect. The recognition of a "miracle" as a sign of divine intervention is no longer a matter for medical doctors, but for the Church, which judges it by the religious context and the fruits it produces. (Laurentin and Lejeune 1988a, 62)

Contrary to what one might suppose, this represents anything but a return to religion divorced from science, something that would be anachronistic and "unthinkable." Rather, it is a call for autonomy, which in any case appears to be in accord with the way science itself is developing.

> The science of today is less ideological, less pretentious, less absolute, less hasty in saying "A miracle is impossible." It begins with statistical arguments in terms of probability, including the physical sciences. Today's science has renounced absolutism. It integrates the concepts of relativity, uncertainty coefficients (Heisenberg), and conclusions in statistical or probability terms. (Laurentin and Lejeune 1988a, 65)

Professor Gildo Spaziante, medical director of the Istituti Clinici di Perfezionamento of the University of Milan, takes a similar position.

Today absolute determinism is powerfully tempered by the stochastic interpretation of phenomena at all levels of reality in the cosmos. The appearance of exceptional events does not *per se* contradict the order of known natural law which, instead of a rigid immutable "fixity," more and more tends to allow for a dynamic, variable, and changing reality open to evolution, novelty, and unpredictability. (Spaziante 1988, 282)

By this logic, science allows as possible (hence, literally normal), exceptional events in a nondeterministic order. Thus it is ultimately powerless to make any judgment on miracles. How could one possibly deny that the exceptions could be miracles? Any science that speaks of "exceptional events" is stymied when it comes to denying the attribute "miraculous."

From this perspective, as soon as contemporary science legitimates the possibility of miracles, the Church takes over. In a scientific system so open to wonders, religion can safely return to *making decisions* about the miraculous and theological strategies can take precedence over scientific ones that have "statistically" or "stochastically" unraveled their own rules. Evidently this approach does not seek to de-legitimize science. While it does severely limit the possibility of scientific intervention, it also finds new ways for science to encounter religion. But on what basis?—that offered by the third protagonist, the "technological."

In fact, this supposed meeting of science and religion, which seems to strengthen the latter, leads to a reorganization of both by means of the technologization of miracles. The devout posture that holds a scientific idea of the world in which exceptional events are *possible* expects evidence that events have actually *occurred* that one can eventually label as miraculous. Hence, they expect evaluation. The result is the aseptic listing of experimental tests as mere technological procedures that prove the supernatural.

Consider what Laurentin notes in his chronicle of events at Medjugorje for June 16, 1986.

Professors E. D. Mor and P. Ameglio, radiation experts, begin to test the ion density at Medjugorje. There is a notable density of positive ions on the order of 1000, and negative ions on the order of 700 ions/cm3 in the apparition chamber, without there being a significant change at the moment of the apparition. It is as if two distinct sources of positive and negative ions kept this phenomenon constant and continuous. Other

studies are being carried out to place this as yet unexplained phenomenon in a wider context. (Laurentin 1986a, 189)

The test found unexplained ionization in the place where the Madonna had
appeared. Contrary to what one might suppose, there was no expectation of
proper scientific explanations, which would only affirm something plausible
in the context of scientific knowledge of the *natural world*, and hence would
contradict the hope or cause for the ionization that was *supernatural*. If a
plausible scientific explanation for the phenomena was proposed, the entire
construct of the experimental verification of the existence of the apparitions
would collapse.

Consider the way Laurentin asks for help in the examination of facts about
prodigies of the sun: "I have collected abundant material on it (date,
testimonies, pictures, video cassettes) and I am waiting for a team of
specialists, both competent and *open to the supernatural*, who would be able
to exercise a judicious judgment on the matter" (Laurentin and Lejeune
1988a, 69, my italics). The wonders require tests that will confirm them as
wonders but not insert them in the framework of general scientific knowledge. Even more explicitly, Laurentin asks the doctors who pronounce on
prodigious cures to stop using the phrase, "unexplainable in the present
state of science," but rather to declare "in what sense this cure is unusual,
extraordinary, prodigious" (Laurentin and Lejeune 1988a, 61–62; 1988b,
64). The doctors and scientists are asked to speak directly about the
exceptional event as prodigious. They are not asked, therefore, for a
scientific *explanation* but rather a certification of the miraculous, the same
thing that Dr. Vergez provided at Lourdes. Hence the unusual absolute value
attributed to the test—detached from a framework of scientific thinking—is
expected to verify the supernatural. It is clearly requested to evaluate a *state*
of the world of the prodigy, not to furnish dynamic material for scientific
explanation.

In this regard, let us consider the test that Dr. Stopar once applied at
Medjugorje. While the seers were having visions, Stopar placed himself in
front of Marija in order to determine whether she could see under these
conditions. Afterward, he told Marija about it: "'Today you saw nothing. I
was between you and her.' She answered: 'Oh, that's why I saw her today as
though through a slight fog'" (Laurentin 1988d, 32–33).

It might appear that Stopar's test, which records one state of the world of
the prodigy, could become normative because it could certify that "when a

man is interposed between the Madonna and a seer, there is created, without the seer knowing, much less desiring it, a thin haze." From this observation might not one then extract a scientific hypothesis on the order of "always when. . . ."?

In fact, this test could never permit the formulation of a rule of this kind. Indeed, another test showed, on the contrary, that a blindfold "did not impede the visionaries from seeing the apparition" (Laurentin 1986a, 144). Note that this inconsistency is not the result of a confusion due to overlapping voices. In both instances it is Laurentin, the prominent theologian and most authoritative supporter of the apparitions, who speaks. The result is paradoxical. The test, completely blind and "dumb" since it is outside of any framework of hypothesis or scientific mode of verification (how might one take as a hypothesis the presence of the Madonna, and how might one verify it according to scientific principles of knowledge of the world?) shows one time X and another, under the same conditions, Y.

It is evident that the prodigy test is not a laboratory procedure for scientific knowledge but rather the *staging* of an experimental verification of a supernatural prodigy. It seems to certify the *existence* of a supernatural event but in fact creates the event, providing it with both a phenomenology and a statute that are *local*. By local I mean that the fact certified cannot be extrapolated to scientifically verifiable general circumstances because, as we have seen, the test at one moment contradicts an analogous test at another moment. The test thus serves to show that the prodigy does not constitute a blatant anomaly for scientific reasoning, not because science explains it but because experimental technology, with its origins in science, registers it in its sensory verifications of the "state of the world." Here it seems clear that the explicit physicalization of the "spiritual" by Lipinski reappears in a less explicit way, but a way no less clear. The entire visionary culture trusts in tests of the supernatural in order to demonstrate, not the scientific congruity of miracles, which would be impossible, but rather the possibility of recording them technologically.

In conclusion, a quite "odd" situation is generated. Science is accorded no greater legitimacy to intervene: once it has affirmed the "normality" of "exceptional events," it has done its job. It cannot, for example, go on to say that exceptionalness is always part of the natural order, because exceptionalness is now subject to the supernatural dimension. Technology has the next word, for it is attributed a greater instrumental flexibility in regard to religion and has a safer capacity for subordination. The test, an expression of science no longer directed to a scientific audience, seems to have become a useful tool of the apparition, about which it speaks and provides elements of scientific explanation. But, as we shall see in the section about the "on-stage" perspective of the actors below and in the final chapter about *mediating* images, the test surreptitiously imposes a totalizing power on the outcome of visions and visionaries and *its own* kind of replication of events, which depend on the technical instruments that *capture* the hard data.

Symbolic Horizons and Actors

The *world created* by the apparitions is not a totalizing, constricting, exclusive structure but rather a horizon—an ensemble of symbolic possibilities to which the actors have access. The nature of this symbolic horizon—common to other kinds of contemporary symbolic production—is that it tends toward impermeability and incomensurateness in regard to other horizons, other *stages*, toward a relation of otherness in terms of what is signified and the practices that develop within it. The actors enter and exit from the *stage* of the apparitions and go on to another stage without any problem. This is perhaps the most "odd" aspect, and that which betrays the *modernity* of the phenomenon of apparitions. To consider them byproducts of cultural archaisms would be short-sighted, for it would miss the component of contemporary culture.

The apparitions of Lourdes had an aspect of opposition to the modern world in general, including science, morality, politics, and customs (Apolito 1990, 18–19). Contemporary apparitions take place in a scenario that is completely different than Lourdes—at the same time impermeable and myopic in regard to other scenarios. Here a condemnation of the modern, if there is one, concerns only the ethical side of life and not, for example, the Galilean worldview. The latter in and of itself does not attract the polemical attention of the cultural products of the apparitions, which on one level, as we have seen, seem to depend on this worldview.

We might expect that by definition the apparitions, as prodigious, repeated, events, would be considered by believers as implicit, sustained assaults on the scientific ordering of the world. For example, in the case of miracles, the questioning of the universal validity of the laws of physics does not affect a rare incident, as with an occasional miracle, which in the *normal* Catholic view is believable precisely because it is rare. In the *normal*

Catholic view it is not impossible to believe in the validity of the laws of physics at the same time as the possibility of a miracle, precisely because of the exceptionalness of the miracle and the conviction that God the creator can suspend his laws from time to time, "in a very few rare exceptions" (Blandino 1982, 231). But when—as with the prodigy of the sun that we will consider below—the suspension of the laws of physics is continuous and widespread, then the compatibility of physics and miracles becomes more difficult. If one adds up the solar events at Medjugorje, at Oliveto, and at the dozens of other places worldwide that continue to report them, one would count many hundreds, if not thousands, of violations of the laws of physics in the last decade.

One might well consider seriously questioning the validity of the laws of astrophysics at this point, given this continuous challenge; or, in Catholic terms, the "createdness" of the laws of nature, if God sets them aside so frequently (Ibid., 231). And yet, no supporter of both the apparitions and the veracity of the solar prodigies has done so. Why? Because they see no conflict between the tacit and obvious application of physical science in daily life (the technological dimension of everyday activity, the obvious evaluation of seasonal weather in personal planning, and so on) and the scenario of the apparitions. A person can plan a trip to Medjugorje by finding out what clothes to take given the time of the year; in other words, live within a code of understanding about the world that takes as absolutes astrophysical laws in which the distance of the sun from the earth, its luminosity, and its "fixedness" are given. They then see the sun lose it luminosity, decline across the sky, and fall toward earth, without noticing any incompatibility between the two, without crying "foul," in terms of the other.

This is the kind of person who exits from the *stage* of the everyday technological dimension and goes onto that of the apparitions, and then exits the latter to go back to the former as she or he goes onto and exits from so many other stages without apparently experiencing dissonance from a personal experience suspended between two universes, two stages on which the units of measure of one are impossible to apply on the other.

A third stage, perhaps the most interesting, turns up in the case of researchers who attend apparitions. Often they are researchers who are also believers. On the stage of their scientific laboratories they are normally led to conclusions that fall wholly within the ambit of natural phenomena; on the stage of their faith they express instead tensions that are absolute and supernatural. Between the first two stages, in terms of institutional activity, there is ordinarily no contact. And here is the third stage, in which they try to mediate between the other two—theoretically science and religion—in concrete everyday personal scientific work and devotion to the Madonna who has appeared. This kind of researcher will then become the actor on the third stage, one who, in the encounter between science and religion, will establish that *this* is an exceptional event (1) legitimated by science—endowed with enough prodigiousness to be considered a divine sign, and (2) recognized by religion. It would seem, then, that the first and second stages are *recombined* in the third, the test, the supernatural experiment. In fact, on the third stage no real mediation takes place between the other two, because there is constituted a joint incompatibility.

On the *first* stage, the scientific one, the rules call for replicability of phenomena and invariance of principles and laws. On the *second* stage, that of apparitions, one expects multiple exceptions and an inevitable deviation from norms, because they come from the divinity. Finally, on the *third* stage, that of the scientific test, a capricious deity is present who ever more often, even daily and without any apparent criterion, enjoys leaving to methodologies and scientific categories the possibility of keeping the world in order, and sometimes frustrates the order.

Hence, on the third stage, the first two stages are canceled out. The first one is canceled because the regularity of scientific procedures is denied precisely when their technological applications are bent to certifying *that* prodigy in *that* moment. The second one is canceled because the divine sign, the prodigy itself, is also bent, reduced to its expression in the testing laboratory. In other words, a faith "tested" with technological instruments is no longer faith, just as a science that systematically proves that there are exceptions unexplained by its laws delegitimates itself. It would seem, therefore, that the attempt to eliminate the contradiction between the two irreconcilable stages on which the researcher's experience separated has resulted in the production of a third stage that did not in fact mediate between the other two but rather produced a new incomensurateness and thus added one more fragmented sphere of action to the experience of the fragmented subject.

There is yet another stage whose internal laws are irreconcilable with those of the prodigies of the sun and that, so far, has not caused those who enter onto it after exiting that of the prodigies to cry "foul." I refer to a central aspect of the Catholic religion, that it is a religion of faith and "nonvision," "swaddled in darkness" (Galot 1985, 21, 25). From the most orthodox point of view, faith implies freedom to accept the divine message, while the vision imposes itself in a certain sense as an obligation since it shows visible evidence of the transcendent invisible. This problem is marginal when it is a question of extraordinary phenomena that are exceptional. "The need to insist on the exceptional nature of extraordinary manifestations of the supernatural perceptible to the senses is due to the fact that the present life of the Church remains in the realm of faith, a realm that could be defined as nonvision" (Ibid., 29).

But this attitude becomes more relevant when the manifestations come to "be a part of the daily life of the seers" (Ibid., 30) and involve hundreds or thousands of persons. The problem then takes on devastating dimensions on the "stage" of the religion of faith if—yet again—we multiply the hundreds or perhaps thousands of solar prodigies in the last decade by the thousands of persons who have been present, arriving at a total of several hundred thousands or even millions.

But that is not all. If to this number, already disquieting, we add those who, even if they did not directly witness the phenomena, may have watched it on television, given that perhaps thousands of videocassettes reproduce the phenomenon, we would surely have many millions of persons. And even more: theoretically, on television the vision of the solar prodigy could be shown to all the billions of human beings on the planet, and hence could translate the religion of faith into the religion of visual evidence. The theological problem is daunting. Yet not one person, not even the most authoritative supporters of solar prodigies, theologians, scientists, or clergy on every level, poses this problem *when they speak of apparitions*. Surely the clergy, when in the arena of theology, are quite aware that Catholicism is a religion of faith and everything that this implies. But in the arena of the apparitions this awareness is eclipsed by other self-evident truths that the apparition scenario presents to them.

This is another exceptional sign of the modernity of the apparition phenomenon. A new scenario that opens in collective life does not neces-sarily nullify or infringe on the others, even those most contiguous, but is added on to them, without the actors noticing difference, incomensurate-ness, or unthinkableness of one in terms of the other. Each scenario has its actors; each person is an actor in various scenarios that fragment his or her sense of unity. The behavior of the boy seers, described in *"It Is Said They Have Seen the Madonna,"* does not seem exceptional to me. They saw the

Madonna, and as a result were ill, wept, and fainted. Then, when they recovered, they began to laugh at, sneer at, and make fun of the pilgrims. And then, after a while, they had a new vision and again felt bad and began again, repeating the entire cycle twice in front of me (Apolito 1990, 218). I wrote then of a "casual or even cheeky attitude toward the sacred." I would now recast the description to say that they shifted their attitude because they shifted scenarios. There is no substantive difference between their kind of multiple subjectivity and that of scientists or theologians who recognize the scenarios of science, of technology, of theology, and of the prodigies of the sun, and who move, shifting mental attitudes as a result of the shift in practice, from one to the other. What changes is the relative value that the subjects place on their own scenarios and those of others.

THE CREATION OF THE WORLD
OF THE APPARITIONS

Definitive Signs of the "Presence"

IN ORDER TO ELIMINATE ANY RISK OF ERROR, the first weeks of the visionary phenomena at Oliveto Citra were devoted to verifying the presence of the Madonna. This was the time of the construction of the context, in which proofs of the veracity of the apparitions were sought and produced. The problem was to decide collectively whether what was before the seers' eyes—though for most people invisible—was something external and real that would warrant public attendance and merit attention to the unfolding events described. Only after the presence was verified could people go on to listen to it, to scrutinize its signs.

One episode marks the collective transition from the verification of a *possible* presence to the interpretation of the meaning of the presence fully *verified*. The way this episode was reconstructed in the *Bollettino* is evidence for this transition. On July 2, 1985, the Madonna appeared to a young girl seer, Serena, who was questioned by an Oliveto doctor. The doctor put his questions for the Madonna to Serena in German, and Serena was expected to provide, in Italian, the Madonna's answers. In the *Bollettino* the episode is reconstructed as follows:

1. Are you the Mother of all men? [in German]
   Reply: Yes.
2. What message do you want us to give mankind? [in German]
   Reply: Pray, pray, pray.
3. How old are you?
   To this question there was no reply; it was an idle question. (B 1, 4)

In the account that was drawn up the same day as the event, Fulvio Piranese notes that after the second reply the doctor "went into shock—babbling, he told us the meaning in Italian of the phrases he used and almost broke into tears" (pp. 2–3). But there were details different from the version in the *Bollettino*. To the second question, the precise answer was "Peace and prayer," and to the third answer, the response was not missing, but was "Pray, pray, pray" (that is, the response to the second question in the *Bollettino* version). According to Piranese's account, then, the Madonna's response to the third question was not appropriate. This could have placed the success of the test at risk. Hence, Piranese interpreted the response to the third question not as that of the Madonna, but rather as a comment by the seer. Piranese writes: "Editor's note: Serena, very irked, virtually ordered us to pray."

In a conversation in February 1986, the doctor in the "experiment" confirmed to me that two questions received responses, and that after these other questions followed in German as well as replies that he no longer recalled. He did recall one detail, which had caused him to remain skeptical. Precisely in order to get rid of his remaining doubts, he decided to ask, in Italian, a series of questions about the physical universe—whether it was finite, infinite, and why. To respond, the Madonna would have to use the terms of physics, and at that point, there would be no more doubts. But the response, "It depends on you," disappointed him—it was as if the Madonna had not understood his question.

The role of this doctor from Oliveto, which appears to be self-contradictory, can be broken down into at least two *positions* ("by *positions* I mean the representations [self- or public] of thoughts, opinions, and attitudes of individuals on a given subject or context as they appear to the group" [Apolito 1990, 288]): the one he presented to me in our conversations and the one he presented to the devout of Oliveto. Recognizing me as a scholar critical of the Oliveto phenomena, he tended to present himself in our conversations as skeptical and disenchanted. He often used the pronoun "we" when he wanted to emphasize that he and I could not be satisfied with the proofs that the various seers offered because they were always ambiguous and incapable of resolving doubts and perplexities. The doctor had a different *position* with believers. It is patent in Fulvio's account of the emotional crisis after the experiment and also in the doctor's own written declaration for the Committee archive. There he repeats the language of the parish priest in the *Bollettino* and admits that his questions after the first two "might be considered idle." In all fairness, he also presented himself to the Committee as inclined toward skepticism; but there his presence, rather than marked by skepticism, seemed to involve the dramatization of a gradual abandonment of doubt, a kind of public representation of the itinerary of conversion.

The most significant point of this episode is that expressed by the *Bollettino*, which emphasized that the third reply in the experiment was lacking because the question was idle. The Madonna, through a seer, subsequently confirmed the *Bollettino*'s attitude toward the question because, she declared, she had come to the world for more important matters. It is this interpretation that marks the transition from *the verification of the presence* of the Madonna to the *reasons* for a presence *already verified*. In short, the momentary *doubt* of the Oliveto doctor—the questions the Madonna did not answer—is reversed by the *proof* that by then the time for the verification of the presence of the Madonna had come to an end. The Madonna did not want to reply to pointless questions, did not want to waste time on experiments. Her job on earth was quite different. It is noteworthy that this conclusion is borrowed from the attitude that exorcists are generally instructed to adopt toward the Devil: "In the *Rituale Romanum*, and other Catholic treatises, the priest is warned not to ask the Devil unnecessary, curious questions" (Walker 1981, 8; cf. for an example, C. Balducci 1974, 32).

At Medjugorje, there was a similar prohibition. After the first month of the apparitions the seers told those around them that the Madonna did not like "curious questions" or "any old things" (Laurentin 1986a, 129).

The episode of the German-Italian dialogue has real significance in the evolution of the events. It was devised as a test, almost a scientific experiment, to produce irrefutable results. But in mid-course its meaning changed radically from an experiment to a rejection of experimentation when consensus was reached that the Madonna was on earth for more important matters. In this way a major phase of the collective perception of the events came to an end: the verification of the Marian presence. Once this presence was held to be certain, it was time for a collective effort to interpret *her* signs, for other objectives, other experimental procedures.

It is possible to distinguish between the Committee's objectives and those of the majority of the pilgrims and devotees. The Committee directed its hermeneutic effort above all to the meaning of the Madonna's presence— that is, to her intentions, to the celestial design for her coming to the world. Most of the pilgrims, in contrast, were trying to take the measure of the variety of sensory phenomena that the supernatural outbreak provoked in people: visual images, silhouettes, scents, air currents, sounds, feelings,. and so on. There was no clear distinction between the two interpretive tasks since for the Committee sensory phenomena could be signs for divine intentions and, conversely, for the pilgrims divine intentions could be verified only by through matter or persons. But it is nevertheless true that the Committee and, above all, the parish priest were watching for a meaning that was more religious, properly speaking, while the pilgrims were engrossed in the daily wonders and healing. It is also true that both these hermeneutic efforts served implicitly as an ongoing response to doubts about the Madonna's presence, whether in the form of sustained skepticism from diocesan officials in Salerno, which affected the Committee, or hometown ridicule, which affected the pilgrims. The Committee maintained its own kind of pro forma skepticism in order to satisfy, the leader Michele confided to me, the exigencies of outsiders and strangers, those like me who came to investigate {June 14, 1986}.

Signs are the dominant theme of all apparitions. Those who do not see, that is, all those who legitimate the "truth" of the events, often ask for signs, expressing their need to corroborate their nascent belief (or justify their disbelief) through some extraordinary manifestation (or its absence). The seers, in these cases, speak to this collective necessity and ask the visions to show themselves to everyone through some great sign.

At Lourdes, it was the parish priest in his skeptical phase who told Bernadette that he would believe her if the vision caused a wild rose on which the seer said the Madonna appeared to bloom suddenly before the crowd (Estrade 1934, 157). Bernadette more than once repeated the request to the Madonna, who only smiled in response. A similar request at Fatima was more successful; there the Madonna upon request for a sign, performed the prodigy of the sun discussed below.

At Medjugorje, the youthful seers asked the Madonna for a sign several times. At first the Madonna's reaction was one of annoyance; indeed, she did not reply, would begin to sing, or even disappear (Laurentin 1986a, 129). At this time the youths were under pressure from a crowd, part of which was incredulous. There are tape-recordings in which one can hear the youths asked for a sign to convince others that they were not liars (Bubalo 1987, 30). (This was also the phase in which the youths were as yet unable to control their relation with the increasing numbers of pilgrims.) But then the Madonna replied and promised a great, sudden, sign; some said that a great shrine would spring up in an instant (Sala and Mantero 1986, 36), like wonders in fables (or medieval tales of demonic action) in which palaces appear out of nowhere in a night. The seer Vicka herself led people to believe that a great sign would suddenly appear, although she did not specify what it would be (Ibid., 170). Many sick persons would be healed. The seers even talked about the return of an amputated leg to a boy's body. Once before when the seers had seen it mystically rejoin the hip's stump the boy felt "something like an electric current run through his leg" (Ibid., 184).

The bishop of Mostar in his October 1984 report emphasized that the deadline for the sign promised by the Madonna was constantly being postponed. It had been announced for August 27, 1981, and when it did not occur was postponed to two days later, then three days more, then another three. Then it was postponed yet again, until December 8, the Immaculate Conception, then to Christmas, then New Year, and so on. "Naturally, when nothing happened, the seers said, 'We didn't say that!'" (Ibid., 34).

At Ezkioga, predictions of a great sign that would prove the truth of the visions were spreading just three days after the first episode. There the prophecies were spread out among numerous seers and charismatics attracted to the site of the events and, as at Medjugorje, once a predicted date proved to be false, another was immediately produced (Christian 1987, 153).

Also at Oliveto, quite soon there were demands for both an unequivocal sign by those who saw nothing and an assurance that a sign was imminent by those who were seeing visions.

Prodigies of Light

One sign, first announced and then sent by the Madonna, struck the collective imagination more than any other. An eight-year-old seer, Mauro, received a message from the Madonna that on July 20, 1985, there would be a great sign to all present. In the second edition of Faricy's book, the appendix was edited by Luciana Pecoraio, a devotee from Rome, who used interviews to reconstruct the message.

> The Madonna had announced to him the prodigy of July 20, showing him three doves that flew down toward the castle. One of the doves that was black attacked and drew blood from the side of another, which was white. The blood formed a circle within which were inscribed the words "July 20." (Faricy and Pecoraio 1987, 117)

After this first message, a number of seers confirmed with messages the arrival of an extraordinary sign on July 20. Fulvio spoke of it in his report, recalling that, on the afternoon of the dialogue in German, Serena asked the Madonna, "What will happen on July 20?" The response was, "It will be a memorable day" (report cited, p. 2). Don Giovanni wrote about it in his diary, recalling a vision of Aurelia. The Sorrowing Madonna "spoke to her about July 20 as a day of prayer and of particular importance" (AC, June 26, 1985). Ada also asked the Madonna, "What's all this about July 20?" and received the response, "It is a date to remember" (AC, declaration of Ada). The rumor of the predicted wonder spread, strengthening convictions and raising expectations. On July 20, an imposing crowd waited at Oliveto for the Marian sign.

> Several thousand pilgrims filled the little plaza of the Castle and the Plaza Garibaldi, coming to Oliveto in around eighty buses and hundreds of cars. Many affirm they saw the Madonna that day; others noticed the presence of the Virgin from the usual mysterious and very pleasing odor. (B, r, 68)

But the sign consisted of neither the mass visions nor the mysterious scent. One of the many written testimonies of the celestial sign that occurred recounts:

All of a sudden, at about eleven o'clock at night, while we watched the sky, there appeared some white clouds that circled over us. At the same instant could be heard cries from people that they saw the Madonna. Those who saw her were mainly children, and a few adults. The latter fainted from the emotion, while some children pointed to where they saw the Madonna. Suddenly, the place where the Madonna usually appears turned red. That was due to the clouds that we had seen shortly before, which had turned from white to red. (AC, testimony of D. E.)

So the sign here appeared as a group of white clouds that become red. In his book, Faricy writes ambiguously of "a cloud colored bright red and lit up by the reflectors that light the ruins of the castle" (Faricy 1986, 34), where the conjunction "and" gives one the impression that the red color was independent of the reflectors. The *Bollettino* admits that the cloud was "colored bright red *by the spotlights* that light up the castle" (B 1, 3; my italics). For the *Bollettino*, the sign seemed to be a cloud that "began to circle over the castle and the nearby houses, while from the apparition gate there came the message: 'This cloud has been sent by me as a first sign'" (B 1, 3). The witness D. E. placed less emphasis on the scenery: "Later, the town priest told us that a seer had reported that the Madonna had said that this was the first sign she had given to the people assembled at Oliveto" (AC, testimony of D. E.).

The manipulations of written accounts of this message in order to bolster the idea of a prodigy are remarkable. The *Bollettino* merely said that the message "came," without specifying how (logically it should have specified, "reported by the seer who heard it from the Madonna"). Faricy, in contrast, maintains that "many persons heard the voice of a woman, coming from the castle" (Faricy 1986, 34). And Laurentin even suggests there was an "apparition" in the sky of the same message, evidently in writing (Laurentin 1988a, 121). In short, Faricy and Laurentin, the two most authoritative proponents of the apparitions, disagree. One emphasizes a miraculous public locution; and the other, a miraculous public vision. Neither cites his sources. To summarize, a sign from the Madonna was announced by some seers for July 20. *The plaza* constructed symbolic associations and isolated one in particular.

Here we see clearly how, in the first months of the apparitions, the story developed as a result of "inductions" of the seers (and of some particular seers), was elaborated and negotiated with the leaders and believers, and was often clumsily "glorified" by prestigious outside supporters. But some-times in the accounts there subsists a number of interpretations of the same phenomenon. Such is the case for the cloud on July 20. In an interview a few months later with two journalists, who in fact were the members of the National UFO Center we cited earlier, the parish priest declared: "The cloud . . . yes. The extraordinary fact is this, . . . not the color of the cloud, but its 'presence'" (Carione and Serrone 1986, 12).

A few days after talking to the priest, the same interviewers talked to the mother of twins who were among the most important seers. She articulated, combining them, the opinions of her two sons and her own in this way: "Ah, I saw three . . . that passed above the castle. They passed and the color . . . that is, it wasn't the clouds that were strange, but the color" (Ibid., 30).

The event of July 20 is important not only because it was received as a sign but also because it introduced a typology decisive for the development of other wondrous phenomena. The declaration that the cloud was the sign of the Madonna, which originated with a seer and was spread by the parish priest, produced a connection, extremely fruitful in the following months, between the Madonna and certain atmospheric and astronomical events considered prodigious or unusual.

The connection between apparitions and sky, which seems fundamental in contemporary apparitions, was not so obvious a century ago. Catherine Labouré had her visions in a closed chapel, as did Alfonse Ratisbonne, whose experience derived directly from Labouré's visions of the Miraculous Medal. The two shepherds of La Salette had their visions against the backdrop of a valley, while Bernadette had hers in a grotto near Lourdes. Although the dimension of sky was never excluded in the nineteenth-century apparitions—as is obvious in a religion like Christianity with uranic symbolism—there is no particular emphasis on it. On the contrary, the Lourdes grotto harks back to the archaic complex of the chthonic rediscov-ery of sacred images common in the foundation stories of European shrines, which does not include the characteristic and almost exclusive connection with the *physical* sky that became prevalent in the visionary phenomena of this century.

The July 20 prodigy at Oliveto centered, as we have seen, on a cloud. At Lourdes there was also a prodigious cloud, but not in the sky, for it came out of the grotto of the apparitions before the Madonna let herself be seen and disappeared with the Madonna (Estrade 1934, 64). Hence, it was a "chthonic" cloud that came out of the grotto and went back into it.

At Fatima, there occurred a clear *ascending* sequence. All the testimonies did not agree, but the predominant version of those present was that of a white cloud taking shape out of nothing *on the ground*. It surrounded either the holm-oak of the apparitions or the three shepherds and then, after about ten minutes, went away *toward the sky* and disappeared (Da Fonseca 1987, 48, 85). At Fatima, everyone—seers and spectators—*systematically* watched the sky during the apparitions.

It is worth noting that at Fatima, between the third and the fourth apparition, the cloud phenomenon occurred even in the absence of the seers, who had been prevented from attending. Witnesses declared they saw the cloud become colored "with all the brilliant colors of the rainbow. . . . 'The Madonna appeared.' No one had seen her, but the extraordinary phenomena showed that the Virgin, for her part, had not missed the appointment" (Ibid., 49). But there are also significant differences between Fatima and recent apparitions. At Fatima, the cloud seemed above all to have the role of concealment. For example, during the fifth apparition, the white cloud hid the holm-oak and the three seers from those who were watching (Ibid., 65).

In contrast, at Medjugorje, the model for contemporary apparitions, the cloud seemed to disclose the apparition of the Madonna. Father Umberto Loncar, a Yugoslav Franciscan, first saw an "incredible pink-violet cloud," then distinguished in the cloud

the magnificent figure of a woman [who] came out from the pink-violet clouds. . . . This most beautiful figure arose majestically in the sky and disappeared on high, losing little by little its splendid pink-violet color. At the end, I saw a white veil remain slightly below its feet, fluttering elegantly in the air for about a half a minute; then it faded away and disappeared. (Kraljević and Maggioni 1988, 83)

The cloud that seemed to be the vision gave those around the central seers an intimation of what the seers were seeing and hearing. It was the instrument by which the Madonna gave all the onlookers a glimmer of metahistory.

Interpretive scrutiny of the clouds was extraordinarily widespread and frequent at Oliveto, as at Medjugorje. Everyone tried to see something meaningful in the disorganized movement of clouds, and, while the Committee generally discouraged this practice, many had the chance to reach a lower-to-middling *level* of vision by interpreting with others the cloud forms.

Yet cloud phenomena pale in comparison to the most extraordinary and exciting celestial wonder today available to almost all pilgrims to apparition sites: the prodigy of the sun. Here, too, Fatima provides a model. The seer Lucia had requested from her vision a sign so that all would believe. The Madonna had promised one for her last apparition, on October 13, 1917. Here is how on that day the sun began to spin

> dizzily on its axis, similar to a wheel of fire, throwing in all directions shafts of yellow, green, red, blue, violet light . . . that colored fantastically the clouds in the sky, the trees, the rocks, the earth, the immense crowd. It stopped for a few moments, then started again its dance of light like a very extravagant Catherine-wheel made by the most expert designers of fireworks. It paused again, only to start a third time, with more variety, more color, more brilliance. (Da Fonseca 1987, 86)

Malanga and Pinotti drew up a list of thirty places where solar phenomena associated with the Madonna had been reported between 1901 and 1970. After 1970, there have been a very large number reported at Medjugorje, at Kibeho in Africa, and in almost all the Italian apparition sites.

In the matter of solar prodigies as well, there have been changes in the apparition prototype since the nineteenth century. There were luminous phenomena of a prodigious nature at that time, but quite different in nature. At Lourdes, the parish priest Peyramale told of having seen a shaft of light one Sunday in church, which shined around Bernadette's head (Estrade 1934, 216). At La Salette, the children told of a luminous phenomenon, "a floating glare," a kind of globe of light from which the vision took shape (Masson 1988, 23). Catherine Labouré saw a small golden globe in the hands of the Virgin, who said it symbolized "the entire world, France in particular, and every person in particular." According to Guitton, who cites the passage, "This brings to mind the chariots of light, the bushes that now and then turn up in the Scriptures, like the receptacle, the tabernacle of the presence of God. One thinks of the burning bush, of Elijah's chariot" (Guitton 1976, 58).

In these examples there is an obvious, time-honored metaphoric matching of light and divinity, one with biblical roots that deeply affects even the figure of Jesus. But there is no particular emphasis on the concrete, physical, role of the sun as occurs, in contrast, in the twentieth century, when there is an articulation of religious symbols with exceptional visual concreteness and transcendence is presented as a kind of uranic spectacle.

What is interesting in terms of ethnomethodology is precisely the linkage between the sun and Mary, which, properly speaking, has no doctrinal basis. Often believers refer to the passage in Revelation 12:1 that speaks of a pregnant woman, dressed as the sun with a crown of stars and the moon at her feet, who cries out from the pains of childbirth. Theological interpretation of the passage, as we shall see below, varies. Some theologians consider it an image of the Church; others, a reference to the Madonna. In any case, in the context of apparitions the symbolic dimension of the passage becomes transformed into a flat connection with the sun as a physical object. Laurentin himself (1988b, 65) calls for this kind of concrete connection when he refers the Gospel passage of Luke 21:25, in which Jesus announces sun signs in the context of the prophecy of the ruin of Jerusalem. We shall see that the visionary culture is generally able to make plausible the notion that the end is at hand and hence tends to refer to apocalyptic passages in the New Testament, which it reads as an account of events about to happen.

One would like to work with the original documents of the Fatima apparitions (and those of Tilly-sur-Seuilles, France, in 1901, which was apparently the first case of solar prodigy) to try to understand more precisely the origin of the nexus between Mary and the physical sun. According to most of the pious accounts, at Fatima there was no explicit indication from the Madonna that the solar prodigy was a sign from *her*. The Madonna promises the children a sign to convince people of her coming but is never explicit about what that sign will be. Da Fonseca, the author of the classic pious account, writes that during her last apparition the Madonna, "when she took her leave [. . .] opened her hands that reflected the sun, or, as the two little children put it, pointed to the sun" (Da Fonseca 1987, 85). In the preceding apparitions as well, when the Madonna's open hands gave off light, it was said that she reflected solar light, but it was only during the last apparition that Lucia asked people to look at the sun. Hence, according to Da Fonseca's account, it was not the Madonna who *defined* the sign but rather the seers, and through them the pilgrims, who *interpreted* something as a sign of the Madonna, creating a *symbol* that then became available for infinite uses in the future. Lucia herself, in the autobiographical writings requested by the bishop of Leiria, wrote almost as if she wanted to dispel the suspicion that she herself had been at the origin of the connection.

Opening her hands she made them reflect on the sun; and as she rose up, the reflection of her own light continued to project on the sun. This, most reverend excellency, is the reason why I cried out for them to look at the sun. My purpose was not to call people's attention to it, for I was not even aware of its presence. I did it only because I was transported by an interior movement, which is what impelled me. (Lucia 1973, 125)

As a result of Fatima, the nexus between solar prodigies and the presence of the Madonna, already present in the lesser-known apparitions of Tilly-sur-Seuilles, was reinforced and became impressed upon the Catholic imagination. We are confronted with the construction of a *symbol*, in the sense that Eco speaks of "a way to *discipline*" mental and affective associations (Eco 1981, 898) selected "to the detriment of others that the symbolic mode decides not to consider" (Ibid., 911). Once it has taken hold, this symbol will appear in other apparitions as obvious.

The connection of sun to Madonna thus became the central issue of the Fatima apparitions, the irrefutable proof, the most accredited testimony of the truth of the apparitions. It was so strong in the collective imagination that even the ufologists, with an entirely areligious explanation for extraordinary phenomena, paid close attention to the events at Fatima and took as real the wonders attributed to the sun (or rather to a light similar to the sun), even though they denied any connection with the Madonna.

Indeed, there are ufological readings of the events at Fatima. In 1982 in Portugal, a book was published by Joaquim Fernandes, a journalist, and Fina D'Armada, a historian, entitled *Intervençao Extraterrestre em Fatima*, that reinterpreted what happened on October 13, 1917, as a visit from outer space. In 1990, Corrado Malanga and Robert Pinotti, two of Italy's best-known ufologists, expanded on this argument (Malanga and Pinotti 1990, 89–111). They compared the descriptions of eye-witnesses at Fatima with testimony of quite analogous experiences explained as encounters with extraterrestrials.

They also applied *other interpretations, derived from ufology*, to descriptions of the sun at Fatima as a silvery disc with precise and shining outline, to its bouncing in the sky, to the lights that were reflected in various colors in rapid succession, even to the fall of flakes similar to snow that disappeared before they touched the ground and, finally, to the fact that rain-soaked clothes were later found to be totally dry (Ibid., 100). In regard to the wet clothes, for example, the two Portuguese scholars use testimony at the time to maintain that not all seers found their clothes were dry, but only those who stood in a given swath of the ground about seventy meters wide. This swath supposedly corresponded to a trajectory of the sun, in the Marian interpretation, but, in the ufological interpretation, would be that of a flying saucer when it came closest to the earth (Ibid., 106).

One cannot conclude that this type of interpretation is independent of the "objective reality" of the phenomena or that, if one changed the interpretation, the phenomena would in any case remain. In my previous book, I made extensive use of the ethnomethodological concept of the *reflexivity* of social practices, in particular of those of oral accounts. With respect to these accounts, "when one speaks of the reflexive nature of storytelling one means that the stories (the justifications, explanations, discourses) of the social actors are constituent elements of what the stories refer to, of that reality about which the stories speak, furnish descriptions, explanations, connections, evaluations, etc." (M. Wolf 1979, 129).

One can easily grasp the effect of reflexivity if one considers that for those who claim a connection of sun to Madonna, a hypothesis relating solar events to flying saucers is not simply another hypothesis about the events but the negation of anything miraculous about them, hence, their negation pure and simple. No believer would have any interest in defending the objectivity of the phenomena if the Marian interpretation were rejected.

Similarly, for a ufologist, the sun-Madonna connection is meaningful only because it provides access to information that can then be explained by a different model. If, in the meantime, the ufological hypothesis loses its power for the ufologists themselves, the "objectivity" of the phenomenon disappears, leaving only the "subjectivity" of human error. In both instances, the aspect of *symbolic* organization of the reconstructions and the testimony is decisive. And the symbol, we know, is a "way to *discipline* mental and affective associations" (Eco 1981, 898). We recall in this regard that no astronomical observatory registered any solar phenomenon, which leads Aubert in the Catholic *Dictionnaire d'histoire et de géographie ecclésiastiques* to conclude that "one must therefore consider it a phenomenon of the atmosphere, and not, properly speaking, of the sun" (Aubert 1967, 680).

This interpretation, "a phenomenon of the atmosphere," has the advantage of scientific-experimental prudence, but it is unlikely to account for the specific details of the phenomenon as well as the other interpretations. Here there is a new symbolic connection, this time with the symbolic reference to the prestige of scientific experimentation and the observation of reality based on natural law.

The solar prodigy has become extremely common since Fatima, reaching the point, at present, where one can watch it on videocassette. The position of the Church toward these wonders is very prudent, but it allows both the maintenance of doubt and active involvement based on faith.

On the one hand, as Aubert points out, there is no mention of a prodigy of the sun in the decree of the bishop of Leiria who in 1930 solemnly declared as worthy of faith the visions of the shepherd children of Fatima and authorized the cult—almost as if the bishop wanted to leave out but also leave ambiguous something of major importance. On the other hand, there is talk of a solar wonder that Pope Pius XII himself witnessed. During his discourse at Fatima at the close of the Holy Year of 1950, Cardinal Tedeschini, the envoy and a personal friend of the pope, mentioned that Pius XII had an apparition of the Virgin in the Vatican gardens in the last days of October 1950.

He is supposed to have looked toward the sun and seen the portrait of the Virgin, surrounded by rays. The pontiff is said to have been able to have looked at the sun without its light blinding him [. . .] The sun was shaken, moved, transformed into an image of life, a spectacle of celestial motion, an intermediary for messages that were at once silent and eloquent for the vicar of Christ. (Loewenich 1956, 225)

In the pontiff's case, the sun-Madonna connection, which as a problem must have been fully present though latent, is part of the very content of the prodigy. Indeed, Pius XII sees *in the sun* the portrait of the Virgin, and then sees colors, movement, and so on. In the formal account of the pope's vision, the problematic association is not made by a human agent but expressed in the very content of the vision.

René Laurentin's attitude is one of eloquent ambivalence. In a publication of 1984, he defended the possibility that God might want to provide signs by way of lights.

Should we forbid God to give humble signs by way of light, using a simple symbol preferred in the Bible for the manifestation of God or of Christ? Why would God not express himself in a living language accessible to the poor? [. . .] At Medjugorje, these exceptional signs made a deep impression. They played a determinant role at the beginning. They drew the people of the parish to the place of apparitions. They inspired conversions and confessions. (Laurentin and Rupcic 1984a, 109)

Laurentin's justification of this effervescence of visionary phenomena is implicitly qualified by his reference to the inception of the visions. Later, when the solar phenomena proliferated widely, the French theologian denied this connection between luminous signs and conversions. In 1987 he wrote:

First of all, these signs in the sky are not essential; what is important are prayer and conversion. These are the best and most important miracles. Secondly, it is dangerous to stare at the sun looking for signs. To look at this blazing star and to interpret the agitated reactions of the eye as extraordinary phenomena is to tempt heaven. (Laurentin 1988d, 41–42)

However, in 1988, he returned with greater emphasis, opening the section "The Sun as at Fatima?" of the latest of his innumerable books on Medjugorje with a reference to the passage of Luke 21:25 on the "signs in the sun" (Laurentin and Lejeune 1988a, 68).

By the time of the Oliveto apparitions, the sun-Madonna connection was taken for granted. But when people reflected on the reasons for the connection, problems arose. The leader Michele explained to me at length how the prodigies of the sun occurred. But when I asked him whether these were signs of the Madonna he was quiet for several seconds, as if stumped, and then explained:

{8}

Because in the other apparitions that's it + like this—the first thing that occurs to me + because in the other apparitions she did it the same way ++ I believe. {June 14, 1986}

At Oliveto, experiences linked to the sun were countless. They were considered the elementary level of seeing, the one all reached sooner or later, and they were quite diverse. The *Bollettino* pointed out that "the sun, punctual as always when we have a special gathering in honor of the Madonna, made spectacular signs with a fiesta of colors and extraordinary movements" (B 13, 29).

As time passed, seers reported numerous messages in which the Madonna announced the prodigy of the sun as her sign of pleasure at the arrival of pilgrims, and many pilgrims saw the Madonna and other holy beings in the sun; for example, a group of pilgrims from Naples in a signed statement on April 17, 1988.

> We were four adults and four children. At that point I and my wife had seen the face of Jesus in the sun, first head on, then in profile, then we saw the Madonna, first from the waist up, then entire with her hands raised, and then with the Baby Jesus, for about 20 minutes. While I and my wife and the son of my friends S. P. age 13 saw the figures, the others only saw the sun rotate and give off colors. (B 13, 14)

The same people then saw a gigantic host in place of the sun. This vision was a frequent one. According to the *Bollettino*, sometimes in the host of the solar discs could be read the letters IHS (cf. for example, B 11, 8).

Generally, the phenomenon occurs in the following sequence. Some- one—as at Fatima—shouts: "Look at the sun" (often it is someone using a video camera, which, as we will see, is quite significant). At that point all look at the sun, which they perceive as spinning, some say counterclock- wise, producing circles of red, yellow, violet, and green. A woman seer from Salerno explained, based on Marian messages, the symbolism of the colors of the solar circles. Yellow, for example, referred to "underdeveloped countries," where faith would be born {May 17, 1986}. Some then saw a rain of light falling, sometimes composed of crosses, other times hosts. Almost all claimed that the sun in these instances did not dazzle them, rather it is as though its light "imploded." Others gave different details. Three seers from Portici declared that the light did not disappear, but rather that the sun "was very bright, blinding, and that nevertheless they could look at it without any problem" (B 15, 11).

One interesting testimony describes indirectly, not the prodigy of the sun, but another miracle. The day after a woman from Aversa saw the Madonna at Oliveto, she witnessed the prodigy of the sun from her house and watched it for "about two hours" because she saw "crosses, weapons, and other things." When she finally looked away she had lost her sight. After a few days she went to the oculist who diagnosed a very serious "photo-coagulation from the sun." A specialist in Rome confirmed the diagnosis, fearing it was irreversible. But the woman "miraculously" regained her sight, (cf. Faricy and Pecoraio 1987, 105). The point is that the "prodigy" of the sun was so taken for granted that, as in this case, one could seriously damage the eyes because of it.

At the time of this writing, the solar prodigy has reached a remarkable level of triviality. It is occurring just about as often as there are pilgrims at apparition sites, not counting the hundreds of video cassettes that circulate with taped versions of the miracle of the sun presenting as an obvious fact the technological-supernatural "marvel."

Malanga and Pinotti performed a definitive experiment related to the videotaping of the solar prodigy. Trying to understand if luminous phenomena related to Marian apparitions could be explained as UFO activity, the two authors studied

some films of Medjugorje and other Italian sites near Trieste, Milan, and Cosenza. In all of these films the result was the same: the sun pulsated or seemed to pulsate, with very precise frequency above the scene of the appearances of the Animated Entity of the Blessed Virgin Mary, as reported by the different seers. (Malanga and Pinotti 1990, 72–73)

The authors were struck by the presence of two different phenomenologies of the prodigy: those pilgrims who declared they saw the sun rotating, and others who spoke of pulsation of an intensely green sun. It was the latter that was visible in the films. The authors wondered whether those taking the videotapes might have been an influence on the general testimony of visions of the second kind, since an analysis of the films indicated that the believers present shouted the prodigy was occurring only after being alerted by the camera operator.

The first thing that occurred to Malanga and Pinotti was that it might be an indirect effect of the videotaping of solar light. After a few tries, they confirmed their idea. The pulsation did not occur when one simply focused the sun but when the aperture of the lens is set at less than 1/150 of a second and one second after focusing. This is why it does not always occur, but only in certain conditions of videotaping during an event that is held to be miraculous [. . .] In plain words, when too much light hits the electronic circuits of the video camera, it tends automatically to close the electronic shutter which in automatic mode remains closed, but in manual mode reopens, returning to the conditions set by the operator, which produces the phenomenon cyclically.

What would be the reaction of the many thousands of faithful throughout the world, who have been presented a tape of this kind to lead them to believe it depicted a miracle of the Madonna? This is how the only scientific proof of the Miracle of the Rotating Sun, famous from Fatima on, was disproved. (Ibid., 76)

The association of sun and Madonna, as I have said, although new in its concrete, physical details, is based on the deeper, ancient association of light with Jesus, which extended to other celestial beings including, obviously, Mary. Also in the case of the more general association of light with the Madonna, there is a displacement from a metaphoric and allegorical plane to a concrete, physical one.

The apparitions of Mary are often presented as breaches of intense light in the dark of night. A memorable instance was recorded in the *Bollettino* with the title "A Woman Dressed in Light": During a terrible storm in which a lightning bolt caused the lights to go out and the little plaza to suddenly become pitch-black, a group of persons saw "the figure of a woman all dressed in light break through the shadows and descend from the castle toward the plaza" (B, r, 8). On other occasions, the Madonna uses specific signs of light, like "a luminous disc that for a few minutes was spinning through space" (B, r, 32). She has herself announced by a very bright light, or shows herself in lights in a "luminous sphere that descended from the clouds. As it came closer it opened, and there in the center the Madonna appeared, most beautiful in the midst of so much light" (B, r, 66).

There is a suspicious resemblance to depictions of extraterrestrials in movies, and, by and large, the image falls within the general phenomenology of unidentified flying objects. At La Salette, Maximin and Mélanie discovered a kind of "sun," a "floating glare" in which they distinguished a person (Masson 1988, 22). At Ghiaia di Bonate, the child Adelaide Roncalli, who in 1944 said she saw the Virgin, observed in the sky a globe of intense light coming from the east (Cazzamalli 1951, 44). At Fatima, the vicar general of Leiria said that, during the apparitions of the three shepherd children on September 13, 1917, he saw

> distinctly a luminous globe, that moved toward the west, shifting slow and stately through space. My friend looked too, and was fortunate to see the same unexpected and enchanting Apparition. Suddenly, though, the globe with its extraordinary light disappeared before our eyes [. . .] The little shepherds, in a celestial vision, had contemplated the Mother of God in person; we were allowed to see the vehicle—so to speak—that had brought her from heaven to the inhospitable Serra d'Aire. (Da Fonseca 1987, 63–64)

At Medjugorje, the seers affirm: "First there came a great light, then, in this light, appeared the Madonna" (Kraljević and Maggioni 1988, 44). From these descriptions one could understand why, in ufological circles, the idea that Marian apparitions were appearances of UFOs from other worlds took shape.

But the Madonna of Oliveto could appear herself as light, or rather as an "entity of light," as a seer from Salerno put it {November 29, 1986}; as "a light in the general shape of a human form," as Benedetta recounted (Faricy and Pecoraio 1989, 51); or even, as light that gradually takes shape. "Near the gate I prayed intensely, and all at once I saw a strong light, so strong it dazzled me. In that light little by little there formed the image of the Madonna" (B, r, 54).

One notes that in the places where the sun no longer dazzles, these unnatural lights dazzle like the sun. Another seer declared:

{9}

> It was very far away—because—I think—if it was close it would have blinded us. {May 24, 1986}

In any case, the point is that in some instances there was an identification pure and simple of the light with the Madonna, a *materialization* of the metaphor.

In addition to being identified with light, the Madonna could also become light in the form of the moon. While the sun was the Madonna's *sign*, the moon could be the Madonna herself. This is one of the possible meanings of an extraordinary episode of collective vision in which I was, literally, a participant observer.

Approximately one hundred pilgrims gathered in a side street near the castle, away from the eyes and the microphones of the Committee. In various sectors of the group shouts arose in waves that rippled across it. Every once in a while there was a pause in the excitement, and people described what they saw and commented on it. Then the shouts and wails started again. They watched the Madonna appear and disappear behind the clouds.

As a rule, for each episode of weak visions with a hermeneutic basis, I attempted to recognize in the play of light and darkness the possible shapes identified as the Madonna. This time the only shape I made out among the clouds, as I was invited to do so by those around me, was the crescent moon. I had trouble grasping that for the pilgrims who were "seeing," the Madonna was the moon itself. In the meantime, my tape-recorder caught the following fragment of dialogue of two women between visions:

{10.1}

(1) fv: I didn't see anything—but the other ladies saw—but I only saw the moon + and I can't say I've seen the Madonna— but you have seen the Madonna—I only saw the light.

(2) fv2:   That is the light but + then came out—the moon with the Madonna in it.

What I gathered was that someone had seen the Madonna in the moon, but also spoke of another "light" that I was not able to fit among the things that I was seeing. All of a sudden the shouts got louder because the clouds had broken up to form a kind of net in which now and then the moon appeared and disappeared. I noted that the shouts increased and decreased exactly when the moon appeared and disappeared. So I asked those next to me:

{10.2}

(1) res: But isn't it the moon?

(2) mv: If it were the moon every once and a while it should come out!

(3) res: But that is because of the clouds.

(4) fv:	Some see the Madonna herself and some don't.
(5) mv1:	It is not the moon.
(6) fv2:	Of course not—what do you mean, the moon!
(7) f child v:	But it is the moon ++ look—it has the shape of the moon.
(8) fv3:	What do you mean, the moon!—I saw the angel be quiet.

For a few minutes this kind of exchange went on, along with shouts. A woman with a thick accent of Ciociaria then said:

{10.3}

fv: But it seems strange to me—it is a strange moon—if it were—uncovered we should be able to see it clear sharp [she "sees"] there it is even more clear now—brighter ++ the outline of the moon is not clear—yet + I don't know—let's see—let's see [she looks] ++ there now the light decreases—decreases and shrinks, gets smaller—if it were the moon at a certain time + the clouds should cover it and make it reappear—look there now it is resting—at the same place.

What I thought I understood was that the emotional climate of the visions in progress pushed people to see the moon as the Madonna and that the moments of commentary between one vision and another allowed unease about the identification to emerge in conscious reflection.

All at once a *strong* seer, Giorgio di Frattamaggiore, showed up, and some of those who recognized him immediately asked if the moon was the Madonna. After a moment's meditation, Giorgio declared that what the pilgrims were seeing really was the Madonna. Here was an instance of mutual reinforcement. The seer, not well-regarded by the Committee, took advantage of the situation to have his leadership recognized, while the pilgrims took advantage of the seer's consent to confirm their own uncertain and dubious visionary experience.

A few minutes later, when the period of collective excitement was over, I asked some women what they saw.

{10.4}

(1) res: Signora—but wasn't the moon in the sky before?
(2) fv: No, I didn't see the moon.
(3) fv2:   Yes, it was the moon—but it made itself visible in a
                different atmosphere.
(4) res: In what sense?
(5) fv2:   That is, it made itself visible.
(6) fv3:   The moon got smaller—got mangy—got reduced in
                size + and went off in the clouds—then it came out
                again. {March 15, 1986}

The Hermeneutics of the Apparitions

The July 20 episode of the cloud opened a new phase, one characterized by "public" consensus to move on from the verification of the presence of the Madonna to the interpretation of the ways she presents herself and communicates. The collective hermeneutic work produced a general profile of the Madonna that included (1) an external zone of almost indistinct perceptions with a maximum possibility of error admitted collectively, (2) an intermediate zone of rough identification of "something" with a rudimentary character of certainty, and (3) a core, more official, of sharp definitions and total certitude.

With the arrival of pilgrims from all of Campania and, in particular, those of the northern part, the number of seers grew impressively. The testimonies to the Committee multiplied, and every evening people said they saw or perceived something; on Saturdays and Sundays the numbers sharply increased. Not everyone saw with clarity, much less spoke with, the Madonna.

One can now elaborate a distinction, indicated above, between *strong* and *weak* seers. The former told of seeing her with great clarity, of speaking and of interacting with her, and they initiated cycles of visions that took on the nature of a *story*. They became central figures in the cult, while some became dangerous for the Committee because of the influence they gained. We have seen that Don Giovanni was quite alert to this aspect, co-opting into a small group the seers who could be assimilated, and marginalizing the others by every means.

The great mass of seers, however, were *weak* ones. Their perceptual connections with the Madonna were varied—a whiff of perfume, the awareness of a presence through a rustling sound, a shadow glimpsed while a *strong* seer was having a vision, a statuelike figure, a silhouette, a movement in the dark, an "odd" light, a tunnel of light and wind, unusual movements of the sun or moon, and so on. These were visions that might involve scores of people simultaneously, maintained by a collective effort to make perception more precise. They occurred almost daily in productive moments of great emotional tension. These collective visions took place above all in the evening, and were based on a kind of interpretive scrutiny of light and shadow.

The *strong* seer was able to reshape entirely the real, the usual in its everyday clarity; the *weak* seers, in contrast, could only work in the shadows. Neither in light, indisputable in its obviousness, nor in total darkness, unassailable in its opacity, but rather in the penumbra, chiaroscuro, was where they had visions. These seers were not given visions with clarity— that could be problematic, difficult, and would demand interpretation. But just as in classical hermeneutics there is sure to be a meaning in the text to be brought to light, so in the Oliveto visions the Madonna was sure to be there. The point was to catch her exact trajectory, interpret her signs correctly, and decipher her ciphered evidence. There was a hierarchy of visions, as there was of visionaries. On the one hand, there was an operant conviction that "she can't let herself be seen by everybody," and on the other the certainty that "something about her can be noticed by everybody: a shadow, a scent, an outline." Here perception was clearly *recognition* (Geertz 1973, 271), symbolically oriented by the context of the apparitions.

One consequence of the mechanism of collective production was that the certainty of the seer generally depended on the *others*. The proof of the phenomena was to be found in the experiences of *others*, which created a general emotional ambiance as well as a considerable strengthening of conviction. Even the *strong* seers had moments of doubt about their own experiences, and at these times the collective consensus was there to back them up and reassure them, as we saw with Ada, the first seer, and Nello, one of the most important (Apolito 1990, 150–51).

Once the context of the apparitions had been defined, every subsequent testimony, emotional outbreak, or shout was a *proof* of the Madonna's presence. There were no longer critical thresholds for credibility. The Committee and, above all, the parish priest constantly applied their own filters and thresholds of doubt. But while the Committee did not consider much of the general excitement credible and simply gathered and filed away the accounts of witnesses, this material nevertheless supplied much of the content of the *Bollettino*.

The formation of the context of the apparitions affected the believers' definition of the world in that it identified a place where the Madonna appeared, an arena for encounter between heaven and earth. It then became a question of the type, manner, and duration of the presence—but not of the presence itself—once any seer affirmed it. According to the most wide-spread and prevalent hermeneutic attitude, each individual testimony contributed to the phenomenology of the presence. This attitude was contested by the Committee, which refused to give up its role as a central filter of truth, but the attitude created the homogenous connective tissue of *credence* that simplified and made automatic the spread of *evidence* of the events.

On a cold evening of March 1986, an argument between believers pro-vided me with a clear contrast between two positions: one inclined to constant "supernatural testing" and another inclined to a passive under-standing of the events as one continuous global prodigy.

A group of pilgrims thought that they could see an angel on a chimney pipe above a house near the castle. Gigino, a thick-bearded youth from Grumo Nevano, challenged the authenticity of the figure since, in his opinion, it was the result of a shadow, which could be shown by looking at it in daylight, a time when one would see the natural discolorations that the pilgrims took to be an angel. The Grumo youth was not a skeptic, in fact he was one of the most convinced supporters of the apparitions, and in particular was one of those who took photographs that had captured a celestial phenomenon that many pilgrims declared they had seen. A woman from the group of weak seers retorted that she had been at Oliveto since the afternoon and had not seen any stain on the chimney pipe. Here is their written testimony of the prodigy:

Saturday November 30, 1985

We, the undersigned, who went to Oliveto Citra near the gate of the apparitions about 1:15 P.M., suddenly noted the following phenomena:

1) a rosary with very large beads which at a certain point were transformed into birds which we counted and there were 59

2) The aforementioned birds began to outline in the sky a number of things

a) at first they formed a V, while three birds that broke away from the group went to the center of the V, forming one after the other the word AVE. (AC)

Their testimony was accompanied by a drawing of the prodigy. Gigino had also taken photographs, which he showed, maintaining that one could distinguish a demonic serpent, the number six, and a flame, as well as other signs of the Devil.

In this context, Gigino wanted to show the weakness of the angel vision in contrast to the solidity of his own proofs of the prodigy he himself had observed. The woman to whom he was speaking, however, maintained that one could not say that the vision was an objective phenomenon:

{11.1}

fv: Excuse me—why do you have to raise these
           doubts?—are we to conclude that we should all see
           the same thing? + The Madonna means to say she
           wants to have herself seen by you and not me—or by
           me and not someone else.

The youth, nevertheless, insisted on the indisputable validity of the photographs in contrast to the subjectivity of the nocturnal visions. The woman then questioned the interpretation of the photographs that he was showing, giving her own interpretations of their forms, colors, and signs, and even suggested that he could have scrawled on the negatives to prove the prodigy. Finally, one argument left the youth speechless.

{11.2}

fv: Either we question everything or we believe
           everything—it comes down to that + believing + there
           is no certainty anywhere. {March 15, 1986}

In a certain sense the woman had raised a central point regarding the legitimation of vision testimony: acceptance of the presence of the Madonna in every possible appearance reported by the pious pilgrims meant *believing*. The problem was not—as at the beginning—whether the discovery of *strong* proofs would remove the possibility of arbitrary judgment and constitute evidence—that is why the woman took pleasure in raising doubts and furnishing other plausible interpretations about the proofs held to be objective and undeniable. The problem was rather whether or not to *decide* to consider things in the ongoing "symbolic mode" of faith.

Here one may note the effects of the effort to examine the proof that, as seen also in *"It Is Said They Have Seen the Madonna"* formed the basis for the construction of the context. Once that work was done, for people like the woman any search for proof was unnecessary, or worse, dangerous and devilish. There was nothing more to verify; one only had to believe. By this time the Committee itself, although indisposed to take everything as good and valid and often in the terrain of "supernatural experimentation," was using a normative criterion, not a critical one. The Committee's criterion was deductive (this yes and that no, this orthodox and that spurious), not empirical-inductive. The initial work of the investigation became superfluous once the presence of the Madonna had been verified and the risks could only come from the credibility of the seers and the interference of the Devil.

The symbolic *decision* was to endow the great mass of pilgrims with the capacity to *see* something. From this perspective it is understandable that anyone (except a leader) who openly challenged this attitude, raising doubts about the perceptions of the Madonna that occurred, would be rebuked. In the following excerpt of conversation, a group of pilgrims sees a kind of monogram of the Madonna near the gate. The second male voice flatly maintains that it is only stones, and he is harshly rebuffed by all around him. If he "does not believe," it would be better if he left. In vain he repeats that he "believes"in the apparitions. For those around him believing is the same as seeing or at least seeing-seeing.

{12}

(1) mv:	To the side—do you see her?
(2) mv2:	Where—in front to the left? + that's a white stone— hardly the Madonna!
(3) fv:	Eh, down there—you see her?
(4) mv2:	Where do you mean? It's a white stone!
(5) mv3:	No—what are you saying?
(6) mv2:	No, listen if someone sees her he sees the Madonna he doesn't see stones + the excitement—near // the wall
(7) fv:	That is really a pattern—why are you talking that

	way? if you don't believe go back // down—if you say they are stones.
(8) mv2:	No, it is not that I don't believe // I do believe—but I think that when he sees her he should really see her, not . . .
#(9) mv:	Hey—now if you say they are stones—then get down and leave room for others.
(10) mv2:	The design doesn't mean anything + boy // don't pay attention.
(11) fv:	What do you mean design? We are seeing the statue, the image.
(12) fv2:	Yeah, I see the image, too.
(13) mv2:	Where are you seeing her // lady
(14) fv2:	Straight ahead—if you can't see it I can.
(15) mv2:	Straight ahead where?
(16) fv2:	Straight ahead.
(17) mv2:	But what you're seeing are stones.
(18) fv:	If you don't see anything why don't you go away?
(19) mv3:	Please don't argue.
(20) mv4:	Do you see her really straight ahead?
(21) fv2:	Straight ahead there.
(22) mv2:	Do you see her straight ahead?
(23) fv2:	I see her straight ahead + to the right and to the left.
(24) mv2:	But near the wall // do you see her?
(25) fv2:	Look more carefully if you don't believe us // because . . .
(26) mv2:	I believe more than you do—there are a lot of people here getting upset over nothing.
(27) fv:	No, I'm not getting upset.
#(28) fv3:	No, it's really the Madonna + you can really see her. {June 13, 1986}

When a leader raised doubts, the reactions were not so adamant. In such cases, the others become became silent. But I have also been present dozens of times when, after a leader departed, the believers once again defended the validity of the vision or the testimony that had been rejected.

There is a recurring phrase that indicates the full acceptance of the attitude that identifies belief with seeing or seeing-seeing. A believer comes to a place where others are watching a point in the sky or on the walls of a house, shouting, weeping, etc. What the newcomer says is more or less, "What?—Is there seeing here?" ["Che?—si vede qua?"] The "Is there seeing here?" objectivizes the individual claim or even the collective convention: this is the place *not* where *someone maintains* they see something, but where *there is something* to be seen. The interpretive exercise then addresses the form and nature of the presence; the presence itself is not at issue, is not an object of hermeneutics.

For months at Oliveto there occurred hundreds of episodes of collective vision in which a spot, a light, a color, a smell, a puff of air, was varyingly interpreted as a sign of the Madonna. The collective dimension of these episodes made them emotionally highly intense. Frequent faints, indispositions, shouts, weeping, and collective crises marked the evenings in Oliveto in the winter of 1985–86. All went home convinced of having taken part in a collective perception of the Madonna; to all she had given a sign of her presence. The sign was never clear or sharp, as with the *strong* seers, never indisputable and unique. Always one had to consult and argue about what it was and meant. Looking at the place in question, each person asked for and provided details to those around them, each identified a shape, tried to describe it, and asked for and provided confirmation. This phenomenon can reasonably be termed *hermeneutic vision*.

I do not mean to say that all became sure they had perceived the presence, or that everyone could perceive it everywhere. Doubts remained and the skeptics, those in the Committee or influenced by it, were numerous. But these were not the people who constructed the collective *focus*. I saw that even at the start of the visions (Apolito 1990, 181–83) the skeptics, although numerous, were no match for the productive power of the believers, which derived from the construction of collective practices that became established institutions. Even though by then the Committee was intensively mobilizing to promote *procedures that were orthodox and official*, it could not stem the increase in opportunities for collective seeing at different places and times. If a skeptic's criticism of one sighting was successful, another sighting would take place that would overcome all doubt. Eventually, these episodes dwindled almost out of existence, but as a result of the Committee's repression, not of a conviction that the hermeneutic visions were baseless.

Moreover, the phenomenon was so general that no one could be sure of herself during situations of collective seeing—someone who criticized the visions in one spot might find himself defending them in another. In any case, it was an automatic reaction to try to expand the normal, distracted, capacity for perception by following the lure of the semantic risk of an interpretive proposal that anyone nearby might offer. In the Oliveto nights when the pilgrims considered the Marian presence obvious, all visible forms around the castle were incorporated into the game of celestial attributes. It was as if the obviousness of everyday perception underwent a drastic overhaul and the world appeared composed of new presences in old forms.

At night, the play of shadows from natural and artificial sources of light did not form a motionless backdrop for human action as in the dull everyday round. Rather they became a vivid focus of human attention as places for barely perceptible movements of the divine presence. Those present for these moments of collective production helped redesign the world. Even outside observers were swept up. Adele Cambria wrote an article for *Il Giorno* in which she recounted her own experience.

For a while now people have been pushing behind me; all spasmodically fix their pupils on the darkness and light beyond the gate. I imagine from this experience that hallucinations are more than likely. Indeed I (yes, even I, with my poor eyesight) see at a certain moment a clearly-defined point of light moving, the precise round light of a portable flashlight. Then, in the light, forms the shape of a white bird, but one that does not take flight but instead creeps up and down along the ruins of the wall. Of course I keep quiet, nobody has as yet "seen" anything this evening, but then here are the first voices: "The dove, the dove of the Holy Spirit . . ." "No, it's the Madonna, now she is getting bigger." "You're crazy! that is the dove of the Holy Spirit, but She is coming down on the other side, from the ramp, don't you see her, with a black mantle." (Cambria 1985)

Not even the researcher could remain aloof from this detailed exercise of scrutiny, in which everyday objects of the world no longer were called by their everyday names—clouds, moon, smoke, chimney, plaster, bricks, walls, etc.—but were spoken of as long or short, growing or shrinking, circles or squares, gradations of light and dark, colors and thicknesses, points and planes, movement and suspension. Doubtless, the collective interpretive intention was to recognize the Marian sign, but in the long phase of definition what was observed was the enormous job of collective reshaping of cultural ways of perceiving the world. Often the final definition never arrived and the effort at redefinition stalled in mid-passage. Instead of crystallizing in an epiphany, it simply dissolved the consoling self-evidence of the world. At these moments, a universe of childhood fears of the dark seemed to spill out disquietingly and then, especially on the dark streets far from the little plaza, someone would make the sign of the cross and quickly call the others to go back to the safety of the plaza spotlights and the Committee microphones.

A group of women and children were in the lee of a precarious old bell-tower in a street running from the side of the castle. While they were trying to decipher shapes and profiles of the fallen arch, night fell and they saw new things. One woman even asked me what I saw:

{13}

(1) fv2:   You can see something like a picture.

(2) fv: Yes, like a picture.

(3) fv2:   Like a picture it is.

(4) fv: And then it's arranged I can't say.

(5) fv3:   I'm not sure about it

[PAUSE]

(6) fv: Do you see that brown spot?

(7) fv1:   That is the bell.

(8) fv: No—over here down here to the...

(9) fv2:   What are you seeing?

(10) fv: With a hood plus a black strip around like a kind of head—of a monk, understand? I see it like . . . with a hood on and a bow in the back [the woman turns to me]

(11) res: A hood, like a hood with black ribbons?

(12) fv: And a the bow in the middle.

(13) res: And what could it be?

(14) fv: Well, everyone is seeing it; now either it's an image . . .

(15) res: That woman saw clearly the whole picture.

(16) fv: Well, I didn't see the picture.

(17) fv2:   Hey, everyone here is seeing that white strip.

(18) fv1:   Maybe it's a sculpture made by the . . . over so many years certain things are shaped that seem to be animals, a lion—something or other.

(19) fv: And what is there to see?

(20) fv1:   A lady kneeling

(21) fv: You?
(22) fv2:   Even your mamma sees it.
(23) fv1:   Mamma? Where did you see it?
(24) fv2:   Over there.
(25) fv1:   Where those green leaves are?
(26) fv2:   Yes.
(27) fv1:   In that entrance-way?
(28) fv2:   Yes.
(29) fv1:   Where the hole is?
(30) fv2:   The hole, no, look a little higher up.
(31) fv4:   There is a . . .
(32) fv5:   Good.
(33) fv6:   There is a white spot.
(Then one woman sees a picture, another a stone; one boy says it is the Madonna, another tells his grandmother he has seen something white and green; a little girl says she has seen a kind of image of the Madonna dell'Arco; a woman sees a stone, but in front of it a strange spot that acts like a halo.)
(34) girl: . . . Then there is that little wooden table see an image that seems like it's heavenly?
(35) fv2:   Yes.
(36) girl: With two vertical lines—can you make it out?
(37) fv3:   But that's a spot in front of the stone + it's a spot.
(38) fv3:   Look at that—is it a small stone?—beneath that small stone sort of between the stone and . . . in the middle is there something heavenly? you can see a spot in front of it + that dark spot is in front if it.
(39) fv6:   Yes it's an image . . . that is.
(40) fv3:   It surely is a figure + that's a . . .
(41) fv7:   You can even see a light.
(42) fv4:   Yes, midway up the bell.
(43) fv7:   No, not midway up the bell + I see it . . .
(44) boy: You can see two of them.
[. . .]
(45) little girl: Granny, let's go I'm scared. {July 21, 1986}

In this instance, none of those present made a satisfactory identification or proposed one successfully to the others. All was left suspended between ordinary perception and the possibility that all of a sudden something might emerge from the depths of the unspoken, breaking out of the accustomed surface of things, creating an opening that might suck the everyday order into metahistorical reality—spots, pictures, entrance-ways, arches, holes, tables. Out of there, in an instant, infinity could erupt. But this time the compactness of the ordinary held control. Only toward the end was there a kind of vertigo from the temptation of the transcendent, and the little girl murmured the fear. In situations like this, there is a lack of contingent interpretive leadership that could direct to the collective work effectively.

But there were also persons who proposed their interpretations effectively enough to bring those nearby around to admitting that shapes that were not at first "named" as coming from the Madonna in fact did come from her. The leaders were obviously more effective when those around them could be satisfied with a basic level of interpretation. The following conversational segment may be an instance of this nature; it came at the end of a long hermeneutic effort, with additional kinds of persuasion not indicated in the quotes.

{14}

(Many people weep and cry out after identifying an image.)

(1) fv:	But I don't see anything—where is she? I don't see her.
(2) mv:	Sure you do + up there.
(3) fv:	Where?
(4) mv:	Look under there—at the end of that gutter + down the side of the wall.
(5) fv:	Oh—that little . . . ?
(6) mv:	Yeah—yeah—that white thing—that white light.
(7) fv:	Ah, I've seen her—that's the Madonna?
(8) mv:	Yes, she's going like this + by the wall—she's coming out and going down.
(9) fv:	Ah, I've seen her—(turning to a man a ways off) we've seen her Franco—on that pipe—we've seen her.
(10) Franco:	(murmurs something apparently skeptical that the tape-recorder does not pick up)
(11) fv:	But that's what a gentleman here said—that there is a pipe and there is the image of the Madonna. {February 1, 1986}

This elementary kind of seeing required a segregation from the level of the fuzzy and the unnamed. It was an initial selective configuration to which other signs could subsequently be added. When a shape became a celestial design, the possibility that it might be a casual silhouette—a stain from humidity on a fallen wall or chimney, or the effect of lights on the shadows of streets or walls—had to be eliminated. In these moments emotional tension played a critical role. If a hermeneutic proposition was received with weeping, cries, and exclamations, it had good prospects of being accepted. If, on the other hand, it encountered a chilly mood, it almost always quickly disappeared.

Once the first step of identification of an unnatural shape had been made, the next step was the "naming." A woman from Cardito told me that when a figure appeared near a wall in her village, people first tried to decide whether it was Jesus with long hair or the Madonna {April 26, 1986}. At Oliveto, the name of choice was the Madonna, but it was not unusual to propose others, including Jesus himself, or saints Michael, Macarius, Anthony, and Rita, anonymous angels, and so on. There was also the Devil, as we shall soon see.

The next step was to decide if it was a representation (a sketch, painting, or statue from out of nowhere) or the Madonna herself "in flesh and blood." The levels of vision came to be based precisely on this distinction, which constituted, for this reason, a source of conflict among the seers. Some of them only observed the animation (eyes, mouths) of pre-existing images, especially in the devotional niche of the Madonna to the left of the gate. Some, though, had the frightening experience of a picture that suddenly appeared and then became animated, its two-dimensional features coming forth and taking on corporeal form. A group of believers from Grumo told of having seeing the movement of the eyes and an arm of a statuette of the Baby Jesus that belonged to a fellow townsperson. Moreover, they maintained that the image periodically became totally animated, and its owner would take the "baby" in his arms or have him walk. Once the animated statue even engaged the Devil in combat and came out of it with a broken finger, something that could be seen embodied, as it were, in the statuette. While they were telling me this, the Committee leader, Michele, was listening, and he recalled other episodes of struggles with the Devil that produced signs, commenting that it was hard to reach a judgment one way or another {March 15, 1986}.

Many times this level of vision of images referred specifically to known advocations: the Madonna dell'Arco, the Immaculate Conception, Our Lady of Lourdes, Fatima, Medjugorje, and so on. One woman saw the Pietà of Michelangelo in the sky (AC). At times, the presence of the leader served to define in traditional iconographic terms the result of a hermeneutic exercise. After Giovannina of Salerno listened to the "firsthand" description of a seer, she concluded that he was seeing the Madonna of Loreto and, in order to convince him, offered to take him to see a Loreto image in a chapel {February 1, 1986}.

As time went on, the normative pressure of the Committee had the effect of producing among the pilgrims a sort of canon of *weak* apparitions by which some kinds were rejected and others were accepted. Arguments periodically erupted over whether it was possible for the Madonna to appear in such-and-such a way, as claimed by one seer or another.

{15}

(1) mv: I am sure of one thing about apparitions—apparitions do
             not appear near the wall or on a rock—only in the air
(2) fv: That's not true because many people have seen the
             Madonna on the wall + the pilgrimage on Friday saw
             her on the wall—with a blue mantle and a crown on
             her head—a white dress + something I didn't see—on
             the wall in front of us + so saying the Madonna only
             appears suspended in the air + well we saw her
             also . . . when we were getting off the bus + a lot of
             us saw the statue—I saw the statue of the Madonna of
             Loreto—I've seen other kinds of statues just as I've
             seen . . . + so pardon me but am I supposed not to
             believe anybody?—should I only believe those who
             say they have seen the Madonna suspended in the air?
(3) mv: But it seems to me much more logical . . .
(4) fv: What logic . . . ?
(5) mv: Why appear by a rock. {March 15, 1986}

Here is another example:

{16}

fv2:   No, that is not the Madonna—she does not appear by
             the wall + my husband has seen her in Bellizzi the

> Madonna—but he saw her suspended in the air—in a
> void + now that was the Madonna for sure—because
> he didn't see her next to something + now its
> happening like before when they saw her in the
> alley—next to the wall where there was a reflection
> from the window + then they closed the window and
> they stopped seeing her there. {November 29, 1986}

"Logic" and experience seem to become references in the construction of this canon, which, while it does not block marginal experiences completely, becomes useful in guiding successive hermeneutic visions toward forms that, if not approved by the leaders, will at least be tolerated. But the gestation of a canon of *weak* visions was the first step toward their disappearance; as the possibilities decreased, the fertile interaction of individual interpretation became progressively more difficult.

As time went on, the collective pathos that accompanied the hermeneutic visions tapered off. In many cases, the pilgrims returned time and again to Oliveto and participated in the same experience of collective vision. They were unable to go beyond these weak perceptions and hence became habituated to visual familiarity with a transcendence they could only glimpse, which reduced the likelihood of feeling the shock typical of their first experiences. It was possible then to observe the collective interpretation of signs as routine exercises with little emotional involvement. I shall take up this matter again in the final chapter.

The Seers

What made the experiences of hermeneutic visions especially intolerable for both the parish priest and the Committee was the absence of prior stable external criteria by which the visions could be filtered and verified. The search—in ethnomethodological terms—for plausibility, rationality, and verisimilitude typical of the procedures of the hermeneutic visions was circular and self-confirming. This kind of autonomy was impermissible for an institution whose general criteria for truth were fixed by the authority of tradition and by the Church hierarchy. The rejection of hermeneutic visions was a rejection of the worldview implicit in them. It was not that the Committee itself had a criterion for objective truth in these circumstances, and much less that it rejected the common "symbolic mode" of approaching the events. The Committee, like the believers, had no preexisting *code* in which there already existed an order of differences that allowed *signs* to be identified.

Following the dispositions of Benedict XIV, Catholicism, as a religion of faith rather than vision (Galot 1985, 21), attributed to apparitions only the assent of "human faith." In other words, the Church did not have a specific doctrinal *corpus* it could check to locate a pre-established truth. In short, the difference between the Committee and the *weak* seers was not here. The difference was that the Committee already had *auctoritates* of its own *to decide who ought to decide*, while the hermeneutic seeing was constructed in such a way that the *auctoritas* that *decided* what perceptual threshold was valid and what object perceived was constituted in the very process of the hermeneutic work, hence it was contingent, precarious, and reversible. The randomness and instability of the hermeneutic *auctoritas* were quite intolerable for the Committee, itself founded on the recognition of the eternal *auctoritas* of the church hierarchy.

In any case, it was not easy for the Committee to impose its hegemony. In the space that it attempted to control, that of the apparitions, the discourse that constituted the events was not, in the last analysis, that of the Committee, the hegemonic group, but rather that of the seers. The Committee was constrained to base its own *auctoritas* on that of the various *auctoritates* present among the believers, over which, however, it wanted to exercise its own authority. In other words, the seeing could be delimited, defined, and legitimated only by recourse to the seers themselves: the testimony of some could only be explained, exorcised, or contradicted by the testimony of others. The set phrase in the first issues of the *Bollettino*, which later disappeared, stating that "everything in this report [. . .] is always understood as the meaning and the thinking believed by the seers," had a much more literal sense than its ritual formulation might imply. The universe of the Oliveto apparitions was built entirely from the words of seers, however revised, reformulated, or reordered for plausibility from an orthodox perspective; each time someone said, "The Madonna said" or "The Madonna did," there was the unspoken understanding, "according to seer x." The seers supplied the bricks for the edifice that the Committee was constructing. The stability of the building could not be assured without carefully inspecting the construction material. Hence, the most serious struggle developed over the definition of the status of seer.

In this respect, the Oliveto case is rather atypical, compared to the more famous and "successful" apparitions. When there are few "recognized" seers, one (Lourdes), two (La Salette), three (Fatima), or six (Medjugorje), it is quite easy to set up a collaborative construction of truth between leaders and seers in which the former from time to time mark a perimeter of meaning around what the latter report. It is no coincidence that seers, after their apparitions, end up in convents (first and foremost, with Lourdes and Fatima) or even start off in convents (Catherine Labouré), where discourse is rigorously managed by church authority. But even in these cases, there is, at the beginning, a dispute about the status of the seers.

At Lourdes, a few weeks after Bernadette's first apparition, numerous persons declared they had visions that were, moreover, quite varied in nature. These latter visions, however, were soon rejected as false (Estrade 1934, 190ff.). At Fatima as well, a number of persons said they saw the Madonna without getting any credit for it (Lucia 1973, 59). And around Medjugorje other seers came forward who were rejected by the leadership (Sala and Mantero 1986, 130).

In these disputes, however, the leadership had no difficulty in coming out on top, organizing and defining the phenomena around the first, central seers. At Oliveto, in contrast, just who the central seers were changed with remarkable swiftness. As I have indicated, this changeability was an indirect consequence of the constant endeavor to reduce the charismatic appeal of the seers in order to maintain the authority of the leaders. In any case, this strategy was encouraged by the nature of the first seers. The boys led to their own ouster by their uninhibited speech and gestures. Ada at first was isolated by her own father, then isolated herself by marrying and moving away; others did not have the requisite charisma, and when they did (Aurelia, for instance), they could not be counted on to be orthodox. As a result, no seer stayed a star, much less the only star, for any length of time.

The first seers gained star status automatically, since they were the direct protagonists at the origin of the events. But because of their rapid ouster, the subsequent contest over who were seers became sharper and more dramatic. Formal legitimation was always conferred by the Committee: every person who claimed to be a seer went to the office to give testimony, which was generally taken down. But only some would have their seeing, messages, and condition publicized. A few, rare cases were directly discouraged, others were essentially ignored, while still others were well-received and listened to favorably each time they said they had seen something. Obviously, the ones favorably received expressed their visionary experiences in terms at least acceptable to the Committee. The most valued vision content was so congruent with the Committee's religious concerns that it constituted a kind of inspired counterpoint to the Committee's pastoral objectives. These were the visions most often published in the *Bollettino*. The seers who declared them were those most frequently mentioned on public occasions and in informal conversations with Committee members.

Yet, and this is the point, the Committee alone did not determine who was a seer. A seer may simply have been a person who had a fit, who fainted, or who wept while gazing fixedly at the sky or at the castle, and who afterward reported what was seen. In the informal gatherings that took place every evening, it was not difficult to be recognized as a seer. If the person in question went to Oliveto frequently, she or he may easily have been considered a seer even without the Committee's accreditation. Margnelli and Gagliardi similarly observed, based on interviews, that it was enough to "glimpse" something and mention it to others in order to become "automatically pointed out as a 'seer [*veggente*]' " (Margnelli and Gagliardi 1987a, 36). There were great numbers of seers of this kind; they spread out in the zones around the castle and often started promoting themselves in their hometowns. While the Committee could have with relative ease controlled the visionary enthusiasm of these seers in Oliveto, it found it difficult, if not impossible, to do so in their towns of origin. With this in mind, the Committee published in the *Bollettino*, starting in the seventh issue, a challenge. "The faithful are urged to consider as true only the messages distributed by this Committee. Since many persons, without the knowledge of the parish priest, say they are seers at Oliveto Citra, you are asked to find out whether they are or not by telephoning the Priest Mons. [Giovanni Morano]." Indeed, the proliferation of seers who attracted groups of believers in their home towns was extraordinary. Oliveto acquired such an elevated status in the visionary piety of Campania that any aspiring "charismatic" could easily gain credibility by a vision at Oliveto.

Once the status of seer had been acquired, a person became a point of reference attesting to the validity of the phenomena, explaining what the Madonna wanted, and constructing the process of events. The status of *strong* seer in particular conferred the ability to intervene in the development of the apparitions. The *story* of the events of Oliveto was generated by seers; any new developments in the relation between the Madonna and Oliveto always implied a declaration from one or more seers, which effectively constituted the event. The Committee kept for itself the job of accepting or rejecting the seers' input and, naturally, of orienting the process; but it was the seers who fueled the engine of the *story* (consider, for example, the July 20 episode). Naturally the Committee was able to create the conditions that might generate a certain kind of visionary input. If the Committee expressed hopes for a given content in the Marian messages, for example, the seers who sought recognition for it may well have modulated their visionary experiences in ways that fit these hopes.

All the seers wanted the Committee's recognition. But after a while, some tried to escape the control of the Committee and, in particular, of the parish priest. Indeed, the seer recognized by the *plaza* was truly a free and independent protagonist. The seers who were controlled by the parish priest, in contrast, found themselves in the situation of the female somnambulists of the "somnambulist medicine" of nineteenth century Europe, as Clara Gallini describes.

> The somnambulist is at this point a personage with all her power. But these powers are never absolute, not even when she has achieved the autonomy of her *trance*. Like that of the Sibyl, her discourse is frequently obscure and requires interpretation. And here is where the magnetist comes in, apparently as an interpreter, but in fact as the codifier of a magma of information over which the somnambulist seems to relinquish control to the leader. (Gallini 1983a, 42)

The seer who was a Committee favorite knew, as the episode with Benedetta illustrates, that his or her testimony would always be *translated* before it was made public. If their messages were too frequently dubious, then the seer was dropped. Only a few seers enjoyed a stable recognition from the Committee. Over time this number had declined by attrition because it was all too easy to take on a tone, report messages, dare to make comments, or describe visions in which heterodoxy became preponderant. Some rebelled because it was just as easy to chafe against the interpretive strictures laid down by the parish priest. The leadership was harder on these open rebels than on the seers who had only occasional heterodox, or simply folkloric, "lapses."

We often find folkloric themes in the fragments of messages that have been ignored or trimmed by those in charge of maintaining orthodoxy and providing the events with rationality and plausibility. Ubaldo, an especially certified seer, wrote in a section of his testimony that the Committee never released the "fact" that the Madonna "predicted that the next day [he would] see a falling star and that [he] should make a wish" (AC).

Another noteworthy example can be found in the way Faricy censors the testimony of Tommaso. The Irish Jesuit states that he transcribed "faithfully from these documents" which, he emphasizes, "are written on two pages torn from a note-pad, which Tommaso gave to monsignor [Morano]" (Faricy 1986, 44–45). Faricy does not say that the handwriting of these two pages was not that of Tommaso, whose irregular penmanship was available in other, signed documents.

More important, Faricy makes some significant textual omissions. The first is at the end of a phrase from "Tommaso" in which the lad referred to secret messages from the Madonna: "In effect these are warnings for humanity, about which I was informed" (Ibid., 47). The full text continues: "[about which I was informed] one week before they occurred, as with the Mexican earthquake and the volcanic eruption in Colombia, [and] another warning will take place not long from now [. . .]" (AC). The most significant omission in the two pages attributed to Tommaso, however, is the entire paragraph that follows the above quotation.

> One time she appeared to me and she had at her feet a plant, she told me that this plant would cure a disease that afflicts the world, she further told me that I must find it and that She would help me. The next evening she told me that this task was too difficult for me and that she would pass it on to another person whose name I will not say for the time being, She said that She would help this person to find the plant. (AC)

The search for a plant or a magic healing herb is a well-known folkloric motif that, according to Stith-Thompson's *Motif-Index of Folk Literature*, falls under sections H1324 "Quest for marvelous remedy" and H1333 "Quest for extraordinary plants (fruits, trees)." It is a motif often seen in television cartoons. The orthodox credibility of Tommaso, which Faricy vouches for, is constructed by leaving things out that could cast him in a bad light.

Similar operations were performed on the messages of other "official" seers. Serena's unfulfilled prophecy of July 2, 1985, was not circulated. It stated that Fulvio would be a seer. The other child seer, Mauro, who the Committee backed strongly, was one of the authors of the prophecy of three days of total darkness on earth that would occur at the end of March 1986. The failure of this prophecy became the pretext for the sudden demotion of

Remo, the seer from Frattamaggiore. Nello, another major seer, reported extraordinary stories of blood, of the Devil stabbing the Madonna, and so on (I go into them in the next chapter) that were not mentioned in the official accounts. Giovannina, a highly respected seer from Salerno, told of her bilocations, during which she visited the earth below the castle and located hidden treasure and a spring that sooner or later would break through to the surface (testimony by Fulvio {February 1, 1986}). In the *Bollettino*, the official organ of the Committee, more questionable aspects and compromising experiences of visions were edited out, but without raising doubts about the accredited seers who reported them.

In addition to censuring or silencing the unorthodox words or deeds of the seers, it was common among the leaders involved in apparitions to concoct plausible interpretations for these kinds of words or deeds in order to avoid calling the seers into question. At Medjugorje, the bishop of Mostar, who, as we have seen, was quite critical of the visions, did not hesitate to expose a number of episodes in which dubious messages from the seers were "rescued" by the leadership. The bishop maintained that he laid out the seers' "lies" in a private conversation with Laurentin. The French Mariologist, according to the bishop, counseled him not to reveal the facts so as not to damage the conversions of many pilgrims. Laurentin subsequently denied he said anything of the sort, but the bishop insisted on his version and essentially called Laurentin untruthful.

Laurentin, among others, has tried to contextualize incongruent aspects of the messages reported by the Yugoslav seers. For example, he explains the bishop's statement that the youths said that at the end of June 1981 there would be three apparitions more, whereas they continued years later at the time of this writing, as a message that the seer who first reported it "believes she has understood" (Laurentin 1986a, 56). In any case, he adds in another book (Laurentin 1988d, 18), even canonized saints have been mistaken at times. Here again the issue arises as to who decides whether a message is authentic or simply "believed" by a seer. Basically, what was useful in the seers was the channel they established with the Madonna. Communications on this channel was always subject to filtering, but rarely, at least for the accredited seers, was the channel itself questioned.

The status of seer carried with it a high degree of social attention that many people in the apparition community would have liked to have achieved, even if this meant, as was often the case, denigration and ridicule from nonbelievers in the hometown. If, in addition, the seer was recognized by the Committee, then this social success was even more substantial. The effort to achieve this status meant that, on the one hand, the Madonna came to be involved with messages directed to the Committee or the pilgrims in order to get them to believe the seer who transmitted them; on the other, conflicts developed between seers who were more or less on the same level. In contrast, seers of lower rank tended to agree with seers higher up in an attempt to rise in public esteem.

The hierarchy among seers made the events, as an arena of conflictual relations, particularly mobile and unstable. When a seer at a high level announced an important message, confirmations from seers lower down often followed. Other seers with prestige then had to decide whether to confirm or deny the message, an action that could lead to rising or falling in prestige, a clean sweep of an entire group of seers, or the elimination or confirmation of "opposing" seers.

The prophecy of a sign on July 20, 1985, was confirmed by all the Oliveto seers at the time. In that phase the need to confirm the apparitions was even more pressing than the incipient conflicts between seers. But, by the following March, the prophecy of three nights of darkness led to a schism among the seers—some backing, others rejecting, it. Consider how an accredited seer, Giovanni of Agropoli, tried to liquidate with one message an entire echelon of seers who had approved the prophecy. The Madonna told him on May 24:

Enough of these things, I don't want you to fall into error again. To you have come in the past, are now coming, and will come in the future many persons claiming in my Name to bring messages that provoke panic. These persons, even if they seem to be ripe fruit, have gone bad. Dear friends, I will now explain in detail how you are to distinguish between false messages or false prophecies and true ones so you will never fall into error again. False prophecies, O dear children, are fatalistic prophecies, that is, that within a day, a year, a month, certain things will happen. (AC)

Before Giovanni, Giovannina had raised the same arguments in conversation with me:

[. . .] When they give a date they are false prophets—because the Madonna no + Jesus never says . . . —says always be prepared—like the Virgin—always keep your lamp lit + we don't trust them because these days so many false prophets are born and we must send them away—the false prophet is the one who gives you dates. {May 17, 1986}

If a mistaken prophecy was not cause enough for a seer to lose prestige, it still might lead to an increase in prestige for other seers if they could present themselves as free of the error.

The reciprocal *moves* constituted an extremely varied and risky game for each seer. One had to intuit what moment to seize, which alliance to make, the pretext to use. In general, it was hard for seers to keep up their standing exclusively on their own. Some seers worked in tandem, although it was rare for an alliance to last long. Others depended on the approval of the pilgrims; still others on that of the Committee or Don Giovanni.

Those seers who depended on the approval of pilgrims produced many messages that fed the hopes and devotional preferences of their constituency about predictions of the future, petitions for healing and jobs, and millennial hopes. Every once in a while, other seers tried to delegitimize this process. Ubaldo passed on a message in May 1986 in which the Madonna asked people not to make "mistaken requests" nor ask for "jobs or girlfriends because I have not come for these things" (AC). But apart from rare attempts at resistance, it was hard for seers to avoid, sooner or later, giving in to the expectations of the believers. These expectations included (1) concrete needs for the resolution or reassurance "about problems in the here and now" (A. Rossi 1969, 108); (2) direction of meaning in "marvelous" terms deriving from folklore and television; and (3) strongly apocalyptic and millenarian configurations, stimulated by a layer of believers attuned to these issues through the international visionary culture. It was this last group of believers who were capable of making connections among Oliveto and Fatima, Medjugorje, and other worldwide sites, thus completing a circuit of Marian intervention in the world that they understood as a sign of the coming end of times. The seers alternated among the different fields of expectation according to the varying rhythms of collective consensus. As a result, at times they found themselves intensively delivering messages of questionable orthodoxy.

The seers closest to the Committee generally reported messages useful for the purpose of regulating the cult, for which the Committee was grateful. But even these seers were unable to avoid totally the constant demand for configuring the transcendent in accord with the hopes of the different groups of believers. The difference lay in the emphasis the seers put on one kind or message or the other. Hence, the problem was not so much whether the seer should refer to these matters, which were in any case expressions of cultural levels that the seers themselves often shared. The problem came if and how the seer did so in relation to the pilgrims—whether the seer accepted the leadership of the Committee and became a charismatic spokesperson for its agenda or a direct intermediary for the Madonna without going through the Committee.

Consider, as a prime example, the contrast between two seers from adjacent towns, Giorgio and Nello. Giorgio, an accounting student, was educated, spoke Italian, and was reserved. When he felt weak after a vision he simply collapsed in the arms of those around him without uttering a sound. Nello worked part-time in his brothers' small shoe factory, was almost illiterate, and spoke a dialect that was only slightly Italianized. When he saw the Madonna he had sharp nervous fits, with loud screams and convulsions. Between the two men there was a fierce, hidden rivalry, often expressed by mutual back-biting.

Of the two, the Committee recognized Nello longest, precisely because he always remained obedient to its authority. Giorgio (the seer in the episode with the moon cited above), on the other hand, was trying to become an overall leader of the groups of pilgrims that came to Oliveto. Moreover, Nello was able to eliminate the emotional and theatrical aspects of his visions, explaining the transformation as a response to the Madonna, who asked him not to weep or feel bad when he saw her lest she be obliged not to appear to him again. Nello's transformation and the desire that the Madonna expressed to him constituted for the Committee a *model for*, that is, the source of, "rooted 'mental' dispositions" (Geertz 1973, 123), a way to modify the expressive aspects of the "Neapolitan" piety.

The "game" played on the apparition field had three groups as players: the leaders, the seers, and the believers. *Visibly*, the seers were the intermediaries with the transcendent. The Church leadership could tolerate a modest reduction of its institutional prerogative of mediation with heaven only if the visible mediation of the seers confirmed and did not attack its own fundamental and institutional mediation. On the other hand, the believers who came to the apparition site demonstrated by their very presence that they were drawn more by the new charismatic mediation than by the traditional kind of the institutional Church. The seers responded to the conflicting demands of the leadership and the believers by alternately leaning toward the former—and jeopardizing their charismatic momentum—or toward the latter—and risking a crippling encounter with the institution.

At Medjugorje, this three-way game became less dynamic when a fourth player was added who radicalized the positions of all the players: the bishop of Mostar. By all accounts, the local Franciscan leadership had used the apparitions in their decades-old conflict with the bishop of Mostar and the diocesan clergy (Bax 1990, 1995). It was not by chance that the bishop at first was cautiously sympathetic to the apparitions, as Franciscan supporters pointed out. In a declaration of August 1981, the bishop defended the honesty of the seers and the clerics who had guided the seers, emphasizing: "We are convinced that the youths have not been instigated by anybody, much less by anyone in the Church. For the time being there are no reasons to believe the youths are liars" (*La Madonna a Medjugorje*, Cittadella: Bertoncello Artigrafiche, 1985, 181).

It is probable that in this phase the bishop considered himself part of the third player, the institutional leadership. The bishop told Mart Bax that initially

> he had been in favor of the movement and the visionaries, and he still is convinced that the Church in general may benefit from the devotion to Our Lady. Only when the youngsters in Medjugorje (allegedly supported by the Madonna) began to criticize his diocesan policy publicly he was forced to take "other steps." (Bax 1990, 73 n. 13)

At that point the bishop became aware that the local Franciscans were trying to use the apparitions as a new resource in their conflict.

> One of the first messages was for the bishop of Mostar. Our Lady stated that the prelate had wrongfully excommunicated a number of Franciscans. She encouraged the bishop to perform a "public reconciliation" with these "sons of the Church." The diocesan priests are also frequently urged along this "heavenly" course toward reconciliation. The numerous messages and instructions did not remain secret for long. It became widely known that the Madonna reprimanded the bishop and his priests and supported their adversaries. [. . .] This open stigmatizing has turned into an institution of sorts. On the mountain of the apparitions and in the church, weekly "intentions" are prayed for the bishop and his priests, who are referred to by name. According to

the visionaries, the Gospa has urgently requested these prayers in a special message. (Ibid., 68–69)

The bishop, who found himself to be the fourth player in a game that he must surely have seen he would lose, had no other alternative than to mount an all-out attack on the apparitions. In 1990, he obtained an undeniable victory. The newspapers of January 4, 1991, gave ample coverage to a document of the Yugoslav bishops of November 28, 1990, which they had prudently kept secret, in which the bishops declared that the supernatural character of the Medjugorje phenomena "cannot be affirmed" (not "affirmed," but not "excluded" either, commented Laurentin [Giacomini 1991]).

While the case of Medjugorje, in which the game became one with four players, cannot be generalized, it is not unique. Bax cites analogous situations of apparitions used to defend religious orders under attack by dioceses (Bax 1990, 71). Carroll (1985, 73) refers as well to the use of apparitions to boost the autonomy of national churches in subtle tension with the Vatican. In any event, the Medjugorje case makes it quite clear by its relative exceptionalness that because apparitions are visibly charismatic phenomena they have the potential, when accepted by the Church, to become a powerful means for strengthening institutions. It is for this reason that the efforts of the leadership were above all concentrated, at least at the start, on the seers, who were apparently intermediaries with heaven: In fact, the leadership was trying to get the seers to become intermediaries between the faithful and the Church.

There is no doubt that, in the eyes of the faithful, seers at Oliveto, as elsewhere, served as intermediaries with the transcendent and could procure special graces, request predictions, and get responses. There was a standard set of ways to mediate with the Madonna that varied slightly for each apparition site, and the Oliveto case stands for many others. The Oliveto seers were always besieged by throngs of believers desperately seeking contact with the Madonna. Sometimes the seers protested: a little boy became annoyed because everyone was handing him rosaries to be blessed by the Madonna {March 22, 1986}; often Nello took evasive action to avoid being cornered by believers; Tommaso learned to adopt a brusque, distant attitude. In other situations and at other times, the same seers, when told of the circumstances of believers standing nearest to them, took advantage of their close relationship with the Madonna: Donato told a sick man that the Madonna wanted him at the gate at a certain time (Faricy 1986, 29); Nello took a perfumed handkerchief sent her by the Madonna to a woman believer {April 26, 1986}. Often various seers separately appointed themselves intermediaries for the same person, and each asserted the role, causing confusion and embarrassment. A little girl received from the Madonna a message that a blind man present would imminently be healed. The girl hurried to tell the man, only to find that the Madonna had already spoken to the person accompanying him {May 3, 1986}.

The mediation of *strong* seers during their own visions permitted believers to have weak perceptions of the Madonna. Often believers surrounding a *strong* seer saw a shadow, a silhouette, noticed a dove in flight that might have been the messenger of the Madonna, noted a warmth, a scent. Sometimes the body of the seer gave off a scent, or an unexplainable heat, especially in the case of Nello after his visions. Nello sometimes told of "having" some friend or relative "see" the Madonna. On such occasions he would pause at the gate with the person in question, and in a climate of intense emotion urge the person to pray and to see. At the end he would faint and subsequently explain his state of prostration from the enormous effort necessary to "have someone see."

A *strong* seer might reach the same plane of extraordinary visibility as the Madonna. One woman had her first vision of Mary after a preliminary vision of a female seer {February 1, 1986}. *Strong* seers had different ways of advertising their capacity for mediation. Consider this eloquent passage from a message reported by Benedetta: "I am in the midst of you, I walk with you, I talk with you through the heart of this sister of yours who is my servant. You do not see or hear, but you will see and hear all from the person who reveals it. Trust the person who speaks about Me" (B, r, 18).

In the following testimony cited by Faricy, Tommaso proposed himself explicitly as an intermediary: "She also tells me to help my neighbors because I who have been fortunate to see her can help others to believe through me" (AC). On another occasion, Giovanni acted as an intermediary in "real time." A certain message warned of punishment if there were no prayers. The people said a prayer to avoid the punishment, and soon after Giovanni reported this message: "The collective prayer has been accepted by God, who has promised a modification in the threats of chastisement in the prayer continues" (AC). In contrast Serena, in a message of December 16, 1985, proposed herself as an intermediary on a much higher level: "You will carry faith to the people" (AC).

As consensus, collective attention, and emotional participation focused on a given seer, the seer began to consider her- or himself as a central figure in the plan of divine providence. There quite clearly developed an attitude that we might call *narcissistic*, one that Gramaglia describes very well in the seers of Medjugorje (1983, 43). The Yugoslav seers, different only by degree from seers elsewhere, believed they had been assigned a worldwide mission having to do with the salvation of all humanity: "The future of the world depends somehow on what happens at Medjugorje," declared one of the seer girls. The Devil knew this so well that he asked God for Medjugorje in exchange for all the rest of the world (Rooney and Faricy 1988, 75).

Not only on a cosmic level, but also on a concrete historical one, events in the lives of the seers were closely bound to world events. On January 6, 1986, the Madonna asked Vicka if she was willing to renounce the apparitions until February 25, "as a penance in order to put into effect a particular plan. The proposal was accepted and put into practice. There are those who speculate that it may have had to do with the return of democracy in the Philippines without painful upheavals" (Juarez 1987, 186). As compensation for agreeing to take on this historical and cosmic role, one of the girls was answered by the Madonna that "the graces that you and your fellows [seers] have had, have never been had by anyone in the world" (circular of the "Regina Pacis" prayer group of Turin, 4, p. 5). She promised them: "At the end you will be happier" (Kraljević and Maggioni 1988, 48).

Doubtless so central a role, which in terms of self-perception became narcissistic, was the result of the overpowering devotion that the seers received from the millions of pilgrims who went to the Yugoslav village, a devotion encouraged by the local leadership. Some seers took on the role of spiritual directors for the prayer groups that formed around them, in the guise, as they termed themselves, of direct "microphones" or "mail carriers" for the Madonna. The following quotation is the Jesuit Robert Faricy's description of a prayer group session on January 1, 1986, at Medjugorje. It centers on Jelena, a fourteen-year-old girl who, from December 15, 1982, on had "interior locutions," that is, "real" internal dialogues with the Madonna.

Pero [the chaplain of the group] and Lucy [Sister Lucy Rooney, with whom Faricy wrote the book] and I met in Marijana's bedroom with Jelena, Marijana, and nine other young women, most of them about 14 to 17 years old. They all seemed like ordinary girls, dressed in jeans or skirts, sweaters and the other things girls their age all over the world wear. Jelena and Marijana both wear small gold crosses around their necks. The prayer meeting lasted from about 4:05 until about 5:10.

Jelena began it by reading a message about love that she had received from the Lord the night before. She had written it in a note book. Then they shared how they felt about the message, sharing one at a time with no comments or discussion. Next they sang a hymn. Immediately after the hymn Jelena gave what sounded like a prophecy, even though in the car afterward Pero called them "interior locutions." Lucy thinks maybe she's really hearing interior locutions and then speaking them. I would call that a form of prophecy.

Jelena began the prophecy with the words "Jesus says" (*Isus kaze*), and the content, brief, followed. Another sharing, on the prophetic message, took place. No comments on what each said, no discussion.

Then another hymn. Another prophecy by Jelena, starting with "Jesus says." Another sharing in the same way.

Another hymn. A prophecy by Marijana—beginning again with "Jesus says." Another sharing. Then we all stood and sang the *Our Father* while holding hands in a circle. At the end of the prayer we fell to our knees and said a *Hail Mary* and a *Glory be*. The meeting was over.

[. . .] Pero and I talked in the car about the meeting. In these days, Pero said, all the messages are from Jesus. But often, in other times, it is Our Lady who gives messages through Jelena and Mirjana. (Rooney and Faricy 1988, 71–72)

At Oliveto, in this respect quite the opposite of Medjugorje, the priest was always careful that the seers were not overly prominent. Nevertheless some seers tried to institutionalize their charisma. The following is a telling example. A blessed set of rosary beads breaks; as a result the owner becomes upset, and the seer Giovanni di Agropoli is brought over. Here is Giovanni's subsequent written testimony:

> As I am a seer I went at once to see what had happened, my aunt right away asked me if in the presence of the Madonna the rosary could be rejoined, I went to the gate, I saw the image of the Madonna and the rosary was rejoined. This is a sign of the Madonna addressed to those present as a sign of conversion. (AC, my italics)

The most important context for mediation was the suffering to which the strong seers were called. Here, too, the situation at Oliveto was like that at other sites. Tommaso writes, in testimony cited several times already, "I suffer a lot for humanity" (AC). Aurelia di Contursi writes in her testimony that she must "suffer for the people and for sinners and in fact I do I always have pains in my back" (AC). Luciana Pecoraio, Faricy's collaborator, was a witness to Aurelia's mission, and has declared that the girl accepted all her suffering for the sins of mankind. Nello relived with his body the pain of the Passion during Holy Week, with stigmata and bloody sweat that disappeared after Easter. During a mystical journey with the Madonna, which we will return to in the next chapter, Nello underwent the Passion and told the Madonna, who was sorry, "Do not worry I want to suffer I will save humanity" (AC, May 9, 1985).

Intermediaries can identify with divine beings to the point of "positive" possession. If possession, following Rouget (1980, 281), involves public identification with the divinity, there can be no doubt that there have been various cases at Oliveto, sometimes denied but other times even publicized as "ecstasies" by the Committee. I cannot say whether these symptoms occurred in an "altered state of consciousness" (Bourgignon 1979, 297–343) as measured by neurophysiological indicators.

In this regard, Margnelli and Gagliardi, in their clinical research on a group of Oliveto seers, found that only one of the seers, Ubaldo, experienced enough changes in physiological indicators for them to be able to say an altered state was "very likely" (Margnelli and Gagliardi 1987b, 61). Ubaldo, in addition, displayed states of possession. I was personally present at episodes of altered states in the form of culturally stereotyped *trances*. Descriptions of other similar episodes lead me to believe that such episodes were quite frequent. What is certain is that the community experienced and interpreted the recounted phenomena as if they occurred in altered states of consciousness.

In general, the "ecstasies" of the seers, like altered states of consciousness with or without possession, are considered by the supporters of the apparitions irrefutable proof of the authenticity of the apparitions. In this regard, visionary Catholicism is no different from many religions in which an altered state of consciousness is a proof of an extrahuman or divine presence. When at Lourdes Dr. Estrade came up against an altered state in Bernadette, he concluded, "the time for discussion is over" (Estrade 1934, 116).

As I explained in my preceding book (Apolito 1990, 233), at Oliveto, Ada's trance was considered an irrefutable proof. Christian remarks on the same criterion for proof at Ezkioga (Christian 1987, 144). Laurentin, based on his studies of Lourdes and his observations at Medjugorje, observes that "a certain lack of contact (incomplete and finely modulated) with the external world is a condition for the personal encounter with the Madonna" (cited in Kraljević and Maggioni 1988, 5).

It is precisely the altered state of the Medjugorje seers that brings the ecstasies of apparitions to the more general ecstatic typology studied by anthropologists. Margnelli and Gagliardi note that in the first phase of the apparitions the Yugoslav seers did not have "ecstasies" and that these began only later on. "One could conclude [. . .] that ecstasy can be learned, and this would not be a negligible finding" (1987b, 39). In fact, anthropologists and students of religious history now take it for granted that ecstatic states are subject to learning, initiation, and control (cf. Rouget 1980, 52ff.).

At Oliveto, some phenomena of altered states of consciousness became part of the official routine. The *Bollettino* described what happened on May 24, 1986, the first anniversary of the Oliveto visions, as follows:

> The most moving and spiritually rich moment of the celebration was when the seer Ubaldo, as the Madonna had notified him in advance, received the charism of being able to read the consciences of many of those present. Toward 4:00 p.m., as he paused in prayer before the apparition gate, he went into ecstasy and in that state—he says he remembers nothing—by an inner impulse he began to tell some of those present to go to confession. Then he sort of fainted and was accompanied to the office of the Queen of the Castle Committee where he repeated the same phenomenon and the seer invited one by one many of those present to confess themselves without, however, revealing their sins. (B, r, 33–34)

In general, in the devotional context of Oliveto one can observe the conditions for the inducement of states of hallucinatory *trance* in the monotonous and repetitive prayers. A woman from Frattamaggiore told me that in one evening at Oliveto she had recited at least seventy or eighty Rosaries, that is, 3,500 to 4,000 Hail Marys. When she reached home, in spite of the late hour, she took up the rosary again and during her prayer she saw a "lady, half-length, with a mantle over her head" {February 1, 1986}.

Clearly, the most interesting episodes are those of "positive" possession. As is well known in Christianity, since the heresy of Montanus in the second century positive possession has been excluded from the range of possible encounters with both the divine and good spirits, while the possibility of "negative," diabolical, possession has been preserved. But, in fact, in Christian history, possession by good spirits has never been absent. Walker presents telling examples from the sixteenth century (Walker 1981). In popular Catholicism, the possibility of positive possession has a long history, and episodes of this nature have been frequent.

Annabella Rossi documented, for example, a case near Salerno in 1951 of possession by a benign spirit, as well as the case best-known in Campania in recent times, that of Giuseppina Gonnella in the village of Serradarce, near Campagna, quite close to Oliveto. At Serradarce, the soul of a youth thought to be blessed who died tragically entered every morning the body of his aunt, who was then transformed from a humble housewife into a great charismatic personage (A. Rossi 1976, 62–64).

At Oliveto, even the *Bollettino* reported cases of positive possession, although it does not recognize them as such. For example, here is the testimony of Margherita F:

All of a sudden Nello went into ecstasy: with a faint voice he repeated the words of the Madonna: "Dear children, how I take pleasure in you, for the way you are praying and for these prayers that are reaching me in the Glory of Heaven [. . .]." At the end she thanked [everybody]. The Madonna spoke other words, and no less then twice Jesus spoke, but I cannot remember any more. When Nello's ecstasy was over we started praying again. (B 12, 13)

Episodes of more or less evident *trance* possession by the Madonna were relatively common in the little plaza. A woman from Naples, named Adele, often had fainting spells during which she would be taken by her friends to a corner of the plaza. There she would partially waken from her faint and begin to talk. Here, for example, is a segment recorded in May 1988, in which Adele spoke with a distorted voice purported to be the Madonna's:

{17}

A: I know you are afraid of bodily ailments + and that
          you fear spiritual ones +++ why do you always ask for
          material graces? + ask for the spiritual ones that

last—in eternity my son will return—my son—
sweet-smelling + will return. ##several people: Father
Gino (?) will return!

A: Alfonso thanked me.

[PAUSE]

fv: She has a wound in her hand.

fv1:   Did she have it before?

fv: No.

[PAUSE]

A: All my children have the charism + some will discover
it sooner—some later + some will use it for good—and
some for evil. {August 5, 1988}

A woman from Sarno went into *trance* and her declarations as the Madonna
were recorded and distributed in the restricted circle of her devotees. At
Bellizzi, where the Madonna appeared after the events began in Oliveto and
in the same guise, a girl every evening went into *trance* and spoke like the
Madonna and Jesus.

The seer Giovanni had a *trance* that opened with an extremely brief
segment of glossolalia, followed by a declaration made by him-the-Madonna.
Then the seer said three or four words in French and finally moaned in his
own voice as he awoke. This episode was not reported in the *Bollettino*, but
it was described in a hand-out, and the tape-recording of the *trance* was
played for whoever wanted to hear it in the Committee office, in this way
permitting the identification of the episode as *trance* possession. Another
episode of glossolalic *trance* was reported in the *Bollettino*, which transcribed a long message of a group of Sicilian pilgrims, interrupting the text
periodically with the phrase "there followed a short intervention in tongues,
and then it continued" (B 6, 8–10).

The cases of altered states of consciousness verified at Oliveto (and at
Medjugorje as well) even include—following Rouget's classification—
episodes of "shamanism," which are just as frequent as those of possession.
I shall treat them in the following chapter.

THE COSMIC DRAMA OF THE
APPARITIONS AT OLIVETO CITRA

The Marian Apocalypse

ON THE EVENING OF MARCH 2, 1986, a violent downpour drenched a few, chilled pilgrims praying in the plaza of the apparitions. All at once a seven-year-old boy left the group and went up to the gate. He said the Madonna was calling him, and started going up to the gate and down again many times, until he finally knelt on the cobblestones at the foot of the steps, facing the wall along the steps.

Six days later, a woman told me what happened, becoming upset as she remembered that after a few seconds blood was observed running down the wall in spurts. It was living blood, quite visible since it was red. The boy explained that it was the Madonna's blood, and that it came out after the Madonna had stroked the wall, as if caressing it. In the driving rain many of those present went up to the wall to moisten their handkerchiefs in the blood of Mary. The woman telling me the story had framed her handkerchief and regarded it with devotion. She assured me that the blood was bright red when it issued from the wall; now on the handkerchief it was rose-colored. But when she was talking to me, the woman did not know what to think and was afraid, for a man had just told her that the blood was possessed by the Devil. The woman intended to burn the handkerchief when she got home.

As we spoke, the man who told her the blood was possessed approached. He is the father of Nello, a seer from Grumo, and he said that on the evening of the blood Nello was in Oliveto and witnessed a tragic scene. The Devil stabbed the Madonna and blood came from her body. But the blood of the Madonna was "bedeviled" because the Devil had touched it with his hand as it issued from the wall.

Later, Nello was unwilling to answer my questions on the incident, and I had the impression that his account was told in part under pressure from his father, his convinced and ever-present supporter, and in part as a necessary product of the situation. As a general rule, the simultaneous presence of two or more seers did not lead to overlapping or contradictions because there were so many people that every seer could choose his or her own reference group. But due to the rain, on that evening there were very few people, and in these circumstances a famous seer such as Nello could not admit ignorance about something so exceptional as the emergence of the Madonna's blood from the wall. The demonic interpretation might then have been an effort to get in on the event and diminish the boy's proposed *strong* vision. In any case, others had already spoken of bloody clashes between the Madonna and the Devil.

Six days later, there was a breach in the wall at the place of the event, the result, according to my informant, of an action subsequent to the moment of the prodigy, when the wall was intact. Above the breach could be seen a large, dry red spot. Michele, the Committee leader, told me that at first it had been moist, but it had been dry for several days. The Committee had decided to have the substance analyzed by a well-known laboratory in Naples.

A few days later, I was told that nothing more would be done because the price asked for analysis was excessive—forty million lire. But it seems a preliminary analysis was performed by a less expensive chemist and had been negative. The Committee did not know about the demonic explanation or had ignored it. In any case, since there was no official version of the story, the various circles of oral diffusion multiplied interpretations in a variegated manner, so that in a short period there were versions of the story so diverse that they seemed to refer to different events altogether.

But let us return to the evening that I was told the story.

Nello's father commented that at Oliveto there were two forces, Good and Evil, struggling. An elderly woman reassured us that the Madonna could not lose—victory was just a matter of time because the Madonna was stronger. For now, unfortunately, the Devil had succeeded because he had fooled everyone with the blood of the Madonna that he had touched.

The narrative and symbolic constellation that developed around the blood of the Madonna expressed in exemplary fashion the profound way in which the collective experiences and the symbolic products of the pilgrims took shape at Oliveto. Right before the eyes of the devout and the seers, and in their very lives, there was a *cosmic drama* underway—an infinite experience of sorrow and joy, of defeat and victory, of fear and certainty, the expression of a struggle (as Nello's father had clearly indicated)—between the opposing forces of Good and Evil.

A *dramatic* interpretation of the events was sanctioned first and foremost by the parish priest Don Giovanni, who often said that wherever the Madonna was, the Devil was as well. Indeed, the presence of the Devil was considered a proof of the presence of Mary. "If the devil were not here I would not be sure that the Madonna was" (Apolito 1990, 302). Commenting on the Marian messages, Don Giovanni wrote, "God's own bitter struggle in earthly paradise between the Immaculate Conception and the devil goes on uninterrupted, but it will end with the triumph of the Madonna who will crush his head" (B, r, 24).

A dramatic conception of life and the cosmos is part of the very essence of Christianity. Edith and Victor Turner have observed that the Catholic Church has

conceived of the struggle for salvation as a life-long drama played out essentially in the individual soul but involving a huge cast of actors, some visible, some invisible, some natural, some supernatural: God; Mary, Mother of God; the angels; the saints; and the three divisions of the living Church, the Church Triumphant of the invisible souls in heaven; the Church Suffering of the invisible souls in purgatory; and the Church Militant of living mortals beleaguered in the world by flesh and the devil, and by human adversaries. The individual soul is seen as dramatically involved, until the moment of death, with all these persons, personages, and corporate groups. (Turner and Turner 1978, 16)

Some of the documents of the Second Vatican Council also take up the theme. "Human history in its entirety is [. . .] pervaded by a tremendous struggle against the powers of darkness, a struggle than began with the origin of the world and will last, as the Lord says (Matthew 24:13; 13:24–30 and 36–43), to the last day" (*Gaudium et Spes*, 37). Along with collective history, the lives of individuals are part of this dramatic scenario. "Hence man is divided within. For this reason all human life, individual or collective, shares the features of a dramatic struggle between good and evil, light and darkness" (Ibid., 13). One of the key works of the late, well-known theologian, Urs von Balthasar, is entitled *Theo-drama* (1988).

Thanks to the polyvalent nature of religious language, the official Church is able to maintain an equilibrium between a backdrop of drama and the prospect of redemption (indeed, the document cited is entitled *Gaudium et Spes*). But there is a strong current of devotional Catholicism that pays special attention to the cosmic drama, emphasizing it as opposed to the context of redemption usually maintained by the official Church.

Modern visionary Catholicism has an important role in this dramatic current. The Turners cite a book by John Beevers, *The Sun Her Mantle*, "a very noteworthy study of the phenomenon of postindustrial pilgrimage," which is pertinent here.

Beevers cites (p. 5) two texts as prophetically interconnected and centrally related. The first of these texts is the verse which we have already quoted from the Apocalypse ("And now, in heaven, a great portent appeared; a woman that wore the sun for her mantle, with the moon under her feet, and a crown of stars above her head"). The second is a statement by Pope Pius XII, from his *Evangeli Praecones* (1951): "The human race is today involved in a supreme crisis, which will end in its salvation by Christ, or in its dire destruction." Beevers (pp. 9–10) links the modern appearances of the Virgin (often cloaked in the imagery of the apocalyptic vision with the "supreme crisis" referred to by Pius XII. "From 1830 to 1933, the Blessed Virgin . . . appeared at nine places in Europe: at five in France, one in Ireland, one in Portugal and two in Belgium. At two of these places, she appeared only once. At the others she made several appearances. At all but one she spoke, sometimes many sentences. . . . On our response to her messages may depend our temporal and eternal future." (Turner and Turner 1978, 209)

Beevers well expresses the apocalyptic mood that weighs on Marian apparitions. In line of thought that Beevers represents, the woman of Revelation
12:1 is Mary, and her evocation in the apocalyptic struggle with the Dragon
recalls, closing a prophetic circle, the condemnation of the serpent of God in
Genesis. "I will put enmity between you and the Woman, between your seed
and her Seed; He will crush your head and you will bruise his heel" (*La
Sacra Bibbia*, Rome: Edizioni Paoline [1962]; Genesis 3:15).

Other interpretations widespread at the time of this writing explain the
woman of the Apocalypse as an allegory of the messianic people and thereby
of the Church. It is an open question among theologians (Cantinat 1987,
177–82). In biblical commentary there is a variety of interpretations of the
preeminent meaning to attribute to these famous passages. In the Bible of
Edizioni Paoline of 1962, for example, the woman of Revelation 12:1 is
primarily identified with Mary, and a direct connection is drawn to Genesis
3:15, in which the woman is also identified with the Madonna. In the Bible
published by Edizioni Dehoniane in 1985, with text approved by the
Conference of Italian Bishops and commentary from the Jerusalem Bible,
Genesis 3:15 is slightly, but significantly, different.

I will put enmity between you and the woman
between your descendent
and her descendent
the latter will crush your head
and you will bruise his heel.

In this version, Woman becomes woman, as it refers to women in general,
and not the Madonna. Furthermore, He, referring directly to her Seed (that
is to the Son), becomes "the latter" because it refers to the human
descendants (that is, to the entire human race).

The commentary, in an evident effort at ecumenism, is as follows:

The Hebrew text, announcing a hostility between the race of the serpent
and that of the woman, opposes man and the devil and his "race," but
allows us to see the final victory of man: it is a first glimmer of salvation,
a "protogospel." The Greek translation, which begins the last phrase
with a male pronoun, attributes this victory not to the descendants of
the woman in general, but to one of the sons of the woman: this prepared
the way for the messianic interpretation that many Church Fathers made

explicit. Along with the Messiah, his mother is involved, and the Marian interpretation of the Latin translation *ipsa conteret* has become traditional in the Church. (*La Sacra Bibbia*, Bologna: Edizioni Dehoniane [1985], 851)

This traditional connection between Genesis 3:15 and Revelation 12:1 is strongly emphasized in visionary Catholicism and is an expression of its special dramatic sensibility. The unclear allusions of the references—characteristic of polysemic religious language—become transformed into a complete mirror image of the two texts, which are made to refer to one another. Together they constitute the center of a kind of hermeneutic vortex that picks up papal phrases such as the one cited by Beevers and many spoken by John Paul II, passages from Conciliar documents, and other Church texts, and isolates them from their context, placing them side by side with messages and prophecies of varied origin. The results circulate in millions of copies of devotional pamphlets, newspapers, manifestos, and leaflets.

Furthermore, the welter of catastrophic images drawn from Marian messages and then circulated in the publications connected with the various visionary phenomena is reinforced by the homilies of priests especially imbued by visionary religiosity given in local radio and television broadcasts and by word-of-mouth transmission. In this way, there is a continual enrichment of the apocalyptic *humus* strongly active at the site of Marian apparitions, which from these sites expands out to affect large segments of the Catholic world.

Literary analyses of the Marian messages of Medjugorje, Oliveto, and other places may isolate common themes and concepts, expressions of this *humus*, and even identical phrases and images drawn from a common canon of texts, first and foremost the Book of Revelation. The imminence of chastisements for an unrepentant humanity and the sin-chastisement-evil connection are the major motifs of the Marian messages. In them the call to conversion and repentance are closely connected within a model of faith based on fear of the Devil and God. "Satan insistently tempts you," warns a message at Oliveto, "but do not fear him, fear only God" (B 7, 14).

There is a marked contrast between this religious attitude and another in the Catholic world that emphasizes a clear transition from the Old to the New Testaments, from the notion of suffering-punishment to that of suffering-redemption. I have cited the Jesuit Galot in both this and my previous volumes as representative of a Catholic perspective that, on the whole, is antivisionary. In light of the Gospels, he calls for a reexamination of the section in Genesis considered to be the basis for original sin. This passage is central to the apocalyptic culture of the apparitions. Galot points in particular to the Gospel passage in which Jesus replies to the question posed by his disciples about a man born blind: "Rabbi, who sinned, he or his parents, for him to be born blind?" Jesus' response was, "Neither he nor his parents [. . .]; he is that way because the works of God are manifest in him" (Galot 1981, 433).

One of the conclusions that Galot draws is that

> not even the greatest calamities can be considered punishments; if we ask the question, grace or punishment? the reply must be that a trial is always a grace that tends to endow human existence with a fruitfulness in the order of salvation [. . .]. On the earth, then, there is no sorrow that is inflicted by God as punishment for sin. Retribution is reserved for the other world, in accord with the principle enunciated by Christ. Too many Christians, still now, consider their suffering as a punishment from on high; that means that the value of the redemption worked by Christ has not been sufficiently understood. (Ibid., 443)

This diversity in approach to the problem of evil and suffering highlights the distinctiveness of Catholic visionary culture, a central source for apocalyptic images. This diversity is all the more interesting because it is often not evident outside of the Catholic world; for example, in the lay media that at times tends to consider the entire Catholic world as part of the apocalyptic culture. Here is an example: In his general audience of April 24, 1991, John Paul II spoke of the "Holy Spirit, light of the soul." Among other things, he emphasized that if Christians

> are docile and faithful to its divine authority, the Holy Spirit will keep them from error, making them victorious in the *continual conflict* between the "spirit of truth" and the "spirit of error" (1 John 4:6). The spirit of error, which Christ does not recognize (1 John 4:1) is spread by "false prophets," *always present* in the world, even among Christians. (*L'Osservatore Romano*, April 25, 1991, p. 4, my italics)

The next day *La Repubblica* paraphrased the pope's words, changing the atemporal sense of the phrases so they had a contemporary meaning. The *"continual conflict"* became "there is a struggle *in the world*"; the words "*always present*" became "*there are* 'false prophets.'" For *La Repubblica*, the pope's speech became a crusade and was entirely reinterpreted as part of the apocalyptic and dramatic notions of visionary culture. It would be interesting to reconstruct the reasons why the mass media of contemporary lay culture dwells on the apocalyptic aspects of Catholicism, ignoring or subsuming in it all the rest. Whether due to an eye for the "colorful" or a kind of nostalgia for strong certainties in the potential audience, the coverage that "Catholic life" receives in newspapers and television is predominantly concerned with apparitions, devils, and apocalyptic messages.

That the modern Marian apparitions have conferred, or at least reinforced, a strongly apocalyptic tone on the devotionalism of the great mass of Catholics is indisputable. Lourdes is an exception because this aspect was minimally present in the apparitions of Bernadette. But even before Lourdes, Catherine Labouré in 1830 received a prophetic message about imminent calamities for France and the entire world (Guitton 1976, 44). Our Lady of La Salette has become synonymous with the apocalyptic (Turner and Turner 1982, 156–64). Pius IX summarized for Père Giraud the meaning of the secret of La Salette: "You want to know the secrets of La Salette? Well, here are the secrets of La Salette: if you do not do penance, you will all perish" (Masson 1988, 207).

The sole apparition to the two child shepherds, Maximin and Mélanie, began with the figure of the Madonna seated on a rock, weeping with her face in her hands. When she began to talk she announced the arrival of immense calamities for France and the world because of humanity's indulgence in sins. She announced that if humanity did not immediately repent, there would be a great famine, preceded by the decimation of all children under seven years of age, who would die in their parents' arms, victims of incurable shivering (Carroll 1985, 60). The seers were so frightened that they picked up their shepherd's staves to defend themselves from the menacing apparition.

In twentieth-century apparitions, the catastrophic aspect becomes stronger. There was much publicity given to the catastrophe that was to be connected to the Fatima apparitions, particularly in regard to the famous third secret, so terrible, it was said, that neither John XXIII or Paul VI would reveal it to the world, not even with a call to repentance. Some say John XXIII communicated the contents to world leaders, as a warning. Through diplomatic channels the message supposedly reached a newspaper of

Stuttgart, *News Europa*, that published it in 1963; it was then reprinted in other newspapers. The apocalyptic prophecies of this secret, while officially denied by the rector of the shrine of Fatima, Don Luciano Guerra (Comizzi 1987, 82), were confirmed by the Prefect of the Sacred Congregation for the Doctrine of the Faith, Cardinal Joseph Ratzinger (Messori and Ratzinger 1985, 110). They are worth repeating because they were taken up and imitated in the prophecies of subsequent visionary cults.

> Fire and smoke will fall from the sky, the waters of the oceans will become vapors, and the foam will rise, destroying and collapsing into the abyss everything. Millions and millions of men will perish hour after hour, and those who remain alive will envy the dead. Wherever they look there will be anguish, misery, and ruin in all countries. (Cited in Juarez 1987, 21)

John Paul II, despite his reputation as the "apocalyptic" pope, seemingly sought to reduce the *pathos* surrounding the "terrible" third secret, when, on his trip to Fatima on May 13, 1991, ten years after the attempt on his life by Ali Agca in St. Peter's Square, he stated: "From Cova da Iria there seems to spread out a consoling light full of hope that illuminates the events that characterize the end of this second millennium" (*L'Osservatore Romano*, May 13–15, 1991, p. 7). All contemporary apparitions are marked, more or less, by apocalyptic features. The most common image is that of the Madonna who is tired of restraining the arm of her vengeful son. Each lays out particular catastrophic scenarios. But the almost clandestine model of the third secret of Fatima turns up again and again, even far away, as a demonstration of the strength of the expansion of the visionary culture.

At Kibeho, Rwanda, for example, one of the seers spoke of a fire that would come out of the bowels of the earth and burn everything on the surface (Maindron 1984, 148). At Akita, Japan, Our Lady said that the fire will fall from the sky, destroying, in a chastisement worse than the great flood, a large proportion of humanity and leaving the survivors in even greater suffering (Sala and Mantero 1986, 139). We find analogous images at Medjugorje and Oliveto, along with precise, reciprocal corresponding aspects: one of the chastisements announced the impending destruction of two-thirds of the world population.

At Oliveto, as at Medjugorje and partially in a few other visions, the apocalyptic dimension is affected by the exceptionally long duration of the apparition sequence. While it is possible for apparitions of short duration to describe an apocalyptic scenario in which the dimensions of the cosmic disaster, once designed, remain fixed, it is not possible for apparitions of long duration to escape from their own everyday routine, and hence from a more precise historicity in the referents. In this way, there emerges a double process that renders these phenomena special.

First of all, the *figurative* language of the sacred texts, which in the official interpretation alludes symbolically to a moral encounter expressed in terms of a cosmic encounter, acquires a strictly *literal* sense that changes it from an allegory to a chronicle of events. The cosmic struggle in question is not an image of extraordinary power evoking the precariousness of the creation and the need for a connection with the divinity to be saved, but rather an exact description of what is going on between the troops of Evil, massed under the orders of Satan or Lucifer, and the militia of Good, which includes the angels, the saints, the Madonna, Jesus, and virtuous living Christians.

Second, the cosmic dramas transformed little by little into a *historical drama*, one that is contemporary, with a series of clashes, skirmishes, and battles that involve the superhuman protagonists of the cosmic scene, who have entered the plane of human history to fight their battles once more. "Pray, because the world is at war and the sky is about to split in two" (B, r, 58), said the Madonna at Oliveto. At Medjugorje Vicka reported that the Madonna said that *"this time is her special time* of haste and battle for souls" (Bubalo 1987, 187, my italics).

The theme of a great, historicized cosmic war, which official Church discourse relegates to the background, comes to the fore and becomes the main ideological category for interpreting both historical and personal events: matters of great collective import (from ecology to war, famine to quality of life), as well as private matters (from jobs to love, from health to future prospects). The result of all this is an extraordinary and vital symbolic amalgam that, on the one hand, translates into apocalyptic religious terms everything in the flux of human experience that comes to the attention of the community of the devout, and, on the other, uses religious language to report on the ongoing cosmic-historical war, normally invisible but quite evident at site of apparitions—hence, the stab wound inflicted by the devil (recounted above), the matter of the blood on the wall, and so many daily signs, small and great, of the conflict.

One message of the Madonna at Oliveto places the present historical moment in the sacred history prefigured in Revelation, explaining the precise point of the prophetic book that at which the world is {June 14, 1986}. The numbers 21 and 2 photographed in the sky at Belpasso, on the slopes of Mount Etna, during apparitions to the eighteen-year-old Rosario Toscano apparently refers to the passage of Revelation 21:2 about the descent to earth of the celestial Jerusalem (Comuzzi 1989a, 68). The seers, human witnesses of the war, did not limit themselves to reporting the celestial battles but also took part in them, becoming, as it were, co-stars. The mythical plane of the struggle between good angels, on the one hand, and evil angels—the devils—on the other, is resolved by the historical level of the individual's struggle to remain in the grace of the Lord. This struggle takes on the epic proportions of a psycho-physical battle with the Devil. In some cases, it is transformed into a true physical encounter whose clearest (but not, as we will see, unique) form is demonic possession. Demonic possession "is not a moral ailment—that is, a sin—but a physical one, however terrible and life-threatening, that God in his inscrutable designs allows, like any other tribulation, for a good end" (Balducci 1988, 212).

Moreover, the physical encounter between metahuman protagonists is often expressed precisely through an attack on human protagonists.

> Before arriving at the mountain yesterday I was warned by a woman that something was happening to the picture of Merciful Jesus. I and some of my group quicken our pace and we come upon the face of Jesus bleeding and disfigured and the Paduans on their knees, prostrate, in prayer before Him! You can imagine my profound distress, my emotion! I stayed for some time absorbed . . . and then all shaken, from the depth of my heart I directed to the Lord this prayer, this question: my Jesus, why do you suffer so dreadfully? . . . Who is the cause of such great pain? . . . And for a reply, looking around me, I saw a poor woman who was writhing, tortured by the devil! She was a lady in the group from Padua. In this way the Lord made me understand clearly that Satan was the cause of so much evil! (Sala and Mantero 1986, 136–37)

It is not then surprising, on the one hand, that the daily rhythm of the life of an apparition community is a force for apocalyptic conversions (that is, of existential re-initiations cloaked in the cosmic drama), and, on the other, the locus for the battle between Hell and Paradise *right before one's very eyes*, with the seers taking part. And it should not be surprising that the Devil should be ready to trade his control of the world—for he is the "prince" of this world—with God for Medjugorje (Rooney and Faricy 1988, 74), or that he should declare war on Oliveto (B 3 [1990], 4). The events of the apparitions are thus paced by the incessant reports of the cosmic and historical struggle, with news of victories and defeats, of positions taken or lost, of victims, of tactics and strategies, with commentary on engagements just over and hopes for those about to begin.

In short, the visionary culture moves to the level of symbols and reformulates its experienced conflict between the unforeseeableness, precariousness, and the contingent nature of daily life (configured as the forces of evil), and the desire for stability, security, and well-being (incarnate in powerful and eternal celestial figures that alone can overcome the forces of evil) into the irrefutable mythic scheme of the titanic and unending struggle between Good and Evil.

Through a particular kind of assimilation of experience to what is narrated, a great collective narrative constructs the cosmic events of the apparitions and inserts in them—in the inflections of their daily rhythms— symbolic reformulations of the individual and collective existential problems of the pilgrims, and through them of all humanity. The unproblematic assimilation of *experience*, both individual and collective, to *what is narrated* serves to eliminate the role of historicity and bring the dynamic of *real world events* to the ordinary plane of *structure*. By configuring experience as a sign of the Other (the battle, the enemy, the Madonna), *what happens* is resumed, bent, and explained as an episode of the cosmic drama of the pre-established finale, and human history becomes sacred history. If in this process the daily intervention of evil is not eradicated, then at least meaning has been found.

On this terrain there unfolds a kind of theatrical dimension of this culture that tends to map out as a war in an external and precise location things that in the perspective of post-Conciliar Catholicism (even if held to be in real conflict) are private and metaphorical.

Maria sees the Virgin in her room:

"All of you together go to the meadow at Gumno. A great battle is about to take place. A battle between my Son and Satan. Human souls are at stake."

The seers, accompanied by some 40 people, went to the praire [sic] of

Gumno, 200 meters from Vicka's house. (Laurentin and Lejeune 1988a, 157)

The power of this theatrical dimension is its capacity to affect the collective sensibility to the extent that the struggle it proposes takes place in the *plaza*, so that everyone, collectively, can understand its significance and relieve their anxiety by taking the side of the just. Participation in the struggle (in the plaza and not on a private, personal level) limits the extent to which a response can be internal and requires above all the adoption of the appropriate hermeneutic and participation in the requisite devotions.

The just are asked and taught to read the collective and individual events as consequences of the curse of Genesis and the warning of Revelation, which are anticipated, experienced, and explicated by successive Marian apocalyptic messages, whose call to conversion is almost always preceded or followed by the threat of punishment. The religious sensibility produced in this way is quite similar to that of the Jehovah's Witnesses, the sect so opposed today by the exponents of Catholic popular doctrine because it is a direct competitor. For the proselytists of the Jehovah's Witnesses, as for the devotees of visions, the explanation of collective history and individual lives makes it possible to simplify what is problematic in their own roles, their own life choices, and their own troublesome daily world by enrolling in the army of the Good.

Hence, the just are asked above all to pray a lot, to devote more and more time to traditional prayer according to teachings attributed to the Madonna, who wants to increase the initial half-hour to four, five, six, and up to twenty-four hours each day (Kraljević and Maggioni 1988, 178); to use crucifixes, holy water, holy cards, and blessed salt for defense against the evil one; and to pray triduums, novenas, Rosaries (kneeling and standing), in cars and buses, for the intentions of the pope, for the poor of the world, and for peace. Above all Rosaries, the prayer "preferred" by the Madonna, is to be prayed at all hours and in all possible quantities. The multiplication of the mysteries by three or five can lead to the recitation of several thousand Hail Marys, with effects often conducive to the entrance in *trance*.

The hermeneutic and devotional mechanism set in motion is in essence a new kind of religious option to counter the de-Christianization of the world that it denounces, an option that has attracted adepts by the thousands. Paradoxically, although this option is the expression of a dramatic and apocalyptic Christianity, it seeks to allay the anguish of the historical reality.

But its efficacy for this purpose is unclear. On the contrary, it contributes to the production of this anguish, or at least sustains it, by means of the hermeneutic and devotional mechanism. The drama at these apparition sites is quite intense and derives from the fact that although a powerful symbolic and practical schema has brought the cosmic struggle down to earth and provided certain weapons to living protagonists, it cannot foresee a total collective—and above all individual—victory. The existential danger in this world remains with all its intensity; people can be sure only of a metahistorical victory in the other world, where the just will win out.

But at a given point—we shall see below—even this certainty seems to erode.

The Historical Drama of the Apparitions

The first symptom of the drama that soon thereafter would begin to spread so far from the little plaza of the apparitions of Oliveto was the disquieting worry during the first days that the apparitions might merely be a ruse of the Devil. This worry was rarely made explicit, and persons who raised it would quickly be rebuked by others (Apolito 1990, 238ff.); nevertheless, it was a live possibility, one continuously in mind. Often during the apparitions Don Giovanni and others who monitored the visions performed exorcisms. It was only when the presence of the Madonna was held to be certain that the presence of the devil was openly recognized as a normal, disagreeable, consequence. But there it was: the presence of the Madonna recognized as part of a dramatic dualism of opposing powers. This dualism imposed its rhythm on the events.

The initial disturbing aspect of the Devil's possible presence was precisely the danger of it being linked to a implicit understanding that was *total*. The entire positive universe under construction might be the surreptitious effect of a negative agent in disguise. Later, when this danger was finally declared nonexistent or at least reckoned to have been overcome, there remained only the danger of misunderstanding *within* the positive frame, which poisoned every individual certainty: the Devil might appear to anyone disguised as the Madonna.

To some seers this did not happen, as they perceived with clarity the Madonna and the Devil as distinct figures. But others had the misfortune of having visions of both with the same appearance. Such seers would arm themselves against the Devil in various ways, always carrying a crucifix, as the Madonna herself had advised (B, r, 60), or, like Ubaldo, making the sign of the cross and requesting from the figure appearing a smile in response. Ubaldo maintained that the only distinguishing feature between the Devil and the Madonna, in these doubtful apparitions, were the feet, which in the case of the Devil were those of animals (Margnelli and Gagliardi 1987a, 97–98). Often the Devil betrayed himself because he appeared like the Madonna but then would ask the seer to renounce the Madonna (for a parallel in Medjugorje, see Juarez 1987, 43).

Yet other seers were themselves particularly close to the zone in which both the Madonna and the Devil were present. A "bedeviled" girl, Barbara, was freed by the Madonna and became a seer, but then the Devil had her in his clutches again. Another female seer, from Nocera Inferiore, reported heavenly messages, but then, because she was not well, went to a female healer of Benevento, who discovered that the seer was possessed by the Devil.

The Devil-Madonna might give messages that were red herrings, so the devout worked out ways to recognize their sources. One evening they told me about a woman from Agropoli who did not leave her house for "two months" because she said the Madonna had appeared to her saying that if she went out she would die. A brief dialogue followed:

{18}

(1) fv: That is the work of the Devil.
(2) fv1:   But she said she saw the Madonna.
(3) fv: It's not true—it didn't really happen—because the
              Madonna brings joy. {March 15, 1986}

The continual, obsessive, and hyperactive presence of the Devil performs the well-known role of permitting the expression of the "conflict of humans with historical or natural realities" (Di Nola 1987, 11) and the identification of an enemy, one that is external and the source of all evil. (It thereby implicitly provides the possibility of separating cleanly good from evil and marking off the zone of the elect few from everyone else.) In any case, the canon of modern apparitions, from Lourdes on, includes the Devil. Bernadette heard muffled noises from one direction; with a severe look and a gesture from the Madonna they stopped (Estrade 1934, 81).

At Oliveto, as at Medjugorje, the presence of the Devil supplied the *antagonist* for the daily dramatic representation. By means of the climate of *combat* in which the events were retold and experienced, the devotees adopted a stable frame of reference into which they could push the unforeseeable historicity of their human affairs—including the fear and anguish resulting from the catastrophic worldview activated by these very events, but present as well in the general climate of crisis of the time. Once inside this frame of reference, these human matters could be organized into a schema of meaning in which heaven backs the righteous or removed altogether in a process of continuous de-historicization that protected against the uncontrollable danger of history. Oliveto (like Medjugorje) thus became the setting for an *exemplary story*, experienced as a public show of the forces in struggle. The conversation, reported above, between Nello's father and the elderly woman, is a good example of this symbolic reformulation of *historicity*.

{19}

(1) mv: Here [at Oliveto] two powers are in combat + of
               good—and of evil [. . .]
(2) fv: Note that the Madonna wins—there's no two ways
               about it—she will win because she is more powerful.
               {March 8, 1986}

The daily pace at Oliveto was marked by the rhythm and modalities of the combat between the Madonna and the Devil and the messages that mark its intensity. Mary asked for the help of the faithful in the struggle. The message to one female seer is: "I beg you, pray a lot, only in this way will my immaculate heart triumph. With prayers, humility, and the good works you offer me, I will be able to defeat Satan" (B 7, 23).

As time went by it appeared that the battle involved not only the individual fates of the Madonna's devotees, but the very maintenance of a cosmic equilibrium. At times the messages seemed to reflect a Madonna incapable of defeating the Devil on her own. As at Medjugorje, the Madonna needed her devotees to save the world (Gramaglia 1983, 52). A child seer, Mauro, reported that the Madonna said to him urgently, "Help me, I am the Virgin Mary, my son is in danger because of your [plural you] sins" (AC, November 8, 1985). Serena reported, "Help me, I am in danger, sins are hammering on my heart" (AC, February 1, 1986); another female seer: "Pray, pray a lot, because even I have need of your prayers" (B, r, 51).

The appeals of the Madonna for help for her suffering son seem to indicate a cosmic struggle, renewed in our time, the outcome of which has not been decided. The images of a sad Madonna, common to the most famous apparition sites, appear at first glance to be an iconographic accompaniment to the call to conversion in a battle that above all has to do with the ultimate victories of individual persons. But on closer inspection they might mean, and indeed for some people do mean, that the cosmic battle itself has not yet been decided. The very fact that Satan proposed to God a trade between Medjugorje and all the rest of the world indicates that the contest is still going on and that the players are still trying to get the best of each other.

A report about the Medjugorje seers is prime evidence that the *historic encounter of the metahistoric* appears not yet to be over, and that the cosmic players are still head to head. Long ago, Satan went to God, warning that men would have faith only "while things go well for them" and that "when they go badly" men would stop believing in him. "Then God allowed the devil to take one century to rule the world" (Rooney and Faricy 1984, 52).

It goes without saying that the century of Satan's dominion is the twentieth century. The Devil, even if subordinate in this incident, remains the tempter, even of God, and offers advice and has with God a conversation that is inevitably a kind of struggle, however underhanded and hidden, that shows that he still defies God, that he is still not yet resigned to his eternal damnation, and that the cosmic clash still gives off an infinitude of sparks.

Probably the dominion of this century by Satan derives from the way Saint Paul calls Satan, "god of this century" (II Corinthians 4:4). The role assigned to Satan in the drama is also derived from the Scriptures, considering that the meaning of "Satan" in the New Testament is "slanderer" "accuser" and "enemy of the human race" (Di Nola 1987, 167–68). Here, too, it would be interesting to examine the ways in which the apparition culture displaces and crystallizes in contemporary historical terms biblical text and commentary, giving them a meaning so vital and fresh that they transform Revelation from something *given* to something that is *being given* in the world and that promises to conclude *in* this world:

The present time is being described by the Madonna as "the hour of Satan," that will last until the first secret has been borne out [author's note: for the ten secrets-prophecies that the Madonna has communi-

cated to some seers, see below]. When all of the secrets have been
confirmed, the power of Satan will be destroyed. (Mantero 1987, 182)

It becomes clear that the end of Satan's power, hence of the story of the
redemption, and perhaps the beginning of the millennium, will be soon. The
devotees of the apparitions thus come to follow the events as signs of the end
of times, just as the Christians of the first centuries read the Book of John as
a symbolic preview of what was about to happen.

The news of God's conceding the twentieth century to the Devil was given
by Father Tomislav Vlasić of the parish of Medjugorje to John Paul II
himself (Laurentin and Rupčić 1984a, 142–44). The seers and the local
clergy participate in the same visionary culture, one that explains the
"events" as a renewal of cosmic hostilities, with the ultimate palingenisis in
view. "We have already entered into the great events—the parish priest
himself would say—, there is no other explanation for the presence of the
Madonna for so many years" (Mantero 1987, 177).

It is certain that God, for the leaders and for so many of the devout, will
surely win, but the insistence with which this is affirmed is an indication of
a contagious fear, and furthermore it is made clear that *this* century, the
century of those now living, is a hostage to the new phase of the encounter.

The messages suggest both a language of game theory and the tactics of
game players. It is the Madonna, at Oliveto, who in a message of May 24,
1986, tells her followers: "I want to tell you today what is my Decisive Move,
the one that will win, because my Mother's Heart feels the anxiety and the
urgency of the times coming very soon" (B 16, 21). The Decisive Move is
represented by the devotees of the Madonna.

The bloody clash that opened this chapter is a historically concrete and
emotionally lively instance of the challenge underway, of the game that the
players have begun. But it is also another eloquent sign that victories in the
cosmic struggle seem no longer to be permanently defined but unexpectedly
open to question. The metaphor of this uncertainty of outcome seems to me
to be the blood itself that the devout gathered with their handkerchiefs. It is
blood of the Madonna but also of the Devil. Good is counterfeited by Evil,
and the danger of this imitation cannot even be resolved by a live
appearance of Good. The struggle is still in progress and has reached a
perilous stage in which one cannot distinguish the objects and the weapons
of the two armies in struggle.

At Medjugorje, there is an analogous incident in which blood has a disquieting ambiguity as a sign. A taxi driver was returning after taking some pilgrims there. He was stopped by a man covered with blood who gave him a bloody handkerchief. The man told the driver to throw it into the first river that he found and not to give it to anyone or else something terrible would happen to him. The taxi driver ran toward the river, but was stopped by a lady dressed in black who asked him for the handkerchief. The driver tried to give her his own handkerchief, but the lady asked expressly for the one soaked in blood. He put her off, and she threatened him with something a lot more serious, the end of the world and even worse, which obliged him to give in. At Medjugorje, he worriedly told people what happened, and then a girl seer was asked to find out about the matter from the Madonna. The seer learned that the bloody man was Jesus and the woman in black was the Madonna. If the taxi driver had not handed over the handkerchief, the Last Judgment would have taken place (Bubalo 1987, 90–92). The bishop of Mostar sharply condemned this story in his circular of October 1984 (Sala and Mantero 1986, 33–34), and again in April 1990 in a press conference in Rome, he asked scornfully: "What kind of theological message is this?" (*Il Mattino*, April 20, 1990).

Perhaps it is not a theological message, but it is surely a sign of the depth, tenacity, and vitality of traditional oral narrative. The taxi driver's story is one of a great number of variants on a basic model of a report in which a famous person (a ghost, a monk, Jesus himself) stops an automobile, sometimes asking for a ride, sometimes warning about the next hitchhiker, other times prophesizing an exceptional future event, or threatening one, and then disappears.

At the end of the 1930s, the prophecy involved the imminent death of Hitler, and it circulated in France, Great Britain, Belgium, the Netherlands, the United States, and South Africa (Kapferer 1987, 113). After the earthquake of November 23, 1980, in southern Italy, it involved an old woman predicting another disastrous earthquake, and the story spread through Campania and Basilicata. One of the predicted dates coincided with an earthquake that occurred on February 14, 1981. A new prophecy by the same old woman then circulated that the end of the world would occur on March 7 (Apolito 1983). After the failure of this second prophecy, nothing more was heard about the old lady.

Other well-known stories tell about hitchhikers who have forgotten something in a car and for whom the driver looks the next day in order to give back the forgotten object. With enormous surprise the driver discovers that the person given a ride the day before had been dead for weeks or months (Brunvand 1986, 41ff.). Stories such as this are common, and there is considerable literature about them.

In the Medjugorje story, in addition to the stopping of a car and the prophetic threat, there is an additional element—the bloody handkerchief and the call to wash it—that is especially interesting. Blood is a symbolic feature present in Christianity since its beginning, in the sense that a special connection has been made between the blood Jesus shed for humankind and eternal redemption. Indeed, in popular tradition and learned culture, blood has taken on a number of often radically different mediating roles. The point here is that the blood on the handkerchief at Medjugorje, between Jesus' call to get rid of it and Mary's call to keep it, once more oscillates ambiguously, almost as if it were unclear and undecided whether to assign it a positive or negative role.

In popular tradition, in effect, blood has been assigned a dual value, both as a factor of life and as an effluvium of death (Lombardi Satriani and Meligrana 1982, 290). But in the context of visionary religion, the ambiguous meaning of the blood is precisely in the unresolvable nature of the conflict that is expressed in the ambiguity of the vital substance of the forces of Good. The Committee at Oliveto, the bishop at Medjugorje, the discomfort of Bubalo when he interviewed Vicka on the matter, demonstrate the official Church position that there is a clear distinction between Good and Evil.

But the ambivalence of daily life, which comes through, transposed, in the events of the apparitions, does not permit the safety of boundaries. The factor of uncertainty is brought into the very heart of the epic phenomena. The impossibility of absolute decisions in history is expressed by the similar impossibility of absolute identifications in these bloody incidents. In the last analysis, the mechanism of the culture of the apparitions, which purports to be able to control the collective anxieties of the here-and-now and channel them into a sacred history whose outcome is guaranteed, here reveals its limits and fosters the very precariousness that it wanted to eliminate.

Other incidents extend the trail of blood to the battle itself, calling on humankind to do its duty. A female seer at Oliveto, in the church, saw the Madonna with a sad face. She asked Mary for the cause, and the Madonna told her to look at the consecrated host. Here, the seer noted at the level of Jesus' heart (evidently in the host she saw Jesus as well) a deep wound. The Madonna told her: "This wound has been caused by the sins that are constantly committed in the world" (B 1 [1990], 14).

Hence, the blood calls men directly to take sides. One of the boys of the first apparitions, in the course of another interview four years later, remembered in this way an incident that occurred to one of the first seers, Aurelia.

> Aurelia—began to say—that there was a man who went down the steps—and there was another man who ran after him and wanted to kill him—this man—I did not see him—I heard Aurelia who was not in a conscious state—she was in trance—was squinting and looking toward—the steps—[. . .] and screamed with fear—practically wept— "there is a man running down—and there is another man behind him"—with a sword or a dagger? + sword eh sword—"who wants to kill him" + this man got as far as Aurelia and took Aurelia's hands and—at that point he was killed + and—Aurelia's hands were covered with blood ++ then—she turned toward me—she was weeping—because she had seen a man killed—without mercy. (Marotta 1990, 222–23)

It is interesting that this vision of Aurelia was recounted by others with a different, reassuring ending: the next day the seer saw the same man, rejuvenated, dressed in white among the souls who were singing in a choir to the Madonna. The dual ending is another testimony to the precarious quality of the victories.

In any case, the upshot is that something portentous in the other world that mirrors this one was being decided in front of the seers' very eyes, something that moved sharply, altering the cosmic equilibrium. The apparitions can therefore be read, and are read by some, as a desperate attempt from *beyond* to obtain the help of the devout *here*, in the face of a sharp attack—the twentieth century as time given over to Satan—that appears to be undermining the very bases of the cosmic equilibrium.

The Other World in History

The articulation of a model of *historical* drama in which events are experienced simultaneously as cosmic and everyday and the direct and dangerous participation of heavenly characters in this drama result in heavenly figures, without any particular hesitation, moving completely into a historical and temporal dimension close to that of humans. Above all, it is the Madonna who undergoes this shift.

Through hagiographers, Mary of Lourdes, La Salette, and Fatima without difficulty achieved a fixed profile that was definitive and indisputable. But a Madonna like the one at Oliveto, who appeared to *new seers every day over many years*, could not have a similar fate. Inevitably, her profile changed, her outlines became more elusive and blurred with traits that were contradictory. In a routine that occurred day after day, to which tens and at times hundreds of persons contributed, the outcome was inevitably a compromise and the key to a series of varying interpretations. Previously at Medjugorje there were serious and evident problems of this nature, but these problems were largely limited to a few salient episodes (for instance, when the Madonna's messages went against the bishop of Mostar). At Oliveto, serious contradictions emerged on a daily basis. In the towns of the Salerno region, the hermeneutic procedures of the collective vision, the accounts of the *strong* seers, and the filter of the Committee were the *three* principal elements that contributed, in conflict one with another but as a whole, to the design of the physical-corporeal realm for the Madonna that included the forms and levels of her discourse.

From the moment a *plural* kind of vision was accepted—an indirect result of the Committee's attempts to prevent the excessive increase of charisma in the *strong* seers—the consequence was the implicit acceptance of a variety of visions, even if, at the beginning when there were as yet relatively few, the diversity tended to be denied or ignored. The diversity of images seen, in turn, made it possible for there to be an extremely long list of physical and psychological attributes of the Madonna, many of them contradictory.

The Committee tended to judge the contradictions against the measure of orthodoxy and exclude exceptions. In effect, the changing attributes of the Madonna corresponded to the contingencies of the situations in which they were expressed. They were the products of the dynamics of a given moment—in turn derived from the role and background of the people involved, which provided a meaning to the "truth" verified there.

The *inventio* of the Madonna was always as contingent and reversible as the vein of collective cultural creativity that nourished it. The Committee certainly had a powerful weapon for slowing the word-of-mouth attempt at defining the outlines of the apparition and imposing its own, official, canon of images and words. Thanks to its daily work gathering, elaborating on, and commenting on testimony, the Committee could draw up one or more stereotypical profiles of the Madonna, which then had the effect of molding all subsequent (and even prior) testimony and reconstructions. Moreover, the "fixing," effectuated by the texts in the *Bollettino*, was crucial. Nonetheless, an element of indefinition in the image of the Madonna could not be avoided.

The point is that this indefinition changed over time, from the haphazard blend of descriptions given by the different seers to the normal collection of acts and feelings, some of them contradictory, typical of a human being. Hence, the appearing Madonna was endowed, over time, with markedly human psychological and physical features, which almost ended up canceling out her transcendent dimension.

Much testimony agrees that the Madonna *got tired* from the large number of apparitions she had to make in order to satisfy the pilgrims' requests. She confided to Nello that her legs hurt because she continually had to walk to make herself visible to those who invoked her {February 8, 1986}. In his written testimony, Nello emphasized this fact (AC), and in a preliminary dittoed version of the message the Committee included this assertion. Nello himself, in an interview, said that the Madonna *sweated* as a result of penance she performed for sinners {April 12, 1986}.

The leader Michele cited another testimony whereby the Madonna appeared with white bindings on her ankles, which Michele said was a custom in Arab countries and made him think that the Madonna *was feeling the cold*. When she was seen praying on her knees in the rain she explained that she was doing penance; to some to whom she gave her hand, she begged pardon that her hand was cold, like the rest of her body, from the night air {March 8, 1986}. She appeared to Ubaldo saying explicitly that she was cold (AC, October 9, 1985). In January 1986, in the worst winter cold, she appeared barefoot to a woman seer of Frattamaggiore (AC).

The fullest demonstration of the physical nature of the apparition was recounted by Nello, who saw the Madonna fall to earth in an effort to have herself seen by the greatest number of pilgrims and *bleed from one knee* {February 1, 1986}. According to Giovannina, the blood on the Madonna's knee corresponded to the iconography of the Madonna of Loreto. But Nello saw other blood of the Madonna, shed after a clash with the Devil, as we have seen above.

Furthermore, the Madonna said she *was not capable of performing certain acts*, which confirmed her presence in the realm of physical rather than metaphysical existence. A male seer reproached those around him because, while he was in an emotive crisis, he was carried away from the apparition gate just at the moment that the Madonna was about to embrace him, so that her arms closed on air {March 8, 1986}. Another time, the Madonna wanted to embrace a little girl but, impeded by something invisible, could not touch her, and then a man who was near the girl lifted her up so the Madonna could reach, embrace, and kiss her {January 18, 1986}.

The physical concreteness of the Madonna is demonstrated by other aspects of her presence. The seers had *physical contacts* with the Madonna. When she appeared as "a woman all dressed in light" during the storm of November 20, 1985, a woman stepped forward to embrace her and felt the "soft silk" of her dress (B, r, 8). The child Maria Teresa F. was embraced and kissed by the Madonna (AC), who also shook Ubaldo's hand before going away (B, r, 13, 20; and Faricy 1986, 39). She asked Rosa F. to kiss her feet (AC), touched the head of the unbelieving fiancé of a woman seer (B 13, 23), and touched the hands of two pilgrims, curing them, according to a male seer who was watching (B, 21).

Giulio, one of the Committee leaders, recounted that he overcame all his doubts when through a seer he learned that the Madonna wanted to shake his hand. He put his hand through the bars of the gate and felt a coldness, together with an inability to bend his fingers, as if he were shaking hands with someone {June 14, 1986}. Like Giulio, a believer cited in an article in *La Stampa* on November 11, 1985, reported feeling a coldness on her forehead after the Madonna touched her. On the other hand, Ubaldo maintained that "the hands of the Virgin are normal, with the same warmth as any other hand" (Faricy 1986, 39). But Ubaldo told others he had had the sensation of "touching cold flesh" (Margnelli and Gagliardi 1987a, 23).

At times the Madonna offered the Baby Jesus to a seer (B 7, 6). She left the baby in the arms of Rita from Bellizzi "for a little while," after having given her a message about the Rosary (B, r, 11). Nello, too, received the Baby in his arms, but he gave him back almost immediately because "the emotion was too great" (AC). Giuseppe, speaking of a girl who had said she had the Baby in her arms, said that he saw the girl act exactly as if she were holding an invisible baby (AC).

The corporeality and, one might say, the everyday obviousness of this baby in arms provides a glimpse of a world beyond that is a *mirror image* of this one, one with the same problems and aspects of physicality. This is quite clear in the testimony of an eleven-year-old seer from Palomonte, Maria Concetta. Maria Concetta told the Committee that the Madonna who held the Baby said that she had to leave because Jesus was hungry and might begin to misbehave (AC).

In some cases, the features of physicality are drastically revised. For example, in contrast with the Madonna unable to embrace a seer who had been carried away, there was the Virgin who, by an unknown force, dragged a female seer toward her, saying she wanted to embrace her (AC). In contrast with the Madonna who got tired, there was a more heavenly Madonna who moved without walking, levitating a few centimeters above the ground (Carione and Serrone 1986, 58). This same seer emphasized that since she had the chance of touching the dress of the Madonna, "I was able to feel between my fingers only her dress, whereas beneath, where the body ought to be, she was insubstantial, there was nothing" (Ibid., 59).

It is obvious that a great number of believers wanted to participate in physical contact with the Madonna. While this was easy at Oliveto, given the frequency of visions, at Medjugorje it was more difficult. But there, too, the yearning was strong because, as at Oliveto, the repeated daily visions did not permit people to consider the celestial presence as exceptional. Rather people got used to it as the expected visit of a powerful guest. At Oliveto, the physical rapport with the Virgin was on a large scale; at Medjugorje, where there were a small number of seers, it might have been something of minor importance. But it was in the Yugoslavian town that, at one point, people asked the seers to touch, even though they could not see, the dress of the Madonna. Though they could not see, at least they would have liked to participate through another sense.

As soon as the seers passed the request on to Madonna, she disappeared (at the beginning, at Medjugorje, when the Madonna did not want to respond to something, she disappeared). But a few days later she returned surrounded by a special light and invited people to touch her dress. And then people got in line and one by one put their hands in the place indicated by the seers.

People gave differing accounts of what they felt. Draga Ivanković said she "felt something," but added that after a few days the Madonna let her know that if someone had experienced a physical sensation it was an error, for "all that you feel is your emotion" (Mantero 1987, 57–58). But others insisted that their hands became numb (Ibid., 110; Kraljević and Maggioni 1988, 94). Furthermore, the Madonna herself asked others to let her know if, when people put out their hands, they felt something. There was confirmation of a direct physical sensation in the testimony of Vicka, who recalled that a girl let out a scream after touching the Madonna, because, the girl explained, "her hand got stuck in the Virgin's crown" (Bubalo 1987, 109).

As with the features of physical concreteness, so with the Madonna's capacity for *knowing the future*. At Oliveto, there was conflicting evidence. Sergio C. claimed that the Madonna told him he would become a monk (AC, January 2, 1986), but Tommaso said that the Madonna had asked him, indicating she did not know the answer, whether he wanted to marry or become a priest when he grew up. The boy answered that he preferred to marry, "and She told me that I would be doing the right thing" (AC). Similarly, a girl from Palomonte said that the Madonna asked her what she wanted to be when she grew up. "A schoolteacher," The Madonna replied, "Don't you want to become a nun?" "No," replied the child (AC, December 25, 1985).

On May 9, 1986, the Madonna complained to Tommaso because she had expected "more people to come to be with me" (B, r, 40), an indication that she did not know in advance how many pilgrims would come. A week later, on May 16, she indicated the exact opposite when she told Ubaldo, referring to the upcoming anniversary of the apparitions, that "many would come from afar on that day" (B, r, 42).

Often the Madonna showed *she did not know the present*. On May 26, the second evening of the apparitions, she asked Tommaso for news about Ada, whom she did not see in the crowd (Faricy 1986, 45). She asked Donato why Fulvio had not come to the gate on the last two evenings, and then she asked about Matteo, a boy who was sick (AC, December 18, 1985). She appeared in Nello's home because she suspected that the youth had not gone to Oliveto out of fear of an apparition of the devil {March 8, 1986}.

Here, too, it is easy to find parallels with Medjugorje. In the Yugoslav town, there were encounters that allowed one to think that the Madonna was at the very least *distracted*. After one apparition on the hill, the seers were going down toward the town, accompanied by two or three thousand persons. Suddenly, one girl seer went off to the left of the path and fell to her knees. The Madonna reappeared and asked, "Where are the other girls?" (Kraljević and Maggioni 1988, 23).

Another episode was so paradoxical that the parish priest, Father Jozo himself, was disturbed by it and tried in vain to clarify it with the seers (Laurentin 1986a, 58). As at Oliveto, the Madonna at Medjugorje asked for news about those absent from those present—in this way demonstrating a lack of knowledge about the present but nothing more. One day, she asked the seers about Ivan, who was absent but, at the same time as Ivan later recounted, she also appeared to the boy who had stayed in the town; hence, the surprise and disquiet of the friar (Kraljević and Maggioni 1988, 27).

What is most striking about this historicization of the Madonna is the *psychological profile* that is the result of all the emotions and feelings attributed to her. The emotion most displayed by the Virgin is sorrow, although serenity, happiness, and even great joy are not entirely absent. Yet, if the images that appeared were limited to a Madonna who was sad, they would have come to represent a celestial participation in human tragedy and danger, not a historicization of the world beyond.

For example, the Madonna of La Salette, who appeared *only once*, weeping, indicated the intervention of the celestial will in human history with a moving request for repentance. But since at Oliveto, the Madonna appeared often sad but sometimes happy, she became endowed with a *present-time* psychological existence—a succession of emotions, feelings, and reactions in terms of pleasure or displeasure, joy and despair, deep emotion and irritation, participation and distance—that made her into a being who dwelled not on a metahistoric level but on a historic one, however different and superior it was to that of humans.

The one thing missing on the Madonna's level, however, is death. Apart from that, every other human aspect is present: the world beyond is a mirror image of this one, however perfected and "resolved." There is Evil as well as Good in the same way as in this world. There is joy and sorrow, time for struggle and time for repose, for fiesta. In short, the Madonna's approach to humans—which even in the most orthodox interpretations of apparitions marks a celestial intervention in history—is transformed, in a reintegration of the Madonna in the history of mankind, into a living person among the living; in short, a *heaven on earth*. This idea is confirmed by seers' declarations about the possible presence of the Madonna independent of whether someone might have actually seen her, considered below.

By noting the occasions on which the Madonna showed herself smiling and happy, one can identify her *tastes*. Clearly, when she appears smiling or declares her joy or happiness because of the prayers she receives from the pilgrims at Oliveto (cf. B, r, 28, 70; B 7, 7), we are still dealing with an image based on an instructive purpose. Just as the sad Madonna invites penance, so the smiling Madonna rewards conversion. But when, for example, she shows her particular pleasure for the Rosary, her "preferred prayer" (B 7, 7), what is involved is a personal taste that transforms a rhetorical image into a person whose historical and psychological dimensions appear palpable.

Sometimes she is pleased at the large number of pilgrims who stream into Oliveto. In these instances, she is attributed an attitude that renders her more richly human, with even enough historical connotations to take on a cultural identity, as she speaks of the "honor" that she receives from the visits (cf. B 7, 17–18; B 12, 10), recalling ethnic models of visits and hospitality. The proof that her appearance is often ethnically modulated can be seen in the number of times she appears wearing shoes in the style "of the Arab peoples."

Furthermore, her joy is not the stereotypical kind that recognizes the trip made to the sacred center and looks forward to the conversion, after the pilgrimage, of everyday life in the hometowns. No, rather she acts like the mistress of a house who anxiously attends the guests who have come to visit, one who is unable to repress her disappointment when the visits are scarce (B, r, 40), and who is more pleased when more guests come. She tells Nello explicitly that she is very happy because the seer comes to see her often (B, r, 17). She asks another to come more often (B 11, 22), promising, on another occasion, great things for those who come to be with her (B 12, 15). At Medjugorje, this model of a Marian visit to a home is also expressed in an explanation that Vicka gave for the larger number of apparitions that Vicka received compared to the other Medjugorje seers. Vicka was always in her house (Bubalo 1987, 175).

But the most enthusiastic expressions are on the occasions of the Madonna's feast days. Already on the day before the first anniversary of her apparitions, the Madonna told Ubaldo she was very happy because "the big day is at hand." At the beginning of the day, she then said, "Today I am very happy because there will be many prayers." Once again, at the end of the day, she said she was "immensely happy" because so many people came (B, r, 42, 44). The tone was similarly enthusiastic in 1988, on the fourth anniversary of the apparitions (cf. B 13, 28–29).

From the seers it was learned that the Madonna, in heaven, participates in earth time, inasmuch as she counts the years that pass by celebrating her birthdays, for example, her two thousandth birthday. On that occasion—at Oliveto as at Medjugorje—she appeared to seers dressed for company, full of joy and emotion for the presents that she would receive from Jesus.

On this day, as a present for my birthday, He [Jesus] has allowed me to give much joy and many graces to you, my children" (message in B 14, 14).

It was August 4, but I did not know that on the next day the Madonna would be 2,000 years old, much less that Jesus had promised her many conversions. (*La Madonna a Medjugorje*, Cittadella: Bertoncello Artigrafiche [1985], 153)

The Madonna was also joyful in anticipation of the presents she would receive from humans in the form of prayers and time off from work (Ibid., 105). The birthday of the Madonna was as important at Medjugorje as it was at Oliveto because in Bosnia-Herzegovina, as in Campania, the seers reported that the Madonna had specified that her "true" birthday did not coincide with the official liturgical feast day, September 8, but rather was August 5. She considered this feast day very important, so much so that she ran the risk of a conflict with the Church because of the change in the liturgical year. Dressed as "a princess" (Sala and Mantero 1986, 102), she appeared in order to receive the good wishes of humans. Ivan wished her a happy birthday, giving her his hand, and then was embarrassed by his own boldness, which his friend Vicka did not dare to repeat (Laurentin 1986a, 94).

In spite of the importance of the expressions of joy for the construction of a model of the Madonna that was vivid and credible, the kinds of sentiments most frequently expressed were sorrow, sadness, regret, and disillusion. At modern apparition sites, the most customary image is that of a sad or weeping Madonna. Paris, La Salette, and Fatima, to cite the most important, are apparitions sites where this attitude of the Madonna is most emphasized. The sorrowful attitude is then passed on to Jesus, sad, weeping, or even suffering and bloody as at Golgotha. Even God is seen as sad, as when he appeared to the seers at Fatima in an immense light (Lucia 1973, 97). These expressions, even if inevitably presented as psychological traits, in fact rhetorically function as calls to conversion, and due to their rarity do not cause a pronounced psychologization of the figure that appears.

In contrast, the sadness of the Madonna at Oliveto, as at Medjugorje, is part of an unpredictable, on occasion even capricious, alternation of feeling, as if she were experiencing the present like a historically specific person. The "message of sorrow," a stereotypical model well-established in the tradition of Marian prodigies, is a constant of the Oliveto apparitions (cf., for example, B, r, 48, 58, 71, 73, 74, 75). This message includes Christ as well, whose "sorrowing visage" appears (B 7, 5), or whom the Madonna (in January, without any possible reference in the liturgical calendar) describes

as in agony because of sins (B 12, 14), or who says that he suffers greatly for
sins (B, r, 73), or for the sorrow caused to the Madonna. "That increases my
suffering, above all when I see that you make my Mother weep. I gave her to
you; why do you make her weep" (B 15, 16).

The first apparition of Maria was announced, it will be recalled, with the
crying of an invisible baby. According to the parish priest,

> this crying can reasonably be considered a message of sorrow, just as a
> message of sorrow is the appearance of the Sorrowing Madonna to
> [Aurelia] G. of Contursi; a message of sorrow in the very weeping of the
> Virgin: to [Tommaso] D., to [Ubaldo] G., and to some others She
> appeared weeping and explained that the reason was because people
> blaspheme, because they do not believe, and do not pray (B 1, 2).

The priest interpreted the sorrow as a message, and thus as a rhetorical
expression. But often the Madonna says, "*This evening* I am sad" (cf. B 7,
13) (or, I am bitter, or I am happy), expressing feelings rather than sending
messages; that is, providing an impression of psychological specificity
rather than instructive images.

The alternation of feelings as an expression of experience seems to be a
kind of automatic result of the multiplication of the visions, and the
Bollettino itself, with its scrupulous reporting, plays an important role in that
process. The *Bollettino* reported that the Madonna told Tommaso on April
28, 1986, that she was very happy because the pilgrims were praying. Two
days later, she appeared to another seer, "her eyes streaked with tears" (B,
r, 30). In another issue, the Madonna shed "many tears" on November 12
and was "very happy" on November 18 (B 12, 4). To the same seer, Lucia,
she appeared praising her and expressing her satisfaction for having kept
"her promise," then disappeared, only to return a little later "weeping and
dressed in black" (B, r, 62).

The Madonna's "changes of scene" were not at all frowned upon by the
Committee. Indeed, they too could be molded to organize a rhetorical
function for the images that appear by means of the dual modulation of
sorrowful and joyful models of the Madonna. These rhetorical models of
Marian iconography were useful for restating in the apparitions the message
of the Mary put forward in the popular message of the Church.

The images of joy and sorrow are the two poles of the figure of the
Madonna as Mother, which has an exceptional importance in Catholic
popular discourse. The happy Madonna and the sad Madonna represent an

immediate mnemonic syntheses of a pastoral discourse that calls for repentance for sins, but one without desperation because of the "abyss." Keeping in mind the rhetorical function of the images of sorrow and joy, it is then possible to understand how, for example, the seer T. A. could sign "in faith and full of joy" the declaration of the message of Jesus, cited above, in which he spoke of his horrible sufferings and those of the Madonna (B 15, 16–17). The seer did not seem to be saddened by the message; on the contrary, she was delighted because she had an apparition, even though it was *the sad kind*.

But the collective public experience of the images tends to go beyond the rhetorical function of the models and reconfigures, in the flesh and blood of a person alive and present, the isolated rhetorical images. As a result, in the collective imagination, the Madonna suffers and takes pleasure, weeps and laughs, according to the sequence of her immediate personal experiences rather than the needs of a doctrine of conversion for which the hierarchy uses the apparition.

The psychologizing of the Madonna is reproduced by the psychologizing of the *Devil*. He often laughs when he appears "to lead" mortals "into temptation"; here, we are still within the rhetorical function of the image of the Devil. But he also cries, like a defeated, desperate loser, for example, when the blessing of a statue of the Madonna convinces him that he "can no longer work" the way he used to (Sala and Mantero 1986, 100), or he shows himself "very angered" because, Saint Michael observes, "he has realized that many souls are getting away from him" (B, r, 55).

Weeping as a response to events in the present affects the figure of Jesus as well, contributing to the idea of a world beyond that mirrors this one, a world that watches the actions of humans and reacts to them emotionally. At Medjugorje, it was said that the Baby Jesus was weeping ever more often, and there were those who held the bishop's negative attitude to be the cause. Others, however, with an even more historicized idea of the other world, maintained that Jesus wept because he had by now been missing his Mother for at least seven years (Bax 1990, 69).

Other apparitions of the Madonna round out the psychological profile of a character that cannot be reduced to a traditional rhetorical schema of the Mother of God. There are attitudes of the Madonna incongruent with the official model of mildness and modesty. Sometimes the Madonna was described by the seers as irritated, with an attitude not always soft and sweet. To one female seer who arrived with others at the gate very late, the Madonna said: "They come at this time and they do not pray (referring to the group of pilgrims who came late), I tell you I want prayer from every one of them." But the irritation did not go away after the pilgrims had said the Rosary. The female seer returned to the gate and the Madonna said: "You prayed because you were asked to, but not spontaneously from the heart" (B, r, 37).

The Madonna may even appear as aggressive and haughty. To a group of Sicilian pilgrims she said:

> You cost me tears of blood, you should go out in the world and do things so that everyone comes to know this immense love, because otherwise you are egotists, you only think of yourselves, the Christian is always an apostle, I myself, as soon as I received the annunciation from the Angel, went to Elizabeth's house to serve her and I was the Mother of God. (B, r, 76)

She can also propose that persons be tactical and calculating in their relations with others. At Medjugorje, she encouraged a female seer to be a bit more skeptical about the intentions of others. "She said that I was too naive, that I ought to correct that. I believe everybody too much" (Laurentin and Rupčić 1984a, 61).

She defends those under her protection from "spies" (the Yugoslav police), and even exposes unbelievers who have ventured into the circle of believers, as Vicka pointed out at Medjugorje (Bubalo 1987, 198).

She can also be vindictive and promise revenge. The Madonna once said to Armida, the blind seer from Agropoli, who played an important role in Oliveto for a considerable period: "Don't listen to those who make fun of you; follow me; for they too will weep and, perhaps, you will be able to smile at them. When you wept, they laughed behind your back; they too will shed tears" (Bonora 1987, 54).

Finally, on countless occasions the Madonna *herself* prayed with the pilgrims and seers. Here is how the *Bollettino* reported one such incident: "One female seer affirmed that the Madonna asked her to pray the 'Salve Regina' leading it Herself with a slow and very sweet voice like a celestial harmony!" (B, r, 48).

At Medjugorje, she taught the right way to recite the Rosary (Sala and Mantero 1986, 77), something very common in accounts of apparitions and encounters with the Madonna, although there are cases in which she stopped when the pilgrims say the Hail Mary.

The psychological specificity of the Madonna is not simply an indirect effect of the accumulation of the reports about her. The leaders themselves cultivated this dimension. Father Slavko Barbarić, one of Franciscans most prominent in the Medjugorje movement, told Sala and Mantero:

> A theologian, a philosopher, once said of a message, here there is a total contradiction, for in the message she says, "You have not prayed enough" and at the end, "I thank you." How is this possible? You didn't do [what you were supposed to], and then, "thank you"! Consider that the Mother is the one who speaks, and in a mother's words there are always contradictions—she'll say, "You'll never ever get anything more from me because you are bad," and then "Come on, let's eat!" (Sala and Mantero 1986, 140)

Hence, this is a Madonna psychologically alive and specific, physically marked by the "normal" limits of exhaustion that are expressed in the penance of coldness and physical suffering; a Madonna with the ethnic connotation of Palestinian dress but also socially specified by the elegance of her clothes on festive days, above all on her birthdays, the temporal markers of a life in the here-and-now; a Madonna, finally, some of whose physical signs tell us about her *present-time* activity in the world she lives in. The seer Vicka noticed that the Madonna's hands were cleaner and more delicate than those of the seers (Bubalo 1987, 199); she surely did not do manual labor.

Certainly, at the base of the visionary experiences and the narrative accounts, all these psychological, cultural, and physical features of the being that appears reflect the psychological and interactive experiences of the seers. But the end result is that, for her followers, the Madonna takes on the features described by the seers and legitimated by the leaders. The theoretically indefinable and "unthinkable" lines of a celestial figure become as clearly defined as those of a familiar being in the real world, a world in which men and women, just like the Madonna in her world, are happy and sad, jovial and irritated, manual laborers and intellectuals, Italians and Arabs, and so forth.

Bodies in Struggle

The Decisive Move of the Madonna signaled a new dimension in the cosmic struggle. The apparition site was the location for the Devil's main offensive, for it was there that the most devotees of Maria gathered. The Devil broadened his attack to include them and their bodies, which came to be invaded by his aggressions on a daily basis. The accounts of diabolical attacks became an extremely common part of the Oliveto routine. The habitual pilgrims, after arriving in Oliveto, would be informed by those in the little plaza of two kinds of supernatural news: new messages and new assaults by the Devil. Ever more often the messages of the Madonna announced that the struggle with the Devil had spread to the pilgrims and the Committee. Based on a message, Tommaso wrote, "From now on Satan will pursue you in every moment of your life" (B, r, 41).

The casual conjunction of messages with different tones in the *Bollettino* implied an intermittence in the victories in the struggle, which increased the general impression of a *present* drama because victory was (momentarily) in doubt. On April 26, 1986, Tommaso reported: "Dear children, your prayers are reducing Satan's power; his strength now is limited only to breaking rosaries, to scaring people" (B, r, 30). But little more than a month later, on June 1, Ubaldo said: "Again I call you to prayer, because Satan is trying throughout the world to destroy my plans; he has fooled you many times" (B, r, 49). Less than a month later, on June 29, 1986, a female seer reported with satisfaction: "Satan is losing his strength, the lie has no more power" (B, r, 61). But on the same day a different female seer reported: "Satan has taken power on earth, fooling you; for the last time, listen to me and pray, pray, pray. Help Me in prayer, pray with Me for the salvation of the World" (B 5, 61). Three days later, on July 1, 1986, Benedetta reported on the state of the conflict: "He has become aggressive because he knows that little by little he is losing power so he does all he can to break up marriages, provoke arguments between the Ministers of the Church, and terrify and make obsessive persons who are weak" (B, r, 62).

But the partial optimism of this message had no time to take hold, for the next message in the *Bollettino* was quite alarming. The Devil appeared to little Mauro and said:

"Why did you disobey me? You weren't supposed to come here any more." I answered him, "I can do what I want to, because you're not the one who tells me what to do." At this his eyes became like fire and he went on to say, "I am the boss on heaven and earth and I tell you that in families there will be no peace." Then I prayed to the Madonna to help me and She came right away. She was beautiful, all shining and said to me, "Don't be afraid of him, fight him. I am your Mother, I will appear only if you truly need me and only after you have fought with him."[1]

On the next day, the Madonna appeared dressed in black and weeping (B, r, 62).

Like Mauro, other seers were asked to join the cosmic-historical struggle. All were instructed to pray in order to send the Devil away or defeat him. But Mauro, Nello, Ubaldo, Tommaso, Benedetta, and a few others ended up fighting the Devil physically, or, more commonly, being physically assaulted by him. In devotional literature, the Devil is often considered capable of physically intervening in the human history, first and foremost by means of possession, which, as we have seen, "is not a moral ailment, a sin, but rather a physical ailment" (Balducci 1988, 212), but also with other kinds of physical violence, including homicide, mentioned in the messages of Medjugorje (*La Madonna a Medjugorje*, Cittadella: Bertoncello Artigrafiche [1985], 94).

The idea of physical combat with the Devil has a very long history in Christianity. In contemporary popular religious imagery, this idea is connected to many holy figures known to have battled with the Devil: Padre Pio, Saint Gerardo, Saint Anthony, "the enemy of the Devil,"[2] as well as other military saints, "universal" ones like Michael and George, and local ones like Eustace and Mercury. Corrado Balducci, an Italian exorcist, gives examples of death caused by the Devil (Balducci 1974, 64). The combination of this popular theme and the dramatic climate at the apparition sites results in the displacement of the demonic from intimate temptation to a fear of an actual physical contact with the Devil. The Devil goes from being an enemy of the soul to being an enemy of the physical integrity of the believer.

For the Oliveto seers in question, the Devil prepared veritable ambushes. He appeared suddenly, grabbing Tommaso's lance, chortling, "At last I caught you by surprise" (Faricy 1986, 49). When Benedetta was in bed, the Devil danced next to her, jumping on her, keeping her from moving or calling for help, grabbing her by the wrists and whirling her around him as is done with little children. Suddenly he let go of her wrists but, astonishingly, she did not strike the ground but rather fell slowly to earth like an

1. The Devil and Mauro address each other in the familiar "tu" form.
2. In dialect.

empty bag {January 25, 1986}. A film of the "Satanic" variety, *Entity* (1982), includes this very scene.

Nello, too, was assaulted when he was alone, "without people around," his father told me. Nello was already armed with rosary beads and prayers, while to allay suspicions the Devil was disguised as an angel. In this way, the Devil came close and struck the seer, drawing blood, and then threatened him with worse if he kept going to Oliveto. After many such incidents, Nello decided to stop going. And then the Madonna went to his house and told him: "What do you think—that he is stronger than I am?" {August 5, 1988}. Normally, though, the Madonna intervenes to protect her seers before things get violent. The Devil threatened to kill Ubaldo:

> In front he had a human face, behind that of a beast difficult to describe in detail. The latter said to me, "I'll kill you, I'll kill you, I'll kill you, I'll wait for when you are no longer protected by holy figures to strike you." Then the Madonna appeared, and she crushed this monstrous being saying to me, "I know that your task is very difficult, but have faith in me." And then she disappeared. (B, r, 17)

Children too are involved in the struggle. Claudio, one of the first boy seers, after not seeing the Madonna for three or four months, saw the Devil and challenged him (Faricy and Pecoraio 1987, 116). Even little Mauro was drawn into combat. Once "Satan tried to throw him down, into hell, and he began to shout. The angels were pulling him up, the devils kept pulling him down, and marks from the struggle were left on his legs" (Ibid., 118).

Mauro's mother recounted to me what her son told her about a battle in the house. The tiled floor of a room opened to become a "black hole" in which there was an encounter between "little angels" and "little devils." Mauro told her that while some of the little devils were attacking him, others were advancing in another room to attack her. He then asked the little angels not to worry about him but to hurry and help his mother. At that point, the angels got a second wind, and saved him {January 25, 1986}. For Mauro, the Devil also took on the features of a spiteful trickster (Ibid., 117). A three-year-old boy, the brother of Mauro and Serena, removed the nails from the body of Christ that appeared on a cross; he, too, was asked to fight against the Devil (Ibid., 114).

The seer who most often reported clashes with the Devil is, without a doubt, Tommaso. With him the Devil was involved in an out-and-out duel.

Once the Devil appeared, and as the youth was taking his rosary from his pocket, stopped him from doing so:

> Stop right there, don't show me the rosary beads because I have to talk to you. From the moment you said yes to the Mother of God, you have agreed to combat with me; if you don't wish to die, say that you do not believe in your Lord, I will be after you until you deny your God. (AC, February 3, 1986)

It is not hard to identify material derived from reading about or, more probably, from stories heard about, martyrs and ascetics. But in the following passage, elements from devotional literature are mixed with material from cinema:

> I found myself in a dark place, I tried to get out, and heard behind me something like a being, maybe an animal, that I was unable to see; when I tried to get away I found there was a wall before me, I tried to climb it, but I couldn't; in the meantime I heard the being coming closer behind me. (AC, February 3, 1986)

Here the sources should, once again, be looked for in the cinematic imagination: the flight, the terrifying chase, the sudden wall that blocks the escape, the inability to get around the wall except at the last moment. Once, the Devil played a rough trick on Tommaso: "I find myself in a cage, below there is something that moves, it is dark and I see nothing. The Devil asks me to deny the Lord. The cage tilts and I fall. I close my eyes and return to my senses" (AC, December 25, 1986).

The participation of humans in the struggle with the Devil makes his presence familiar, something useful in the mystical strategies of struggle for leadership among believers and seers. The Devil becomes a frame one can impose on doubters or opponents. Benedetta, for example, saw the Devil in a nun of a Pompeii convent who prevented her from telling her experiences to the girls on retreat there {January 25, 1986}. The result is that the seers, above all, consider their adversaries or rivals as participants, or at least supporters, of the other side of the battle, that of the prince of evil. Their own personal experiences are presented as decisive for the outcomes of the cosmic drama.

In terms of iconography, in some descriptions the Devil at Oliveto was merely named "the ugly one." Other times, he appeared with the traditional attributes of devotional images: the Madonna stepping on the serpent; a red monster with horns; the Devil bound with a chain by Saint Michael, and so forth. Aurelia told Faricy that she recognized the Devil because she had seen him in her schoolbooks (Faricy 1986, 42).

Some described more elaborate images: the mysterious short man with little blisters on his face described by the children on the first evening (even though Dario a year later told me that it was Jesus who had had the little blisters); an enormous man with "some eyes of fire, some large teeth" (Ada) (AC); a serpent with wings (Nello) {April 18, 1986}; an enormous mound of hair and fur (Bernadette) {March 15, 1986} (on another occasion, Bernadette saw him dressed all in black leaping on rooftops "like Zorro"); a man "with a beard who rose up in the air with a pair of wings" (Maria Teresa) (B, r, 56); and a monster with animal-like features who spit fire (Ubaldo) (AC, February 25, 1986). Another time, Ubaldo saw "a black dog with a fiery collar around his neck" (AC, *Relaz.*, p. 4).

In terms of descriptive features, the accounts of Tommaso are more detailed than those of the others. the Devil who took his lance away was hunchbacked and goatlike in his lower half (Faricy 1986, 49), as in old popular prints. Another time, Tommaso specified that the hunchback was "made of fat" and that he had stubby hands and long, pointed, fingernails, a head "hard to describe," and a slobbery mouth with "saber-like teeth" {March 8, 1986}. On another occasion, he maintained that the devil was short and came with "a zoo on his body" with monstrous elements drawn from different animals; when he disappeared he left an odor that was a mixture of sulfur and horse manure {April 26, 1986}.

The Devil, who is present obsessively in the messages, in encounters with the most famous seers, and in the pages of the *Bollettino*, comes to Oliveto almost as often as the Madonna. A great many visions are of the Madonna and the Devil at the same time. We have already examined the important ambivalence with which some seers see the Devil and the Madonna, including a certain difficulty in distinguishing who is who. The two figures sometimes seem to alternate on the stage of the transcendent in a kind of two-sided game.

To one seer, Maria Teresa, the Madonna appeared and gave a message of prayer. The testimony continued: "At these words I was moved and all at once a vision completely different than that of the Madonna appeared before my eyes" (B, r, 56). What appeared was the bearded man with wings. In

Nello's house a statuette of the Madonna was blessed. An instant later the Devil turned up {March 8, 1986}. A young seer, Pasquale, was speaking with the Madonna when behind her he saw "a being with wings, extremely ugly, with a red face," which then attacked him. The Madonna disappeared, leaving him alone with the Devil. Then the Devil too vanished, and the Madonna reappeared and assured Pasquale of her protection (B, r, 36). A week later, the same youth saw again, in succession, the Madonna, the Devil, then the Madonna again (B, r, 40).

The following declaration leads one to imagine a situation in which the Devil and the Madonna are on the same stage fighting over or divvying up the seers. A woman was praying when she saw "a very ugly animal speaking to a (female) seer." She became frightened and distracted from her prayers, but when she looked up again she saw the Madonna standing over the Devil (B, r, 35).

Ubaldo's testimony is quite significant. According to him, the Madonna demonstrated a *disquieting inability to get rid of the Devil*, for when Ubaldo went up to the gate, the Madonna motioned to him with her head to stay back because the Devil was there (Margnelli and Gagliardi 1987a, 98). A female seer told of a similar incident. She let it be known that she had seen the Madonna, who seemed unable to come any closer perhaps because, invisibly, the Devil was holding her back. The Madonna seemed perturbed {June 14, 1986}. Moments like these give the strong impression that a battle is in progress whose the outcome, at least for the individuals involved, is unsure. In the struggle, there is no certainty of relief. Even the Madonna cannot protect from all risks.

After the incident described at the opening of this chapter, in which the Devil stabbed the Madonna and drew "bedeviled" blood, even walls became places for demonic apparitions. The struggle moved out to include all visible locations. On the wall where the Marian blood had appeared, people began to see the outlines of a devil figure with tusks and big ears. When the bearded youth from Grumo tried with the point of his umbrella to efface the outline, it seemed to show up all the more, at which point he stuck his umbrella in the Devil's eyes {March 8, 1986}. The Devil appeared in the photographs of this youth in the guise of strange and inexplicable fiery snakes in the shape of the number six.

As with the visions of the Madonna, those of the Devil spread to other towns, particularly to Cardito, where in addition to an image on the wall that seemed to be either Jesus or Mary an image of the Devil turned up as well.

At Frattamaggiore, a friend of the seer Giorgio was not able to open a window
in his house because he saw a Satanic face silhouetted in the air before him.
Someone else saw the Devil outside a window of the house of the girl
Barbara, to whom I shall soon return {March 8, 1986}.

Mary's lack of power and the riskiness of the conflict stand out above all
in the case of the frequent demonic possessions at Oliveto. A pharmacist
from a Cilento town described in writing a typical instance:

[. . .] I noticed a group of persons that carried in their arms a boy who
seemed to be sick. I went closer to give whatever medical assistance
might be necessary. The little child appeared to have fainted, and I
made the appropriate suggestions, inquiring as to the cause of his
ailment. A woman told me that the boy had seen first the Madonna and
then the devil and *from that moment* the boy showed symptoms *of one
possessed by the Devil* (my emphasis). The explanation did not convince
me at all; instead I thought the cause could be attributed to the press of
people who on that evening more than usual crowded the small site. I
also ask if the boy is normally healthy and if he suffers from epilepsy.
His relatives assure me that he is in good health and has never had any
episodes of epileptic convulsions. I observe him carefully and note if he
drools or grimaces, the classic symptoms that distinguish epilepsy from
other kinds of convulsions. But there was none of this.

Instinctively, I trace on his forehead the sign of the cross and
pronounce a few words of blessing. The boy suddenly opens his eyes and
becomes rigid as a stick, in a position similar to a syndrome of tetanus.
I have the impression that he wants to take a flying leap, from which he
is restrained by strong arms. He looks at me and whines: "You, get away,
you should not be near me." A woman sprinkles him with holy water
while others put a crucifix to his mouth and forehead. The contact does
not improve things, but makes them worse. They tell me he's been that
way for about an hour.

A lady comes and shows him a rosary. The boy with a cat-like swipe,
sudden and unexpected, grabs the rosary and tries to break it apart.
(Strange: he did this only with the rosary, but he did not touch, or try
to touch, the crucifix.) I seize with my left hand his wrist, and with my
right hand try to open his fist to release the rosary and prevent his
breaking it. When I touch him he growls: "Let me go, you burn me. I told
you to go away." Without loosening my grasp I answer him: Let me have

intact what you have in your hand and I will let go of your hand. If you break the rosary I will not let go." Finally, he lets the rosary fall into my hand.

After a while, everyone calms down and his relatives take him into the little garden nearby and sit him down on a bench. I stay near them. I am not afraid and I feel myself tranquil, but also determined to follow the matter through as much as I can. Seeing that he is more calm I ask if he is hungry and wants anything. He only wants water, and I take care of that. A lady, I do not know if a relative or not, offers him a sip of holy water asking him to drink it. The reply is chilling: "I don't want this because it's bad for me. I want that," and indicates the glass with water I am holding. He drinks three glassfuls one after another. He asks for a fourth, but I say I have no more and offer him holy water. I am also worried for his health, as he has drunk more than half a liter, too much for a young child. I observed that he has an unusual way of drinking: when he puts his lip to the edge of the glass, the water disappears.

I make no diagnosis, but limit myself to writing only what I really noted, saw, and heard. To my asking him to drink holy water he replies: "Better thirst that this" (literally, "it's better to explode from thirst," in Neapolitan dialect). I ask him questions: "What's your name?" "Nicola." "How old are you?" "Nine." "Do you go to school?" "Yes." "What grade are you in?" "Fourth." I show him a Biro pen and ask him, "Do you see this object?" "Yes." "Can you tell me what it is?" "A pen." I show him the little crucifix I wear on my lapel and I ask him, "Nicola, tell me what this object is." He looks at it, takes on a expression at the very least bad, indescribable, turns his head away, and does not answer. I repeat the question three times in vain. Finally, he decides to respond: "Now you're bugging me. It is the same as this" and shows me a little crucifix that he holds in his hand. I don't give in, and insist: "I do not want to know what it is the same as. I want to know what it is." This time I pose the question in the tone of a command. No response: the word *croce—crocifisso* does not come out of his mouth. In the midst of tragedy, a comic note. Seated next to the boy is his grandfather, who looks at the ground with sadness, and disconsolate, says, "First the Madonna came, then that shitface turned up and messed up my kid." (AC)

One of the significant aspects of this incident is that the possession occurred right after a vision of the Madonna, almost as if to show *Mary's impotence* at avoiding demonic possession, even in a child who had the privilege of seeing her. In contrast to the official Catholic position, which assigns the Madonna a power that the Devil cannot dispute, in this incident the dominant dimension is one of a *struggle among equals* (between the Madonna and the Devil) that is going on *right now* before the very eyes of devotees. Perhaps the final victory is continually assured but the partial victories—those that concern the historical existence of each devotee—can in no way be taken for granted. Individual *histories* are not guaranteed and the final victory will surely leave many casualties on the battlefield.

Dramatizations of the conflict between Madonna and Devil that extend to the bodies of believers are a sign of a cultural thematization of Evil, the randomness and total irrationality of which mean that no one is safe. An episode of public possession constitutes a symbolic dramatization of the forces in conflict and the impossibility of controlling evil. The boy Nicola had just finished seeing the Madonna when he fell into the Devil's hands. It is a story that exemplifies the blindness of an evil that not even the figures that incarnate good can avoid. Cosmic Evil, the symbolic "distant" displacement of the unforeseeable *historicity* of life, comes down to earth, embodied, in the historical drama, as an evil that is historical, biographical, and individual.

Demonic possession is a representation of this evil. The unavoidableness, unforeseeableness, and whimsicality of *historical evil* are theatrically displayed in a body captured through no fault of its own by the Devil. The disquieting aspect that these incidents communicate to the spectators is precisely a matter of the cultural significance that they express, a reflection on the nature of evil that they provoke. They are *structural* signs that the *structure* itself cannot always foresee and control the *event*, and that the world refuses to be forced into *categories* (Sahlins 1985). In short, the incidents are a way that cultural structure has to express its limitations and inadequacy in the face of the contingencies of history.

Not by chance, an exorcism eventually involves all who are present. The community constructs in choral fashion a bulwark against the intrusion of historical reality, experienced as symbolic irrationality, upon the defined and prefigured plane of cultural categories. And when exorcism is effective there is widespread satisfaction because the level of categories has reaffirmed its own power vis-à-vis historical contingency, and the culturalized world demonstrates its capacity to overcome the horror of the formless. Certainly, there exist techniques of self-defense, above all prayer, the continual invocation of the Madonna—at Medjugorje holy water and holy salt (Juarez 1987, 92; Bubalo 1987, 138)—but at times these, too, must give way.

The choral nature of exorcism, as at Medjugorje (De Simone 1986), involved each person present: prayer, shouts, insults, advice, crucifixes, water, and the imposition of hands. The possessions allowed all the believers to enter into direct combat and play their own part in the cosmic struggle between Good and Evil. By materializing the evil in the body of one possessed person believers could both activate mechanisms that identified scapegoats and constitute physically (and observe) the army of the "good ones" who came to the aid of the Madonna and Jesus. Taking part was a privilege that displaced to the level of *things seen and done* what in the everyday world took place on the level of *interior choice*.

The case of demonic possession at Oliveto that best exemplifies this kind of choral combat involves a fifteen-year-old girl named Barbara. During a pilgrimage she and her parents made to the shrine of the Holy Face (Volto Santo) at Naples, she came down with an ailment that was diagnosed as demonic possession. One of the ways they tried to free her was to take her to Oliveto. But there, too, the girl was taken by evil. She hardly had been escorted to the gate when she began to scream and tried to flee. Forced to continue, she inveighed against everyone and violently shook her head. When she was constrained by force to look at the gate she shouted: "Get away! Get away!" to some figure that only she could see, whom some thought was the Madonna, and others, the Devil. Given the frequency of her visits, Don Giovanni became interested in her case, but he was not convinced of the authenticity of her possessions. At times, the girl did not refuse "sacred things," indeed, she prayed and carried a rosary; other times, she had fits.

In Don Giovanni's opinion, which he gave to the girl's family, it was a problem "of nerves." The doctors who observed her in the little plaza during her fits had the same opinion. The members of the Committee gradually came to accept Don Giovanni's interpretation and talked about the recurring fits as a nervous condition. But Barbara's ailments were collectively followed by all the believers present as possessions, an interpretation that was, to a certain extent, imposed on the Committee and on the parish priest himself, who was prevailed upon to pronounce the canonical exorcisms each time that the girl was carried into the Committee headquarters.

Michele then advised some of the believing youths of Frattamaggiore to keep spiritual tabs on the girl and push her to attend mass and receive the sacraments frequently. As a result, three days each week a prayer group met at Barbara's house to say the Rosary. When she was at Oliveto, generally on the weekend, Barbara was often brought by force to the gate in an attempt to obtain her freedom through the Madonna. Often when Barbara went up between the two rows of believers, people would cry out to the Devil, "Vattene, vattene! Go away, go away!" "In the name of the living God vattene, vattene." They would take out their crucifixes, rosaries, and little images of Saint Michael, and would reach out to touch the body of the girl with devotional objects. Some read exorcising prayers such as "In the name of Jesus all the powers of evil Satan have been destroyed vattene."

During one of her episodes of distress, Barbara suddenly shouted, looking at the gate: "No, another month no," and the people commented that the Madonna had told her that she must suffer yet another month. After a while, Barbara got better and became a seer of the Madonna. Her messages were never published in the *Bollettino* but were well-known nonetheless; it was Barbara who said that the Madonna was displeased when people went to find her in the side streets off the little plaza, and who said that the Madonna was sad because people were not praying with faith. The girl was instructed by the Madonna to tell everyone about her cure, emphasizing in particular the accuracy of the prediction of one more month {April 26, 1986}. Many were disconcerted by her transition from the ranks of the possessed to those of seers, but the confusion increased when Barbara was again visited by the Devil and began to alternate demonic fits with Marian visions.

The prominence of Barbara's case allowed people to identify and follow the shifting fortunes of both sides of the cosmic/historic battle underway at Oliveto. Her fits and her cures were like a barometer. The skepticism of the parish priest kept the Committee partially removed from this interpretation. The visions of the girl were hardly ever recognized and at one point she was even forbidden to enter the Committee office, which until then had been a regular stop on her visits to Oliveto. By its rejection of the Barbara affair, the Committee expressed a model of absolute cultural categories to be used for the events, whereas the popular participation tended to identify the holes in these categories.

For the Committee, the Devil could not win even isolated victories; prayer was weapon enough. For the believers, the Devil could grab hold unexpectedly and without any motive, even if the person was protected by the Madonna, and he might not let the person go in spite of repeated attempts at exorcism. For the Committee, it was impossible for a woman to continue to be possessed for a long time, with ups and downs, even become a seer, and then be possessed once more. But Barbara's experience was considered perfectly possible in the popular view. It exemplified the possibility that each person can fall to the Devil without any cause whatsoever and expressed the open and intractable conflict between real world and categories, between the danger in the real world and the mythic reformulation. The Barbara affair was the physically concrete and visible staging of the cosmic/historic drama. The Committee trusted in a universe that was closed and pre-defined; the believers, in contrast, lived in an open universe in which the symbolic forces in the field did not know—indeed, could not know—who would win. The Committee turned to ritual to order the world; for the believers, the Devil represented the upheaval of history in the order of categories.

Whereas it was possible to dismiss the ambiguity that Barbara represented, given her stigma as "possessed by the Devil," it was not possible to eliminate doubts about seers who were fully certified by the Committee but who had experiences of association with good or evil that were disquieting. Here the case of Nello is a good example.

On Good Friday, 1986, Nello received in his house the "gift" of stigmata. His father and aunt said that the sheet on which he was laid was covered with blood. The phenomenon disappeared the same day and then was repeated for a few Fridays thereafter. They asked the Committee not to publicize the event, but the people in the town nevertheless crowded in to see the prodigy {April 12, 1986}. On the next day, Easter Saturday, Nello was attacked by the Devil in the form of a winged serpent, who left little bloody marks on the backs of his hands, negative stigmata, as it were (we are back to the absolute ambiguity of the blood on the wall and the handkerchief). The youth had a true spell of possession because "twenty persons" attempted in vain to bend his spread-eagled arms {April 18, 1986}. Nello told me that at times he felt nervous, and on these occasions he resorted to the care of his spiritual father in Naples, who exorcised him with canonical prayers and gestures. Often in these circumstances he felt like something went out of his body by way of his throat. In short, an important seer like Nello was "talked about" as having been alternately visited by the Madonna and possessed, albeit not publicly, by the Devil. The omnipresence of the Devil provoked a problem of identification not only of what being was appearing but also of what kind of state the seer was in.

And then some seers came to be endowed with another visionary capacity, that of seeing the Devil on the body of seers in a demonic crisis. On the evening of March 15, 1986, while I was in the little plaza, I saw hurrying down the steps four youths carrying a companion who had fainted. I followed them to the Committee office. A female seer there exclaimed that she saw many devils on the youth's body, put a rosary on him, and began to pray to exorcise him. Then Giulio, a Committee leader, arrived and barely touched the youth, who then stood up. I found that it was Ubaldo, one of the most accredited seers.

The account of the seer who had seen devils on Ubaldo's body was not accepted by the leader, but the incident demonstrates that even the physical crisis of a seer can be open to interpretation, and his body may become a representation of the Devil. This was demonstrated especially during the period in which Barbara, no longer explicitly possessed, became a seer. Even when she saw the Madonna, she had physical crises of presence, with weeping, cries, and partial faints. It was difficult to recognize the source of any particular crisis. Tommaso, among others, was particularly adept at finding the devil on Barbara's body or determining that the crisis was a positive one. But Tommaso himself, in turn, was possessed by the Devil, according to a Committee leader who spoke in the Channel 5 television report.

On rare occasions a body attacked by the Devil might experience dissociation. A textbook case is an incident described by Benedetta, after one of the sudden attacks by the Devil described above. She had hardly landed on the floor, once her wrists were released by the Devil, when she turned toward her bed.

{20}

And what do I see on the bed? + I see myself + that is I see me—sleeping [. . .] so I am seen by me I am seen by me and I say "mama so I am—I am asleep" + and then—I touched myself—I say "but then who am I this one or that one?" [. . .] and I couldn't move on the floor—the only thing that I couldn't do—I couldn't get up + then I called "Pretty little Madonna + make someone come to call at the door to see who is the one getting up—the one on the bed—or me on the floor"—I was making an effort to get up [. . .] and in the meantime I turned my head down like this and looked at myself no + and then I raised my head to look again at the bed + I look again at the bed and there is no one + I wasn't there anymore [. . .] and then little by little

I began to move myself + I saw it no longer and then I say "I should get up + I am me" + and then I got up and went back to bed {January 25, 1986}.

Trips

The preceding episode, which in psychiatric terms would be called external "autoscoping" (Jaspers, cited in Gallini 1983a, 344), is the "negative" form, that is, one produced by the Devil, of dissociation that has a positive kind as well. An example of the positive kind was reported by Tommaso, who in front of the gate had a vision of a green field in which he was close to the Madonna, then turned back and *saw himself* in front of the gate (Marotta 1990, 243).

Tommaso's experience can be defined as a *trip* on which the seer is taken to see something that does not pertain to the normal order of reality. Often the trips are made by seers with one part of themselves, while another part, physically inert and unaware, remains on earth. "It is as if I went out of my body," wrote Tommaso on one occasion (AC, March 23, 1986). In terms of Rouget's classification, these are not possession experiences (whether divine or diabolic), for they are not marked by passivity or absence of consciousness and memory. Instead, they are shamanic experiences, which involve the activity of one part of the subject, the presence of consciousness, and hence the subsequent recall of the experience (cf. Rouget 1980, 32ff.).

As in the case of Tommaso, the visions often take place right in front of the gate, which disappears, replaced by heavenly locations. The locations most often visited are Paradise, Hell, and Purgatory. The leaders accept these accounts and publish them in the *Bollettino*. The typical description of paradise is as a flowery meadow—little Mauro added that the Baby Jesus was playing there (Faricy and Pecoraio 1987, 117), while hell is like "a deep pit," a "crowd on fire" with Saint Michael who is in the air with a bloody sword (for instance, B, r, 21).

The model of hell of the visions, is of course, the traditional one of lapping flames that torment the damned and the devils. The most icastic vision of hell among modern Marian seers was that at Fatima, described here by Lucia:

The Madonna showed us a great sea of fire, which seemed to be underground. Immersed in this fire, the devils and the souls there were like transparent, black, or bronze-colored arms in human form that waved in the fire, carried by the flames, which issued from within them, together with great billows of smoke, and fell from every direction, like the sparks that fall down in great showers, without weight or balance, amidst horrifying screams and moans of pain and desperation that made one tremble with fright. The demons were distinguishable by the horrible and disgusting shapes of beasts frightening and unknown, but transparent and black. (Lucia 1973, 80)

One significant detail of some Oliveto descriptions of hell is that the devils "dance" (Faricy and Pecoraio 1987, 117). The Devil is also presented as dancing in the account of Benedetta excerpted above. Opposition to dancing is an important theme in the visionary religion of this period, a reflection of ecclesiastical antipathy toward behavior considered extremely dangerous in terms of relations between the sexes. Vicka told Brother Bubalo that if the Madonna had not appeared at Medjugorje, there would have been a disco there, whereas now "it doesn't come to mind to anyone" (Bubalo 1987, 254). In this respect as well, Fatima set a pattern. Lucia Dos Santos said that another child seer, Jacinta, loved dancing very much, and for that very reason renounced it immediately as the first thing she thought of, right after the apparitions (Lucia 1973, 30). Lucia herself, a child six years old, loved dancing greatly, and later, writing as an adult nun, related dancing with the Devil: "Above all a passion for dancing was sinking deep roots into my heart. And I confess that if our good God had not shown me a special mercy, the devil would have, with it, have been my perdition" (Ibid., 40). The opposition of the clergy of Iberia toward dancing and the influence felt by seers in this matter are also documented for the seers of Ezkioga (Christian 1987, 160). This opposition affected other kinds of popular diversion. In particular, Lucia's diary was witness to serious opposition to a kind of diversion and ritual profoundly experienced in the popular world: the carnival. The episode is interesting enough to merit a short digression.

The only survivor of the three seers, Lucia entered a nunnery from which she continued to report visions of the Madonna, various saints, Jesus, and even the Holy Trinity, receiving messages through voices she hears or "interior language." It was through voices that she received a message about carnival. In a letter to Padre Gonsalves in December 1940, she wrote:

Our Lord told me on Thursday at 11 in the evening, "If the Portuguese government, together with the bishops, converts the upcoming days of carnival to days of prayer and penance, with public prayers in the streets, and suppresses the pagan festivities, it will draw on Portugal and Europe graces of peace." (Lucia 1973, 160)

Political and here-and-now issues have been a specialty of Lucia, if one considers her request in regard to communist Russia. But there is something here more than a position taken against an avowedly Marxist state. Here "Our Lord" directly attacks the carnival celebrations, entering the centuries-old struggle between carnival and Lent (Burke 1978, 203ff.). Even more surprisingly, the celestial voice supports the scientifically dubious position that carnival is a *pagan* celebration (Caro Baroja 1965, 20). There is a clear echo of the Church's anti-carnival campaign in the divine messages of Lucia. Furthermore, the "Lord" did not merely express a scientific opinion but requested a thorough repression. About a month later, Lucia wrote to the cardinal patriarch of Portugal informing him that

Our Lord desires that in Portugal, in atonement for it and other nations, the secular feast days of carnival should be abolished and replaced by prayer and sacrifice and public prayer in the streets. [. . .] Our Lord wants the government to take a part in this, at least abolishing the secular feasts. (Lucia 1973, 161)

Here the earlier, compromising, scientific position is revised, with the shift from "pagan" to "secular [*profana*]." On the other hand, there is a clear request for repression of popular feasts.

What emerges from these episodes is a Christianity of sadness, renunciation, and suffering in which dancing, diversion, and carnival are the stuff of the Devil. This model is very clear at Oliveto, where the Devil told a seer not to follow the Madonna, who always asked for penance, but rather him, who always asked for fun (B 7, 4).

In addition to the vision trips that do not involve going away from the physical location of the visions, there are also accounts of out-and-out trips. Tommaso wrote:

The Madonna came and took me by the hand, led me to an enormous door where there was someone with a white beard and white hair, he opened the big door and I went in to see the Madonna. I saw an immense meadow, with a myriad of flowers; there were many people dressed in white, among whom I recognized P. R., who, smiling, greeted me. Then we walked across the meadow, and at the end through a blue mist I saw a throne held up by the Angels, on which there was a man with long hair and a beard, he gave me a smile, then we went back, but by another path, along which there were flowers with enormous petals which were gathered by little Angels and put into jars of very pure crystal, and all around was noted a most beautiful odor. Then the petals were put back on their stems. (AC)

In an interview on Channel 5, Giovanni, a seer from Agropoli, told of being taken by the Madonna to see Hell, a deep trench full of fire. They got there through a tunnel near the Oliveto castle, which led down to a door. To the left was a river, to the right a path that descended 237 meters, precisely measured by the Madonna, and that led to three outlets, that went even deeper to a stairs with 237 steps.

Another seer who went on trips that seemed to involve going somewhere was Anna, a seer dismissed by the Committee as possibly heterodox but who distributed handouts with her messages from the Madonna and other saints. Anna told about a trip to Paradise on which she was able to see the Hall of Judgment with God on a splendid throne and twenty-four "old men" seated on benches against the wall. She even attended a post-mortem inquest on a girl who, among other things, persisted before God in not repenting her sins. An accredited seer, Serena, also mentioned the Hall of Judgment. The Madonna promised a kind of museum tour of the other world for those who prayed: they would be able to "visit all of Paradise, even the great hall of judgment" (AC, February 8, 1986).

I did not hear in Oliveto about seers who left on trips and disappeared from public view; but one such instance is described for Medjugorje. The Madonna took Jakov and Vicka to visit Paradise, Purgatory, and Hell. In the meantime, Jakov's mother was looking for him. About twenty minutes later, the two seers returned to earth, and Jakov's mother asked them where they had been hiding, as she had been unable to find them. Their story was believed by the mother and neighbors who arrived in short order. Jakov was somewhat shaken. His mother was terrified, because after the trip the boy felt tired and his skin was even a little swollen (Bubalo 1987, 214–17).

As one might expect, the Paradise of the Yugoslav seers is a place of "beautiful light . . . people . . . flowers . . . angels," and indescribable joy (Ibid., 215). But Purgatory is "a dark space . . . filled with something like ashes," and Hell is the classic location of fire with "a blonde, longhaired slutty woman with horns," with devils leaping at her. These marvelous landscapes provoke a certain amount of perplexity in local leaders and more educated observers. Brother Bubalo, Vicka's interviewer, reminded the seer that the Madonna could not show the marvelous places "except in a manner that could be grasped by you"; Laurentin added that these are "of necessity symbolic visions" because, in terms of Hell, "the pure spirits (demons or separated souls) are not visible or combustible" (Laurentin 1986a, 99).

The trips also involved extraordinary places in this world, more or less recognizable, that could be assimilated to the marvelous sites in the other world. The leaders Michele and Giulio told me that Ubaldo had an experience that another male seer had predicted. He entered a *trance* and felt himself change into a child, then he left for Jerusalem accompanied by a being who said he was Saint Michael. This being was also seen by another seer, Nello; and yet another saw a serpent at the feet of Ubaldo and Nello that was about to attack them, only to have Saint Michael crush the head of the diabolical beast.

When Ubaldo came out of his *trance*, he said he had been to Jerusalem and met the apostles. During his trip, Ubaldo felt like he was flying over mountains and seeing Middle-Eastern landscapes. When he reached the big doors of an unspecified building, he entered with the Madonna. To the side of one room he saw a man dressed in red, and in another room men in tunics sitting around a table. They interrupted their conversation when he arrived. The Madonna introduced them as John, James, Matthew, and so on, and Ubaldo realized they were eleven of the apostles. Ubaldo asked where the twelfth one was, but the Madonna told him she did not want him to see that one because that disciple was supposed to accompany him to Hell. She had decided not to show the seer this terrible sight again, after the scare the seer had the last time he had seen it. As he left he saw two women dressed in black. Then he came to.

Ubaldo's experience involved a loss of consciousness, after which he reported what he remembered. Tommaso, on the other hand, said that his trips were preceded by a sense of feeling strange, of almost fading away {January 6, 1986}, of emptying out (B, r, 27). His body seemed to remain on the ground and someone else inside him took the trip {January 25, 1986}.

The experiences Tommaso reported were limited to the simple observations of the places he visited. But Nello boasted of an episode that was both a trip and an identification with Jesus through a new Passion that Nello himself experienced. One of the Saturdays after Good Friday, 1986, on which he first had the stigmata, while his family members were watching him bleed, he

was already in bed when the Madonna came and said: Now I take you with me, you will suffer, but that is to prepare you for the gift you soon will have and also to keep you away from the Beast. Do you want to come? And I answered, Little Madonna I will always go wherever you want, and then I found myself in a place with many hills and I asked where it was and the vision replied: It is Jerusalem. After saying this the Madonna went away and I did not see her, while in this place there were so many people and they mocked me and began to whip me, tied a rope to my waist and pulled me towards them. I was no longer dressed normally—I had just a cloth that covered my hips they put on my right shoulder a cross (at that point those present saw a black smudge take shape on my shoulder) and I began to follow a long road, as I was walking I fell twice and then they dragged me and mistreated me, I got up on a hill where there were three crosses, and here they put me on the ground and began to nail me onto one of these three crosses (in fact blood came out of my hands and feet that those present saw) the pain I felt was atrocious moving my head I tried to shake the crown of thorns from my forehead, but the more I moved the more pain I felt, very far off from the cross was the Madonna, all dressed in black who watched me and the look on her face expressed all the love possible for me (and she seemed to say I cannot help you) but looking at her I said: Mamma Mamma, don't worry I want to suffer I will save humanity all my brothers, I was so cold it began to rain and I saw a very bright light that little by little got weaker and Jesus appeared floating in the air dressed all in white and on his forehead he had a luminous crown of thorns and he said to me: Never mind your suffering, you will save so many of your brothers, your soul has already departed and is already in Paradise, then I fainted. (AC, May 9, 1986 [Nello and the Madonna address each other with the familiar "tu" form])

"Shamanic" journeys and demonic possessions are opposite ways for the bodies of the devout to participate in the cosmic drama at Oliveto. This opposition is not so much one between activity and passivity, as Rouget would have it, but rather one of individual involvement on different sides of the struggle between Good and Evil. Shamanic voyages, together with positive possession, partake of the former, while demonic possessions signal moments in the defeat and fall of bodies into the Devil's clutches. Although the ultimate outcome of the encounter will surely be victory, involvement is always risky for individuals. None of the seers could feel completely safe from capture by the Devil, nor could the Madonna guarantee to each her continuous protection. The cosmic struggle at the level of individual bodies spares no one.

Enchanted World

Following Weber, I use the notion of "disenchantment of the world" to mean the rational recognition of causal mechanisms that regulate the world. Weber thought of disenchantment as an inevitable and incremental process that, starting with an initial impulse from redemptive religion to break with magical "enchantment," leads to autonomy from religion in other spheres of life, until finally it breaks into the religious sphere itself in a process of secularizing rationalization. While today "the consistency of disenchant- ment no longer has a uniform density, thinning out, even leaving bald, eroded patches in some zones" (Mascitelli 1990, 145), and while disen- chantment is no longer assumed to be a simple and linear process, it remains an irrenunciable philosophic touchstone, "a point of no-return, despite its faults" (Ibid., 146).

> The disenchantment of the world, in any case, is definitive and irreversible, because it represents the historical memory of the no- longer, of the line that separates permanently, even of time immemorial. How can we remember, indeed, the time when the divine dwelt on earth and held men and nature embraced in communion, or the time in which the founding words were those spoken in a face-to-face encounter with God? And how, by the same token, can we forget that time, if the constitution of meaning on the earth abandoned by God implies pre- cisely that communion is a thing of the past, that that face-to-face encounter is not believable? (Givone 1988, 4)

In its removed, aristocratic way, philosophic thought as it developed in the West, requires the unthinkability of the enchantment of the world and relegates to pre-thought or nonthought the practices of those who never found out or imagined that "God is dead." The anthropologist who comes into contact with such people observes their practices and discovers that while their rational way of thinking in daily life expresses the impracticability of enchantment, their behavior often occurs in a context totally disposed to a *reenchantment* of the world.

I have emphasized in the section, "Symbolic Horizons and Actors," that it is characteristic of visionary phenomena that those involved need not have total and continuous identification with the symbolic horizon of the apparitions, and they can accede to other symbolic horizons, even ones quite different, without apparent problems of subjective coherence. In this respect, I maintained that

> in complex societies characterized by the simultaneous, nonconflictive presence of various cultural models, by the absence of systematic and hierarchical correlation among the various sectors of social life, and by the disappearance of a Center, individuals experience internal multiplication and fragmentation. The demise of a common *totem* is accompanied by the demise of the indivisible *individual* who was its reflection, and the subject is conceived of "as having different biographies" (Berger, Berger, and Kellner 1973, 67). [. . .] The multiple instantiations of the in-dividual make it impossible for a person to fix on one center for guidance and decision-making. Rather than an internal coherence more or less sustained, one might hypothesize that a person performs an ongoing labor of self-description that seeks recognition for the coherence of her or his own courses of action, that displays coherence to her or himself and to others; this coherence, hence, is not an objective result of individual acts, but rather a rationalization. (Apolito 1990, 287–89)

Indeed, the calculus of personal coherence in an individual (if only as self-description), nullifies, on the conscious level, the possibility of effectuating the reenchantment that, in some spheres of life, is superbly effective, as, for example, with the sphere of apparitions.

Visionary phenomena allow actors to proceed to a reenchantment of the world that is structured around the phenomena, without this implying a radical abandonment of the rational ways in which these actors participate in other spheres of social life. It is as though there came to be created an enclave of fantasy into which the actors entered and within which they moved with ease when they were experiencing the visionary reality, but that they abandon cleanly when they go back to the habitual horizons of daily life. We are not, however, dealing with a traditional symbolic world, one of myth and folklore, to which the actors "return," almost like a cultural reality abandoned by the advances of disenchantment, to which they now go back to live. It is not an identifiable and bounded symbolic territory in which people happily discourse once again with "demons and gods."

What occurs is literally a process of "re-enchantment." Once one has acquired daily concourse with the Madonna together with many other celestial and infernal figures and has discovered many channels by which these figures present themselves, it becomes an everyday experience, not just for the seers but for all the believers as well, to identify the presence of the otherworldly during quite lengthy episodes. Over time, the repertoire of epiphanies comes to be enormous, so much so that the world of the apparitions can no longer be circumscribed and described—perhaps as a partial, limited, "miraculous" exception—with the everyday and "disenchanted" categories used to refer to ordinary reality. Every smell, sound, tone, shadow, color, figure, shape, movement, object; every experience, report, event; every intuition, thought, proposal, comment, theory; every doubt and every certainty can be and are divine or diabolic manifestations. There is no criterion for inclusion or exclusion that enables one to determine what is part of the phenomena and what is excluded. Everything can be a manifestation because the collective practice of reenchantment can be applied to everything.

At the level of individual self-consciousness, coherence implies thinking about the prodigy as an exception, for one cannot jeopardize the rational and scientific legal order that operates in other spheres of life. At the level of meaning of the apparitions, on which one does not think about oneself but simply registers the epiphany, the very way of organizing perceptions and ideas, of registering individual and collective discourse, produces a reenchantment of reality and even leads to a kind of self-evidence. What occurs is always the result of enchantment.

By suggesting some examples at this point, I do not mean to *delimit* the enchanted world, in the way in which, for example, Bruno Bettelheim marks off the confines of the "enchanted world" of fairy tales for young children.

For Bettelheim, it is a pre-existing symbolic world to which children have or have had the chance to gain access, thanks to the process of acculturation (Bettelheim 1976). In our case, there are no designated boundaries but only helpful signs along paths never before explored. The practice of reenchant-ment demonstrates its consistency and potential by symbolic elaborations of the itineraries of experience, those very itineraries that in everyday life the normal ways of considering the world would have "always" interpreted along lines derived from disenchantment. If the practice is rewarded by the success of the collective experience, if the visionary movement goes forward, sooner or later there will precipitate out the particular forms of the extraordinary and the enchanted by means of which it will be possible to experience consistently and recreate that world. Eventually, it will become clear what pertains to it and what does not, and a mythology and a ritual for it will develop. For now, in the formative process, virtually *all* the ordinary world, all individual and collective life, once they have passed through the symbolic horizon of the apparitions, are captured omnivorously by the new ways of interpretation and transformed into signs of the enchanted world that was discovered by the visions and now expands in all directions. The horizon of the apparitions itself stretches out to incorporate new and old extraordinary phenomena, near or far (learned through the media) that multiply the possibility of enchanted events.

The examples advanced here are samples, minimal and fragmentary, of an extraordinary and unconfigured world that awaits its crystals, its patterns, its rules, but that also may disappear before it is found. Once again, in addition to examples from Oliveto, I shall use others from Medjugorje because, in this matter particularly, comparison can give an idea of the presence of a true culture of visions, of the work of a culturally specific product.

The first example is the familiarity with the physical presence of the Madonna and Jesus. The following description is by an elementary school teacher from an unspecified town in Campania.

Often we gathered to say the Holy Rosary in the parish church, near our school. On Wednesday, March 14, the front benches were already occupied by a group of German children meditating with their own priest on the Stations of the Cross. So as not to disturb them, yet not renounce our own prayers, we sat on the bench farthest back in the church. This time we had to be patient, far from Jesus, the Eucharist, and the statue of the Madonna. During the first Hail Mary of the Rosary, a girl saw near us the Madonna join our prayer. Before each decade we expressed a particular intention: For those with muscular dystrophy; for blasphemers. The Madonna proposed the third intention: For the salvation of the world. She said with us the Our Father, the Gloria, and the prayers taught by the Angel at Fatima. She just listened during the Hail Mary. At a certain point the crucified Jesus came off the great cross on the altar and approached us, above. He scattered flower petals on our heads and also on that of his Mother who was with us. Jesus said, "I scatter my blessing upon you." Then he turned again and said to us, "I forgive all your sins and I will keep you from all evil," adding, "I would be very happy if you come again to Oliveto Citra." The Madonna supported this desire of her Son and expressed herself in the following manner: "I too would be very happy." We were 5 in the little group: 3 children—my students, one mother, and I. We all came to Oliveto Citra. (B 3 [1990], 12)

Familiarity with the seers lead the Madonna to talk at length about her life. Over many months, from January 1984 to April 1985, her almost daily appointment with the Yugoslav seer Vicka swelled this narrative to a final result of 635 pages, which the seer, with the Madonna's permission, gave to a priest to publish (Rastrelli 1987, 68). In the meantime, autobiographies of the Madonna circulated in which the Madonna might be involved in declarations like this:

In a recent book (*La Mia Vita a Nazareth* [My Life at Nazareth], Rome: Ed. Salustiana, 1988), the Madonna, telling about her life in Nazareth, says of her Jesus that already when he was barely an adolescent "he had the Majesty of a King and his bearing was regal even in a simple tunic." (E. Mor, cited in *Medjugorje*, a periodical of the Associazione Comitato Medjugorje [Milan, 1991], 53:308)

Even if the particular representatives of the other world were not completely visible, people came to know that they were constantly nearby, by the gate of the apparition, for instance, intermingling with the living in truly extraordinary numbers, as the Madonna herself had let it be known on one occasion, when she rebuked a certain informality shown by some pilgrims.

I would prefer, children, that you respect a little more the holy place that goes from the first step up to the Gate, you know not how much holy ground you traverse and how many holy souls and Angels fill it, because my Presence is not a presence of small importance. (B 12, 16)

But the believers were put on alert that there were infernal, as well as celestial, beings present. The Madonna asked at Oliveto that people always carry a crucifix, "a weapon against evil" (B 7, 12), or rosary beads (B 13, 12), and at Medjugorje that they use as "armor against Satan" blessed objects on their bodies and in their houses (Rastrelli 1987, 119). The Devil himself told Ubaldo and others: "I'll kill you, I'll kill you, I'll kill you, I'll wait for when you are no longer protected by holy figures to strike you" (B, r, 17). The infernal beings may not only be the well-defined devils known in visions. The reenchanted world may include hidden and uncontrollable aggressions. A pilgrim from Treviso was continually bothered by "invisible diabolical beasties" that would not let him rest (B 15, 9).

In the world of enchantment, the distance between heaven and earth is shortened. One evening the Madonna asked Benedetta to sing a hymn whose words had been composed by Fulvio Piranese. But Benedetta had scarcely begun singing when the Madonna interrupted her. At that point, the seer heard the singing of a heavenly choir teaching her the new music that the Madonna wanted for the hymn. Subsequently, there was talk of music dictated directly from heaven, and some newspapers carried the story. When someone objected, a correction was printed that it had been an old, traditional melody that had not been used for years, which evidently the Madonna had wanted to revive. This song has become the official hymn of Oliveto Citra, and is even available on a record on the Citra label.

At Medjugorje, the Madonna gave to both Mirjana and Ivanka a magic sheet of paper with ten secrets about the future of the world, announcing, threatening, and insisting on prayer to avoid chastisements. Mirjana described the sheet of paper in this way:

The page is made of a material I cannot describe. It seems to be paper, but it is not paper; it seems to be cloth, but it is not cloth. It is visible and it can be touched, but you cannot see writing. When the time is right I will give the page to a chosen priest, who will have a special grace to read only the first secret, but not the others. The page comes from heaven. My brother-in-law, an engineer who works in Switzerland, has examined the page, but he is unable to say what it is made of. (Sala and Mantero 1986, 98)

The chosen priest referred to, Father Petar Ljubičić, is to read the secrets (each lettered in gold and numbered and dated) ten days before the announced secrets are to occur. The seer herself, who chose the priest and submitted her choice to the Madonna for approval, will give the secrets. He will announce it to the world three days before the event, and then give the magic letter back to the seers while awaiting the outcome.

It is hard to avoid the impression that the prodigious page, the ten secrets, and the gold lettering are derived from the symbols in the Book of Revelation; for example, the book with the seven seals (5:1), whose disclosure, seal by seal, correspond to chastisements and manifestations of divine power, just as the disclosure of the secrets of Medjugorje is the manifestation of the punishing God. The symbols of Revelation provide a major part of the "strong" elements of this enchanted world, particularly through the spread of the sense that one is living through the events of the "last times." The Devil is so active because he knows that time is short, as in Revelation 12:12: "The Devil has come to you with great anger, knowing that he has little time." This is the Devil we saw described by Tommaso as a "zoo," just as in the book by John he is a pantherlike beast with bear's feet and a lion's mouth (13:2).

As in Revelation, the rhythm of the narration is marked by warnings such as "The first 'Beware!' has passed; now two more 'Beware!'"s follow these things" (9:12), and "The second "Beware!" has passed, but quite soon now will come the third" (11:14). At Medjugorje, the rhythm of the events described by the seers took on the cadence of secrets and chastisements revealed, to be revealed, or already confirmed (at Oliveto, there were just clumsy, desultory attempts, like that of Tommaso): announcements of the first, second, or whatever chastisement—confirmed, avoided, diminished, and so on.

As with the rhythm of the events, so with the punishments. The extermination of one-third of humankind in Revelation resembles the two-thirds mentioned at Oliveto and Medjugorje; similarly, the blood in the oceans and rivers (16), the living who curse God and envy the dead, and so on. In Revelation, there is singing in heaven (14:2–3), like that of Benedetta; a great whore (17), like the "slut" of hell of the boys of Medjugorje; and twenty-four elders seated on their thrones around the throne of God (4:4;

11:16), like those Anna described at Oliveto. These symbolic elements enter the devotional literature and are reshaped in announcements of charismatic events: the three days of darkness announced at Oliveto repeats the same chastisement announced by Domenico Masselli, the charismatic of Stornarella, well known in Southern Italy (Sanga 1979, 58, 64). For Domenico, it was a quarter of mankind that would soon die in the divine chastisement.

But the "enchanted world" is not comprised solely of this apocalyptic aspect, which involves a cosmic stage, unceasing struggle, and drama in the here-and-now. On the contrary, most of the time it is expressed with minimal signs, little, even banal things. The "internal locutions" of Jelena, at Medjugorje, began when once, at school, the girl, bored, asked herself, "I wonder what time it is," and a voice inside said, "Twenty minutes past ten" and it really was 10:20 (Rooney and Faricy 1988, 78). Later, the same voice said to her, "Don't raise your hand, because you won't be called on." Jelena laughed to herself and raised her hand but she was not called on (Rastrelli 1987, 205). Surprised, she spoke about all this to her father, who at once understood, in a reenchanted way, the events and told her that "there are people like that; God gives them a gift to hear voices" (Rooney and Faricy 1988, 78). In this way, the Madonna began to speak with Jelena.

It is not only seers who have these normal experiences of dialogue. Even a theologian such as Faricy came to ask himself, with greater impetus than Jelena's "What time is it?," "Why am I at Medjugorje?" In reply he heard, "I did not send you here to minister" (Ibid., 58). Similarly, the parish priest of Medjugorje, shortly after the events began, came to ask himself, "What should I do?" and heard a clear, external voice answer, "Go out and take the youths in custody, under your protection" (Sala and Mantero, 1986, 20–21). A leader at Oliveto, Giulio, during Ubaldo's *trance* described above in which the seer went to Jerusalem, asked himself, "Do you want to see that there is a devil?" and heard in reply a voice that said: "Don't worry I have him under my feet" {June 14, 1986}.

In addition to internal and external voices, there are other *channels* chosen by the voices of enchantment. Don Giovanni spoke by telephone with Armida, the blind seer of Agropoli, who asked him for news of the latest events at Oliveto. The parish priest complained that the Madonna always promised signs but never sent any. A voice then came on the line, saying reproachfully, "You'll have a sign, you'll have a sign" (Marotta 1990, 308).

One frequently hears of unknown voices that turn up on tapes of hymns, accounts of visions, and interviews made for listening at home. Often the voices are infernal, sometimes heavenly, but in any case are an indirect or direct call to return to Oliveto (or Medjugorje). Once, at Medjugorje, a voice interrupted a tape-recording, pleading to a boy who was listening with his mother, "Quick, go get surgery, because you are in danger," and then faded back to the original recording. It was a warning that he needed an emergency operation for peritonitis (Juarez 1987, 161).

From inner, outer, telephonic, and tape-recorded voices, the zone of enchantment spreads through a number of ways. *Through speeches*: Faricy himself realized that once he spoke, invited by a local priest, to a group of Italian pilgrims in such an extraordinary Italian that it must have been a divine favor, "because I simply cannot speak as well as I spoke this afternoon" (Rooney and Faricy 1988, 23). *Through interviews*: the questions that a group of doctors administering scientific tests to the Yugoslav seers wished to pose to Dr. Frigerio, a supporter of Medjugorje, were useless. Frigerio seemed already to know the questions and the order in which they would be asked (Sala and Mantero 1986, 111). *Through scientific tests*: an unbelieving doctor, examining the seers at the beginning of their ecstasies, began hearing celestial music and decided to suspend the tests and confess and receive communion (Ibid., 114). *Through sources of information*: an American priest asked a Yugoslav priest if the Madonna of the apparitions had given her name. Father Tomislav, the Yugoslav priest, did not know the answer. Shortly after that a male seer, not present at the priests' conversation, arrived with a slip of paper with words dictated by the Madonna: "I am the queen of peace" (Rupčić 1983, 73). *Through photographs*: believers took pictures of scenery, in which people found celestial or diabolical figures.

Nature, in the sphere of the apparitions, participates in the prodigy. During a ceremony in a community inspired by the message of Medjugorje, thirteen doves were released. Instead of flying away, they stopped near the statue of the Virgin and stayed there during the ceremony rendering her homage (Laurentin 1988c, 67). This prodigy has been familiar at the shrine of the Madonna of the Hens of Pagani, near Salerno, for centuries (Villani 1887).

Even objects become active, and not just statues of the Madonna that weep or become luminous, flooding houses with light (B 16, 24); or statues of the Baby Jesus that, as we have seen, come alive and fight the devil; or, at Medjugorje, crucifixes on the mountain that light up or disappear, replaced by the gigantic silhouette of a lady (Laurentin and Lejeune 1988a, 350). Hands of clocks run backward (Laurentin 1986a, 21); petals rain from the sky; real rain falls but does not wet; rosary beads are lost and then found, break apart and come back together, are taken by the Madonna from one person and given to another.

And there are mysterious forces that propel or restrain, that inexplicably increase the velocity of movement of people, or slow them down inexorably; streets always thick with traffic suddenly empty; cars break down that always worked perfectly; blaspheming drivers pray on their knees; woman-chasing husbands are converted; drug-addicted sons are returned to life; and so on through the repertoire of the whole world turned to one continuous prodigy, experienced and retold.

Some great prodigies are reported *routinely*, like that of the sun, since

> *every time* there are significant gatherings for prayer or holy days having to do with apparitions of the virgin, the sun participates punctually with spectacular, marvelous signs: changes of color, rotations and pulsations; often there is noted in the solar disc the host used by the priest in the Eucharistic celebration with the letters IHS, or a gigantic cross and the figure of the Virgin. (B 16, 8, my italics)

Or of the moon:

> To His Holiness John Paul II,
> We the undersigned declare that on July 22, 1985, towards 11 o'clock (in the evening), when the apparition was going on the mountain of Medjugorje (Križevac), the orange moon moved slowly in front of us, going out like a light. From the mountain there came a white light that seemed like a great highway towards heaven. In the night the sky seemed all starry, with a color never seen before. The Milky Way went out from the Cross, traversing all the sky (creating) over the church a very bright white color. Over the mountain the biggest star changed color continually. Signed: Mario, Luigi, Simona, Tino, Emilia, Pina, Carla, Rinaldo. Magherno (PV). (Mantero 1987, 118)

There are prodigies of the polar star, which gets bigger and sends out rays in the form of a cross (Sala and Mantero 1986, 93); of stars that blink out (Mantero 1987, 115), that shine even in daylight (Rooney and Faricy 1984, 22), that all gather in one point in the sky (the Oliveto children on the first night). And there is every kind of light: luminous spheres that slowly go down the sky, then explode releasing thousands of little stars (Bubalo 1987, 83); the word "MIR" ("peace" in Croatian), in the sky in golden letters (Ibid., 117); fires that do not smoke, or crackle, and leave no trace (Sala and Mantero 1986, 23); red clouds at Oliveto.

There are occurrences apparently commonplace, that, however, might be a mask for occurrences or identities particularly spectacular. The weak seers at Oliveto often reported seeing a dove at the site of the apparitions. For some of them, it was the messenger of the Madonna, but for Fulvio it was one of the ramparts that holds up the castle and that at night fools people with its color. But then someone noticed it in the church, and then the *Bollettino* wondered if it might be the Holy Spirit (B 15, 18).

A Neapolitan couple was unable to have children. At Oliveto, where they went with their parish prayer group to ask for the grace of a child,

> the wife was approached by a "young woman" who said to her: You will have a child and you will call her Maria Rosaria; on Sunday October 9, 1986 Mr. & Mrs. M. came to Oliveto Citra with great joy to have their beautiful baby baptized with the name Maria Rosaria. (B 7, 8)

Nothing was said about who the mysterious "young woman" was, but might it not have been the Madonna herself?

The entire universe, which has been discovered thanks to the scientific principle of cause-and-effect, is available for enchanted re-inscription. Astronauts have always remarked on the fact that the earth alone, among all the planets in our solar system, gives off a blue light. The physicist Emanuele Mor noted this in his newsletter *Medjugorje*, published in Milan, as well as the fact that this light comes from the Pacific Ocean. Then he inquired:

> Is it a unique light that wishes perhaps to light up the sky to the edges of the Universe in order to proclaim God's choice of this little blue dot where Christ was incarnate and redeemed us? (Cited in *Medjugorje*, periodical of the Associazione Comitato Medjugorje [Milan, 1991], 53:291)

In addition, there are little prodigies that almost do not get told, they are so common. An Italian woman on pilgrimage to Medjugorje, the director of a travel agency with a degree in psychology, attended the apparitions in the parish house. It was suffocatingly hot, the windows were closed and people were sweating, but when the Madonna arrived a light breeze wafted through the room, refreshing those present (Mantero 1987, 130). Others say said that at the moment of the apparition all the birds started singing. Ultimately, the limits between little and big prodigies become blurred, because, as Giulio said, speaking of the luminous phenomena, "they are strange, incredible phenomena, but by now we are used to them" (Carione and Serrone 1986, 24).

Even the limit between normal events and prodigies becomes invisible because the extraordinary becomes normal and normality partakes of the extraordinary in a mixed terrain in which an account of experience is always enchanted. One group of seers spent the night in a prayer vigil near the apparition gate. In the morning, suddenly there began "a lovely twittering" of "birds of all colors"; one flew up to the gate and "seemed to talk with us." Next, "suddenly everything was over and the most absolute silence returned." But right then "a bead from one of the rosaries hanging from the fig tree behind the gate began to shine with a white light, to pulsate and swell until it became like a little star, with the same intensity with which it lit up, it died down until it became a normal rosary bead." Shortly afterward, the pilgrims noticed a "most delicate odor of incense." Finally, they went home. But after a half-hour on the road they stopped their vehicle because the sun had become active. "It let us look at it calmly, without dazzling us and it was like a perfect circle, golden and empty in the middle" (B 15, 8).

This way of talking about one's own experience of pilgrimage as if it were a journey of wonders is quite common and well reflects the role of the apparition horizon in reenchantment. Important here is the specific characteristic of pilgrimage as a distancing from the everyday world, a new beginning, a liminal or "liminoid" state (Turner and Turner 1978, 34–35). But, in fact, the entire horizon of the apparitions, understood as a symbolic "space," can be considered a "site" of mental pilgrimage in which a pronounced reenchantment is articulated, even if it is destined to remain limited to this "site."

A dermatologist from Naples was called to the bedside of an elderly woman, whom he had diagnosed as having a "suspected folic *penfigo*" (sic), a disease that caused a serious alteration of the skin. Concerned for the woman, he suggested to her relatives that they confide first in God and then in medicine. They acted on his suggestion and prayed to the Madonna of Oliveto. The woman recovered and the doctor commented:

Even if on occasion I let myself be ruled by a miserable attitude of self-satisfaction, given my experience and that I am a specialist, today I have no doubt that a nonhuman intervention had modified what was surely a negative prognosis [. . .] The treatment recommended by me had obtained unexpected, perhaps unlikely, results, but what weight was to be attributed to the treatment and what to a divine intervention?

Then the doctor began to mull over the "coincidences." He himself was born near Oliveto—the first coincidence—where the apparition was going on that seemed to have cured the woman. The proximity to his town of origin allowed him—the second coincidence—to go to the apparition site where he found—a third incredible coincidence—up against the rock wall near the gate, a crucifix "exactly like the one lost by me three weeks earlier because it fell off my favorite rosary, which I had looked for diligently, but in vain" (B 13, 10, 11). It is unlikely that the doctor, like others who told of "coincidences," was *normally* alert to the secret symmetries of daily life. It is in the symbolic space opened by the apparitions that life and world offer themselves in the baroque harmony of enchanted signs.

One can see this baroque enchantment, for example, in the stories that tie together diverse people and experiences. A Genovese pilgrim was praying at the apparition gate. Suddenly, a female seer she did not know came over and gave her a rose, saying it was a gift for her from the Virgin. The pilgrim decided to distribute some of this gift to others. She sent a petal her sister in France to give to her son who was "alcoholic and nonpracticing." The petal arrived on Good Friday. This nephew, said to be "non-practicing," at once kissed the petal and put it behind a picture of Jesus. That afternoon, the youth saw the face of Jesus marked on the petal and called in the neighbors to verify what had happened. He then went to church to confess and receive communion. In the meantime, the pilgrim received a request for another petal from an English friend, Emily, for her unbelieving husband. She gave the petal to Emily's husband herself. The husband ended up putting a crucifix around his neck and began to go to church again (B 14, 22). The Genovese pilgrim probably circulated other petals, and there may have been other prodigies from the miraculous rose.

Baroque enchantment sends us back to the meaning of disenchantment of the world originally proposed by Max Weber. As I have mentioned, Weber pointed to the transition from magic to redemptive religion (Rossi 1981, 154). If we eliminate the evolutionary connotation of the word "transition," for Weber the enchanted world was, broadly speaking, the world of magic. In such a world, rituals, devotions, persons, places, and objects endowed with charisma collaborate in the unity and the control of a world understood as a coherent whole. By the same token, the reenchantment of the world, of which I have given some examples, would be the work of "magicizing" that makes symbols available "in their pure state," as Lévi-Strauss wrote of *mana*, capable "hence of taking on any symbolic content whatsoever" (Lévi-Strauss 1950, lii).

If, in the Catholic Church, there are currents of thought that favor an essentialization of the religious message centered on the "mystery" of Redemption and Salvation, the culture of apparitions seems to belong to other currents that attempt to encourage in Catholicism an emphasis on marvelous aspects of the created world, behind which the creator, by means of his court of relatives, angels and saints, charismatic and seers, believers and pilgrims, immanently activates signs of enchantment. These currents seek to articulate a culture that rejects the secularized canons of everyday perception of reality and substitutes a collective attitude of visual enhancement and participation in a continuous show of wonders, in which the ordinary meanings in daily life are replaced by a new understanding of continuous epiphany. The entire world is pantheistically transformed into a spectacle that bespeaks divinity.

But the reenchantment that the visionary culture proposes is even more complex. The world is not just the voluntary spectacle of the divine, it is also, in an involuntary way, undergone more than it is perceived, in ways that are the result of inexorable processes in which neither heaven nor earth seem to be subjectively involved but instead objectively constrained. I will address this in the next chapter.

This magical reenchantment of the world has precise social utility, but not just a generalized sense of psychological protection and reassurance, although that is indeed present and strong. One social function, I think, can be clearly identified. The Madonna regularly created bonds between people by means of her messages, gifts, and graces. She ordered someone to say something to someone else; asked Tizio to give his rosary beads to Caio; gave Sempronio the answer to a question put by Tullio. While these episodes were common at Medjugorje as well, it seems to me that at Oliveto these bonds were more typical of the networks created by the events.

A considerable number of prodigies create relations among strangers or strengthen relations among relatives or friends. Hence, the apparitions seem to be an unexpected resource available to recreate temporary or stable relations of *communitas* (Turner 1969, 113ff.) in a social structure seriously fragmented in terms of human relations, which are precarious and difficult. The example of the petals is eloquent.

Here are some others with a wider geographical scope. A skeptical Sicilian priest went to Oliveto. With him was a dumb, paralyzed girl, sent by her aunt, a nun he did not know who had asked him to offer her to the Madonna. As he paused at the gate, an unknown youth approached him and told him that a seer said that Jesus had appeared and ordered that priest be told, by the youth, that he should have more faith (B 16, 16). Five people who do not know one another, joined in this bond created by the context; only five as the episode is described in the *Bollettino*, but these five surely know many others not mentioned, all bound in a web of emotion, interaction, and symbol woven around the apparitions.

One result of this *first* social use of reenchantment is an increase, or rather a reinvention, of interpersonal communication. But one soon realizes that the increase applies also to relations with heaven—of which indeed it is considered a consequence—which are rendered easy, objective, and un-mysterious. The whole reenchanted world is a vehicle for this vertical communication. We have seen how the sun greets all significant days and prayers. It is one of the most omnipresent messengers, together with other natural phenomena re-baptized in cosmic language. A woman from Casal-bordino, who at the time believed in Medjugorje but was skeptical about Oliveto, wrote a letter to the Madonna asking for three signs to demonstrate her presence in the Italian town. The third was to repeat "for us in Casalbordino" the prodigy of the sun "splendid as it was for us at Med-jugorje" {July 12, 1986}. The prodigy came and was so "splendid" that the bus of the group drove through the blue disc that fell from the spinning sun. A group of pilgrims from Lucania arrived at Oliveto and the sun expressed to them the pleasure of the Virgin with extraordinary signs. Before departing they asked the Madonna if she was glad for their visit: three waves of "intense and very agreeable" perfume was her response (B 7, 22).

All the examples of prodigies I have given are expressions of this function of communication whereby the entire cosmos is involved. Every object speaks, every word signals the celestial presence behind natural semblance. All that normally escapes the senses, in a universe that has lost unity and coherence, in a world refractory to men, impervious to their suffering, deaf to their desire for comforting, in a life alien to itself and absent for the living, all that is insensate finds in an enchanted way voice through the prodigy. The insensate speaks to those who then hear what they were waiting to hear: that order, unity, and structure are universally present in history, in society, and in the reorganized individual. The inhabitants of heaven, behind the objects, unceasingly proclaim their power. One understands, then, the paradoxically positive and reassuring meaning of all the catastrophes in the world when these have been announced by seers and charismatics and subsequently confirmed.

In 1985, Aurelia saw a dike that was giving way and the alley of the Oliveto castle awash in mud and blood. A few days after her vision, a dike collapsed in the Val di Fiemme (Margnelli and Gagliardi 1987a, 13). Ubaldo, too, had foreseen it: two days before it occurred, he had the sensation of being in the midst of a swollen river. Ubaldo later saw the walls of the Oliveto castle shudder and stones fall out, a warning for an earthquake in Mexico. The Madonna, weeping, had also shown Ubaldo a plane falling and people dead, shortly before a Japanese plane crashed (Ibid., 23). According to the *Bollettino*, on this occasion he heard "the throb of an airplane that was falling and cries for help" (B 12, 8). The same applies to the lives of loved ones: Nello foresaw the day and hour of the death of his uncle; when Nello's aunt was dying, he predicted the date of her death, after successfully announcing a temporary two-week improvement {August 5, 1988}.

The tragic or catastrophic prediction that is positively "comforted" by its confirmation affirms that the universe is ordered, history makes sense, life is comprehensible, death is foreseeable, and all this is within the reach of those in the ranks of the just. This, then, is the *other* use of reenchantment: it permits reconstruction of unitary images of the world, which recompose in the same frame fragments of a sense of nature, society, and life.

We are dealing, however, with attempts at unitary images that are very private and egocentric. They are communicated, certainly, to others, but only with difficulty can they be deeply shared in the true sense except with small groups of pilgrims who are friends, relatives, or close family, or just with oneself. The unitary image of the cosmos offered by the prodigiousness of the world works to the extent that each person hopes to benefit from the marvels with better opportunities and an improved quality of life. The image works as long as a person expects the prodigy. But it does not permit the construction of a world that is ordered and foreseeable and the formation of solid expectations, above all in dealings with other persons. The image's power resides entirely in its arbitrariness. Each person hopes to benefit from it, if possible along with others but even, if things turn out that way, to the detriment of others.

One sees instances in which pilgrims are pleased by the good weather the Madonna granted their pilgrimage, and ignore the bad weather of other pilgrimages before and after their own. A woman asked and obtained the grace of the reconciliation of the marriage of her sister with a husband who had found a lover. For this believer, the Madonna "surely" must have granted the grace because She, our mother, could not remain indifferent when a family became disunited (B 12, 12). This is true given the idea of the relation of heaven and earth that the believing woman had constructed, but it is a configuration shared only with difficulty by the many other believers who could have told of crises in their marriages unresolved by grace.

The most common examples of unitary and egocentric images of the world are the tales of incidents, accidents, personal calamities avoided by a whisker, because something or someone had given a warning, because a disaster was halted a centimeter before it became irreparable: the bus is destroyed but the travelers are unhurt; someone asks to stop just before the curve around which there is a terrible accident; a woman with a babe in arms asks the driver to slow down right on the edge of a ravine; another woman with a child gets out just before a chain-collision—the car is destroyed but the driver, his wife, and children are unhurt and this is a prodigy of the Madonna who appeared precisely to show her protection at last moment in the slip from life to death; her image appears on the hood of a car that has broken down and keeps it from being it by others behind it; the Madonna comes in a dream to hearten the patient of a difficult operation, and the surgery is a success, to the great surprise of the doctors.

The prodigiousness of the world—albeit in an individual narrative that becomes less and less communicable as it passes the first circle of those near and dear—serves to recompose the harmony of linguistic codes, orders of reference, and spheres of life, and to simplify reality.

Evil and suffering are revived in the narrative of the prodigy. The forces of good speak out and come up against those of evil, which are certainly also capable of prodigies but which precisely for this reason are controllable because they operate on a level of action and with a common code of reference. If they were more alien, it would be much worse—they would be indecipherable and unassailable. The *convention* of a prodigy provides an assurance of victory, above all because it shuts out what cannot be figured out, what cannot be converted into prodigy, what prodigy cannot dominate, and that which does not allow prodigy to speak through it.

But what is *this thing that cannot be figured out,* something worse than any diabolic monster? In a certain sense it is the flat and banal daily routine, the obvious side of living totally tamed by contemporary processes of rationalization. This is the locus of suffering and evil, where the habitual immobile and nonsensate backdrop of objects and nature appears to crush rather than serve the individual. The prodigy of the world redeems daily life, transfigures it into an enchanted dimension in which the individual rediscovers mastery and centrality as the privileged recipient of a world that speaks through prodigy and is nourished by reference to just holy beings; this apparition in particular, this particular pilgrimage.

The reenchantment of the world is a *space* of collective imagination, an area of fantasy able to respond to individual and collective problems to the extent that it is not precisely delimited. It is the place of "symbols in their pure state" capable of enabling processes of meaning that respond to even quite particular, personal demands for social actors who have no unitary community language because they have no community, no common centripetal procedures for deriving meaning from experience because they have no center.

The problem is that it is even difficult for each actor to speak to herself or himself with a common language because "when the common totem is gone, with it goes the indivisible in-dividual who was a reflection of it." And then the apparition culture with its power to reenchant the world comes to grief precisely at the level of the individuals for whom it seeks to erect a unitary image. The reenchanted, in this attempt, collides with other spheres of life totally involved in the rationalizing processes of disenchantment. Reenchantment is unable to capture total individuality, which is still irreparably rent between enchantment and disenchantment.

5

IMAGES OF HEAVEN
ON EARTH

Photographs, Visions, Television

ON ONE OF THE FIRST EVENINGS of apparitions at Oliveto, a group of youths from a town nearby, hardly older than children, shouted, "There she is!" Lights were turned on, cameras clicked, and video cameras focused on the other side of the gate in an attempt to capture the supernatural presence. Almost immediately someone wondered whether it was right to turn on the lights, whether it might disturb the Madonna. One of the seers declared that when the lights came on the apparition disappeared. But others maintained that while perhaps when she was in the spotlight the human eye had trouble seeing her, she would come out better on videotape or film. The argument continued until the group decided to turn off the spotlights, shut down the buzz of the video cameras, and instead try an exorcism with holy water: If what was appearing was the Devil, it would go away.

Discussions of this kind arose every time the flash of cameras cut through the darkness of the Oliveto nights or tried to fix supernatural light in the chemical composition of film. Photographs of the Madonna circulated throughout Europe, famous ones from Medjugorje, and on a smaller scale, those of Oliveto and other locations.

The fourth page of the front matter of *Il Miracolo di Medjugorje* by Emanuele Sala and Piero Mantero includes a caption beneath five small photographs that is quite interesting for our purposes.

> The first three photos show an extraordinary event observed and photographed by a group of Italian pilgrims returning from Medjugorje: In the space of a few seconds, the solar disc executed an "impossible" displacement (note the reference points) totally inexplicable in "natural" terms and then returned to its initial position. The fourth photo— taken at night—depicts the Virgin on a little cloud with her hands joined. On the jacket: An image of the Madonna not visible when the photo was taken. (Sala and Mantero 1986)

Here, in this last phrase, is well expressed the idea that an optical instrument more perfect than the eye can catch what the eye cannot. We are, evidently, in the already familiar terrain of "supernatural testing." It is no coincidence that these photographs are quite reminiscent of the nineteenth-century wave of spirit photographs.

> The first examples of what would be known as "spirit photographs" date from 1855, when it was noticed that during some seances photographic plates were marked by strange, whitish spots. Persistent use of cameras by a great variety of European investigators led to results considered more important. Fleeting images, fragments of "fluidic" bodies, in exceptional instances entire bodies, took shape in what were then called "materializations" (understood as the souls of the dead). These "materializations" could be "visible"—that is, leave an imprint on the human retina, or "invisible," affecting only photographic plates. (Gallini 1983a, 30)

From phantoms, photography went on to other repertoires of the invisible.

> Fascinated by the spectacle of the ruins of an ancient city in Asia Minor, a tourist took a photograph; when he developed it, he found to his stupor

three ancient kings with impressive figures and Assyrian beards. I myself personally observed the spontaneous generation and diffusion of these legends: A relative showed me a photo taken in a desert that included the immense smiling face of a prophet. The weekly magazine *Match*, in turn, was able to publish, without denouncing it as a fraud, a photo of the sky in Korea with the gigantic figure of Christ superimposed on bombers in flight. (Morin 1956, 39–40)

A couple was present at a prodigy of the sun in Medjugorje that took place at the exact time that the teenage seers had had their daily apparition there. The husband took two Polaroid pictures of the sun.

> That evening my wife asked to see what we had taken. We noticed that in the photo taken at the moment of the apparition there is an immense halo around the sun and within it, near the church tower, a face of the Baby Jesus with eyes, nose, and mouth, head high, and the Madonna who kisses him on the cheek, in profile. There was even the space between the two foreheads and the veil. (Sala and Mantero 1986, 104–5)

At Oliveto, there circulates a similar photograph of a seer shaking the hand of John Paul II in a general audience, while floating over their heads is a blurry image of the Virgin. It is said that at the moment the photographer took the shot, nothing was visible that would have led him to expect a heavenly presence. The image turned up only when the film was developed and printed. All of this provides "experimental proof" for the idea that the Madonna, the saints, and Jesus are always, albeit invisibly, near pious people and, with the use of mechanical or electronic apparatus, become visible.

One can similarly document the normally invisible presence of the Devil. It will be recalled from the previous chapter how the youth with a beard, taking a picture of the sky, captured images of diabolical little snakes. At Medjugorje, an attorney from Pavia wanted to photograph "the sun, although that day it did not spin." Instead, in the photograph there appeared three Satans "with black horns and tails, one with the pitchfork on the left, one mocking with an arm akimbo, legs crossed, watching me: one was in a blue circle, one in a white one, and the other in an orange one covered by a pink cloud in the sky near the sun" (Ibid., 170).

Even though the leadership was always prudent, though not hostile to the supernatural photographs, there was generally a positive attitude to the phenomenon, and the clicking of cameras became one of the habitual sounds at the apparition site. The significant ethnographic fact is the *objectification* of the physical presence of the Madonna and the rest of the otherworldy figures, which calls for the use of technologies that favor visions that are sensory. As Mantero maintains, the vision experience "has above all a subjective value, even if at its origin there is an objectively mysterious event, documented in photographs and on videotape" (Mantero 1987, 108).

The central ethnomethodological problem in regard to apparitions is *how to understand* the slightly peculiar physical object to be seen. Photography is a collective solution that in one fell swoop does away with all the interpretations of apparitions as "visions of the intellect."

The bearded youth I just referred to saw the Madonna and shouted. His mother, close to him, did not see her, but put on spectacles to see better {March 15, 1986}. Father Janko Bubalo, a well-known supporter of the Medjugorje apparitions, reported that one day, looking toward the mountains near the Medjugorje church presbytery, he could not see the cross on it. Then, since he knew his eyesight was poor, he asked for binoculars to have a better look and made out the figure of a woman with arms outstretched (*La Madonna a Medjugorje* [Cittadella: Bertoncello Artigrafiche, 1985], 141). He then passed the binoculars to a second friar, and a third one took them out of the hands of the second and who in turn had them taken by a fourth (Laurentin and Rupčić 1984a, 148–49).

These "technological" visions are no different in kind from the collective hermeneutic ones. They have in common a radical weakening of subjectivity attributed to the Madonna. It is as though she were not *making herself seen* but rather was *being seen*. But there is a difference between the two ways, "nontechnological" and "technological," of perceiving the Marian presence.

The image in hermeneutic visions is disquieting. It is like a *double* that refers back to a reality that, even when it talks, is mysterious: shadows, profiles, shapes, lights, things vague and hard to pin down. The hermeneutic image refers back to the collective imagination of the invisible and can be said *to leave heaven in heaven*.

Another kind of "nontechnological" image, that of the *strong* seers, is reassuring because, in spite of everything, it does not propose contrasts with people's everyday images and it reduces the gap between the imaginary and living reality, between double and subject. In short, it *pulls heaven down to earth*. But this kind of image is the rare experience of a privileged few.

Finally, vision by technology, above all photography, ends up multiplying the image and making it available to everyone, definitively putting heaven on earth, eliminating any residual dimension of privilege in seers and their connection with heaven.

Does a photograph of the Madonna destroy that "aura" that for Walter Benjamin (1955, 26–27) was ritual and cultural before it was aesthetic? Clara Gallini, studying wedding photos and albums, finds a power of symbolic production and a capacity for ritual in photography and reconsiders the "premature enthusiasm of Benjamin, who believed that the desacralization of social and aesthetic values went hand in hand with the progressive diffusion of techniques for the serial reproduction of objects and images" (Gallini 1988, 690). It certainly is difficult to hold that there was a loss of aura in the case of wedding photography, "the 'ritual basis' for the later ceremony of looking at the pictures. But even the later ceremony constitutes, in turn, a second phase of 'ritual basis' (socially shared) for the existence of a legitimate couple" (Ibid., 689).

Here the aura, that is, the unique apparitions "of something distant, however close it might be" is everything (Benjamin 1955, 25). Possessing a real photo of the real Madonna is not the same as experiencing an apparition of something distant. But there is something of a paradox here. In Benjamin's terms:

> To render things *closer*, both spatially and humanly, is for today's masses a very great necessity, given the tendency for reproductions to overpower the uniqueness of any particular thing. Every day there is an ever more indisputable demand for objects as close as possible to their images, or even better, in effigy, in reproduction. (Ibid.)

It may not be true that getting closer always generates the elimination of a sense of distance. In fact, ritual reiteration expresses at the same time a sense of distance and a sense of approximation, the latter infinitely more vivid to the extent that it alternates with the former, hence the pulse of ritual rhythm. The Madonna in the photo does not cease to be the Madonna, just as the photo of the Madonna does not cease to be a photo.

A photograph of the Madonna does not destroy the sacred around it. Rather, the recourse to technology in order to perceive the presence of the Madonna betrays an extraordinary change in the meaning of relations with the divine: eyeglasses, binoculars, and photography *capture* the image of the

Madonna, as if they no longer let her offer herself to the chosen ones, but instead invade, like *paparazzi*, her "private" realm.

Yet the capture of the Madonna's image does not introduce an entirely new kind of rapport: this Madonna photographed against her wishes reminds us of magical divinities "constrained" to act by humans with the apposite formulae and rites. "Whoever possesses the requisite charisma for employing the proper means is stronger even than the god, whom he can compel to do his will" (Weber 1922, 430).

The inclusion of celestial beings in technological rationalization is a totally novel aspect of the use of photography. The gods become objects among millions of other objects, without anything to keep them from being transformed into repeatable images, reproducible, enjoyable in millions of copies. A pilgrim at Medjugorje was present at the prodigy of light around the cross on the mountain. "At a certain point, then, I began to take photographs, but nothing came out. In my pictures not even the cross was visible, probably because we were quite far from the hillside and I did not have a telescopic lens" (Sala and Mantero 1986, 74).

The problem of supernatural photos is merely a technical one. The reenchantment of the world explains prodigy as the result of the correct gesture that places a vague presence in the sky in contact with a light-sensitive chemical compound. The technological impersonality of the photographic medium—optics, light, exposure, lens, electric automatic mechanisms—changes relations with the divine, which is then assimilated to the world and even subordinated to technique, in contrast to a long tradition of precaution in approaching the sacred, of exclusions and preclusions. Technology assimilates, multiplies, neutralizes, and finally brings the sacred to images, enjoyment, and spectacle.

Are these kinds of magic and technology irreconcilable?

At a certain point, the believers described at the opening of this chapter shifted from electronic technology to holy water. This shift is perhaps the key to an explanation. In reality, technology renders objective and automatic those relations that in Christianity are kept subjective and arbitrary in the same way that magical acts, given their *techniques*, render objective and automatic their consequences.

Walter Benjamin described the differences between technology and magic as "historic variables" (1955, 63). Arnold Gehlen later emphasized the correlation between modern technology and magic, which he called "supernatural technology." Gehlen cited a definition of magic by Maurice Prandines, "an attempt to bring about changes to man's advantage, by deviating things from their own course to put them at our service," and commented, "If one reflects on this definition, one will note that it applies both to magic and to true technology, that is, to both supernatural and natural technology" (Gehlen 1957, 21). Distant and dangerous magical entities can now be controlled and bent to human will with a new ritual activity, photography. Hence, far from irreconcilable, technological "constraint" is the transformation and modern version of magical constraint. The "bound" image of magic is now the "captured" image of photography.

The reenchantment of the world makes the world available for the *technologizing of prodigy* because prodigy has already been the result of effective technique. In the religious realm, prodigy is exceptional because it is an arbitrary and rare act of the divinity who created the rules. In the reenchanted world, prodigy is the mere effect of technological processes. Celestial photography is the complete expression of the reenchanted world in which *prodigiousness is the objective result of the omnipotence of technology*. Discussion of photography allows us to take up a matter left hanging in the air in the discussion of experimental tests of apparitions in the second chapter.

What is the role of divine beings in the tests? Are they able "supernaturally" to avoid a test for the supernatural? Recall Dr. Stopar's test in which he put himself between the seer and the Madonna, causing a "slight haze" in the vision. Is this test imposed on the Madonna? Could she avoid the test if she wanted to? From the way the episode is reported it would seem that she could not. But the other, blindfold, test shows the opposite, that there is no impediment to the vision. The Madonna thus seems to be free to respond or not to the test with positive, measurable information, because sometimes it is X and sometimes Y. Perhaps this is the idea of the leaders of the visionary culture, whether scientists or theologians. We saw, in the case of the laboratory transported to the apparition site, that the test is assigned only the job of "testing" the *state* of the world of the prodigy, the *here and now* of the miraculous event.

But in the collective use of photography, things seem to be quite different. Here, the Madonna does not seem to be able to escape from the chemical reaction taking place on the film. Technology, a new magic, constrains the Madonna to give in to the believers' *desire for images*. They capture her in images, and the photograph, as Morin reminds us, and is *possessed* by the person photographed (1956, 39). In the popular language of the Southern

Italy, the photographer is asked whether he "caught [*pigliato*]" what he was photographing, that is, if he took or captured it.

In this way, one can clearly distinguish photography of the Madonna from traditional pictures of saints. An engraved image, even if miraculous, contains within itself the idea of a copy, not of a perfect reproduction. Think of the common legend about excellent painters unable to complete paintings of sacred subjects because they found themselves incapable of depicting the visage of the holy figure. They could complete the work only with the miraculous help of divine intervention. Think also of the aura of prodigious-ness of certain images held to be painted by Saint Luke himself and therefore are more "true" than others. Such a power of capture, implicitly attributed to photography, can be devastating if directed programatically toward the construction of relations between heaven and earth. Their "objectivity" and "neutrality" even cuts out some of the seers' role as mediators.

It is not surprising that the seers of Medjugorje maintained that the Madonna they saw was more beautiful than the one in the photographs (Laurentin and Lejeune 1988a, 72). But the same seers, in order to reaffirm their privileged relation with Mary, did not reject photographs. They also got involved in the capture of celestial images, even if on terms more clearly in their own interest.

Photographs of the seer with the Madonna on his head and of Vicka's house with the Madonna served to confirm the closeness of these seers to the Virgin. Such pictures demonstrated not only Mary's goodwill toward the seers, but also, and more important, they conveyed a certain control the seers could boast having over her. Jelena maintained that all they had to say was, "Madonna, we want you to come," and she came (Kraljević and Maggioni 1988, 133).

In conclusion, the analogy to the Weberian ideal type of archaic, magical divinity is no longer simply a suggestion; technology seems to imply the disquieting idea of a divinity possessed. The divinity could be considered a kind of converse of demonic possession. All these entities spread over heaven and earth and captured in images from cameras cede their own *double* with the picture, let it be captured. The Devil, however, is not easily taken. Photos of the Devil are rare; mainly diabolical numbers and fire are captured. Hence, demonic possession involves the *bad* double who does not let himself be captured but instead captures the living, in contrast with the *good* double who lets her or himself be caught. Would the latter be a sign of divine love?

The Madonna who lets herself by surprised by cameras no longer decides who can see her, and thereby fosters a perceptive reaction or creates a miraculous one. At this point, she is all "earthly." The seer Vicka declared that the Madonna's favorite place was Križevac hill. Father Janko Bubalo then asked whether the Madonna was being seen there less often. The girl replied: "How do we know! Perhaps she is there and we simply do not see her" (Bubalo 1987, 144).

One might conclude that the Madonna, unseen on the hill, ignores the acts of humans (perhaps she goes there trying to find people). Or perhaps the human presence is irrelevant for the purposes of one of her physical-corporeal dimensions on earth. Her presence, to the extent that it is independent of that of the seers or their visual capacity (how well they can see), has a spatio-temporal *objectivity* that does not derive from celestial—as distinct from human—purposes, an objective existence measurable with appropriate instruments. Humans have thus built a sophisticated technological dimension that heaven is no longer able to evade.

But this affirmation of human power should not become a matter of pride. The test that conquers heaven's dominion has already conquered the person, converting the person into one object among many. And photography itself shows how the subjectivity of the believer is weakened. This is not a special requisite, a distinctive quality, not something that photography *is* and that visions confer upon it, but something that photography *has*. It is not the physical eye, the instrument for connection with the inner world of their subjectivity, that encounters the Madonna, but the electronic eye of the camera that takes her. The believer/photographer does not act voluntarily upon the camera to enter into contact with the Madonna but trusts to the power of technology and to chance in the attempt to capture her.

It is not a matter of the camera's artistic ability in depiction. A painter who saw the Madonna at Medjugorje and tried to recall her in a painting, confesses:

One is unable to render this image; I believe that is impossible. I had the fortune to see her, but I cannot explain it: there is nothing like it in the palette. I can lay out for you all the elements of the palette, hot or cold, but they are not these sacred colors, colors with this special light.

I struggle with all my skill to depict what I have seen, and I am suffering from this impossible task. (Kraljević and Maggioni 1988, 139)

It is precisely the dimension of human subjectivity, with its skill, capacity, and art, that recognizes that it is inferior to the task. But this inferiority disappears when it trusts in the *camera*. The camera captures, freezes, and "catches." The limited powers of humans are unlimited with the camera. Without problem, photography is able to document, in the sense of grasping, a state of the real. With the camera, the power of humans becomes immense but also obvious. There is no pride in the photographer's act, as there would be if a painter were to succeed in depicting the Madonna.

It is not a prayer—traditionally the fundamental act connecting earth and heaven—that will be rewarded by a contact with the sublime, but rather the pressure of a finger on a camera button—a banal act that is one of innumerable banal acts of everyday technology. Furthermore, the aspect that, in terms of the relation of the Madonna and the photographer is a matter of chance—the Madonna was there right at that moment, the believer snapped the photo right at that moment—in terms of the camera is necessary and foreseeable. The causality of the optical and chemical processes *determines* the relation between the believer and the Madonna. *The camera, in short, constructs the relation between heaven and earth.* The seer, then, does not possess the divinity; rather it is the camera who possesses both. The camera is no longer a tool mediating between the two but the locus in which *they produce themselves.*

Consider the problem of authenticity of apparitions. In the absence of the camera, it is the subjective experience of the seers that is at stake—Do they really see, or are they mistaken, faking, dreaming? This authenticity is judged by the nonseers who watch the seers see. The seer is a seer thanks to the consensus of her or his group. Analogously, if we consider the Madonna, she is there because she imposes her evidence on the attention of the seer's companions. When the camera gets involved, the decision that produces the seer and the apparition together has to do with the technical process of fixing light. No longer a matter of the subjectivity of the seer or evidence of the signs from the Madonna, what is at stake is the possibility—to be evaluated in technological categories of analysis and hence neither in psychological nor theological terms—that the camera captures the real thing or, instead, gives a false impression of reality. It is within the camera, then, that the believer becomes a seer and a shape becomes the Madonna.

The omnipotence of the camera has become commonplace and no longer called into question, not even when divinity becomes the object of its processes. In the world of technology, the *artifice* of the camera is replaced by its *naturalness*. The camera then becomes the *very location* in which prodigies take place. Not only the invisible Madonna is revealed in the photograph, but the sun also gives off prodigies of light and movement in the viewfinder of the video camera.

When people start watching the sun and waiting for its prodigy, they have no certainty that it will in fact occur. Indeed, often some people are in the embarrassing situation of saying they see a solar prodigy, only to have others say they do not see anything strange at all. "To this is added an annoying uniqueness. In a crowd's testimony of several "solar miracles," the majority see the phenomena, but some do not see it" (Laurentin and Lejeune 1988a, 68). But when the eye is placed in the viewfinder of the video camera, the prodigy of the sun will be evident and unfailing. Once the television sequence has been filmed, no one can say they see nothing strange: all can see clearly and objectively the pulsing of the sun, its changing color and losing light. Doubts disappear because the solar prodigy is there, evident for all.

Finally, the camera becomes the *auctoritas* that *decides* the first sign of the world's prodigiousness. On many videotapes of solar prodigies—those of Oliveto, for example, one hears the voice of the cameraperson who, at the first hint of a prodigy in his viewfinder, shouts "There it is!" And at once all the people around, even if they do not see the vision, begin to shout because of the prodigy. We know from the experiment of Malanga and Pinotti that "the phenomenon occurs with aperture speeds of less than 1/150 of a second, one second after the beginning of the shot" (Malanga and Pinotti 1990, 76). This last argument leads to another gap caused by the dependence of apparitions on technology or technology's influence upon them: the distancing introduced by *television*, and the consequent, definitive removal of the subject.

First of all, it has been observed that seeing the Madonna—with or without technological resources—has been mostly assimilated to the seeing of earthly objects, depending on a series of impersonal conditions: *when* to look, *how* to look, *where* to look, *what to see*, and *what is being seen*. *Who* is seeing is secondary.

The *when* does not depend on inscrutable celestial decisions: it is prepared, or anticipated or achieved through religious rituals; it is a time impersonally defined as the "usual" time for the start of apparitions—at 6 p.m., 10 p.m., and so on. One goes to a certain place to get there in time for the beginning. In oral news of the phenomena, the question about the time for the apparition is the obvious one used for television programs, shows, demonstrations, and meetings: "When does it start?"

The *how* implies consideration of the right *technique* for looking. One woman told another, who had complained that she saw nothing, "But if you don't look steadily, how do you expect to see anything?" Others, closer to the Committee, maintained that staring fixedly produced illusions. But agreement was almost unanimous about the technical resources that could be useful: spectacles, binoculars, cameras, video cameras, and any technical means of improving vision, independent of who is looking.

The *where* to look in collective visions is reciprocally corrected by adjustments of a half-meter above, below, to the left, and to the right, as if testing a new screen that one expects to use habitually. Sooner or later for the different seers, *strong* and *weak*, there are walls, trees, gates, windows, and angles of sky that are normally themselves but that, at a certain time of day, disappear as objects to become sites for visions. It is surprising how the visual habits of apparitions recall the scientific fantasy of "total cinema."

> There are interesting fantasies to get rid of the theater altogether and project the film onto "the great screen that the sky, the night offers us. We need an inventor to put this idea into practice" [R. Clair]. After René Clair, Dovzenko predicted in 1931 a cinema without a screen, in which the spectator watched the film as if in the midst of the action [. . .] Better yet, Barjavel describes future telecinema: "the waves will carry images everywhere. Receivers will display it on demand." And Henri Poulaille writes: "Tomorrow [. . .] the image will be before us woven with threads of luminous light, without a screen, hallucinatingly." (Morin 1956, 57–58)

Even the *what to see* recalls the rules for seeing earthly objects. What does an object that I have never seen look like? What does one see in order to say one sees a given worldly object among others it is placed with? What must I see in order to say I have seen the Madonna among the other things in my visual field? Not that object, but the other one next to it, that light that you think comes from the moon but instead is from heaven, and so on.

Finally, there is the *what is being seen*. He has seen the Madonna, but I can see something else: an inexplicable cloud, an effect of the sun, a light, a horse, a dove, and angel; an eye in a triangle, saints, and then fierce animals; little green monsters, tall men in white, people who died from hanging, wounded people, processions of the dead, devils, "sluts," and, lower on the scale of visions, silhouettes, shadows, patterns, colors. The scene is enormous when the screen becomes transparent.

Just *who* is seeing is no longer an issue. At Medjugorje, the *true* seers were still distinguished from false ones. At Oliveto, too, the Committee tried to draw this distinction. But the flow of seeing became impersonal. Perhaps not all saw, but all *could* see. In any case, even at Medjugorje, by taking pictures of the Madonna and speculating on her presence on the hill independent of the presence of the seers—hence, by *objectifying* her presence—people eliminated the relation between seer and seen, that is, the choice of the seer by the being that let itself be seen, and worked toward a visibility that was impersonal and universal.

Hence, the Madonna becomes an object among objects. But she is an object willing to encounter an implicit model of reference in the particular earthly object that is television.

A group of pilgrims animatedly discuss the apparitions in front of the door of the church that was damaged in the earthquake, close to the little plaza of the apparitions. Farther off, a group of women look at the sky behind the castle tower. Suddenly one of the women begins to shout. Among the pilgrims a woman says: "Let's go, the seeing is starting." The people move over to be close to the group of women that sees. (Field diary, April 26, 1986)

Note that it is not as though the Madonna were unexpectedly appearing before the eyes of someone chosen by her, whoever that person might be. No, it is the believers who move to a precise place: "let's go" because it is time for the visions to begin, and "there" "the seeing is starting." There is a specific physical location for the visions: a particular piece of sky between the houses that can be seen from a particular corner of the little plaza. It is there that the Madonna, at a certain moment, as if by the activation of a kind of objective and material celestial wave, is visible, potentially by all who decide to go over and look from that point, a point demarcated by looking and by what is seen. One cannot help but recall the particular everyday object for earthly viewing that is the television screen.

Let us then observe how the visions began as generally described by the seers, whether at Oliveto or at Medjugorje. The gate at Oliveto, the wall of the presbytery at Medjugorje, disappeared, and in their place were seen flowery meadows, starry or sunny blue skies, or red sunsets. Normally, people were looking at the same thing—the gate, the wall. Once the vision occurred or became activated, the screen, gate, or wall disappeared, and in its place there was the celestial image and anything else that appeared.

One can make a plausible correlation with the television screen that, once the cathode tube is turned on and receiving, disappears as an object and becomes a window on the world and on the infinitude of the imagination. The visions of the other world recall the forms and the ways of using the images of the world beyond the television screen. But the similarities do not stop here. Television allows seeing what is beyond it through the simple technical action of an on/off switch. There is no emotional complication in the act of starting up the viewing mechanism, before one sees what is absolutely distant.

Some of the experiences of seers and believers at Oliveto indicate that the trip—above all repeat trips—to the apparition town and the subsequent wait at the spot where prodigies occurred worked like a kind of "technological" mechanism, a willing act to see, not so easy but no less obvious than pressing an on/off button. Once the seeing was in progress, it was not experienced as something out of the ordinary, something with an aura, or something troubling.

{21}

(1) mv:	Mario—did you see the Madonna?	
(2) mv1:	No.	
(3) mv:	Lucia saw her.	
(4) mv1:	What about you?	
(5) mv:	No + but now we're going again [he refers to the place where at that time hermeneutic visions were most frequent]. {April 12, 1986}	

Here is a second example:

{22}

(1) boy:	There she is—you see her? you see her?
(2) fv:	No, I don't see anything.

(3) boy:	She's there—on those stones— see her?
(4) fv1:	Oh yes, do you see her? do you see her?
(5) fv:	No, I don't see . . .
(6) boy:	[irritated] Hey, you must be blind—how come you don't see her?
(7) fv1:	Up there—there.
(8) fv:	I don't see her there—there I saw a light.
(9) fv1:	Hey, you're crazy—what do you mean? you don't see her there? {February 1, 1986}

A third example:

{23}

(1) mv:	Do you see her now?
(2) mv1:	Yes, yes, yes.
[PAUSE]	
(3) mv:	Look, look—you can see lower down that she is almost disappearing. {March 15, 1986}

The weak seers' directions for *where* others should look are as explicit as directions for looking at a *screen*.

{24}

(1) fv:	That's the Madonna's rosary—look, you see it?
(2) fv1:	Where is it?
(3) fv:	Look—you can see it now + that sure is the Madonna's rosary.
(4) childv:	I don't see anything.
(5) fv:	Look + look there, you can see it.
(6) fv1:	No + but that is a piece of paper.
(7) fv:	No, to this side—over here [with her hands she aims the woman she is talking to].
(8) fv1:	Ah—yes I see her. {April 12, 1986}

In these examples, there is evidently a kind of removedness on the part of the seers from what they are seeing and from their own experience in seeing. It is as if what was going on in heaven or elsewhere had no direct or personal relation with them, as if it were not happening to them. Here television may serve as a model.

When I watch a televised event, I may be moved or upset, but I will certainly not confuse the event with my experience, as if I were a participant or as if between me and the event there were a relation that was *direct*. My experience of seeing is not a part of the event I see: I may be present at a tragedy without having to choose whether I should intervene or watch passively. I may have various other reactions. Indeed, I might say: "These shows I can't even look at," or, "these shows give me a lift."

Similarly, the *weak* seers, who are habituated to visions and eventually see in an attenuated way what the *strong* seers see better, watch the event without feeling a connection between the event and their experience. As with television, it is not something that happens to them, but something that they attend. They are privileged spectators, but spectators only. They may, as we have seen, be *happy* to have seen the Madonna who is *sad*. One thing is their own experience ("I too have see her!") and another is the content of that experience (the Madonna, sad). The experience is disjointed, as with television. Those who see may be impersonal spectators.

Moreover, the vision (or its surrogate) is taken for granted by those who simply go to or live in Oliveto. The absence of a vision is experienced as a negative sign from the Madonna, perhaps the result of one's sins, perhaps a sign of tragedies about to befall one, or perhaps a sign of the Madonna's displeasure:

> During the greatest influx of pilgrims, in the following months, nonsee-ing was the exception, and impelled the nonseer to wonder why the experience did not occur. It was considered almost a slight from the Madonna, and would lead the nearby seer to point out more precisely the spot where he or she was seeing and where the nonseer, "strangely," was not able to see. (Apolito 1990, 217)

Hence, the vision tended to become an obvious and common experience. A question that captured the general attitude was, "At what time is the Madonna seen?" It would greatly irritate the parish priest when pilgrims would ask the question on the telephone or in the streets. He sensed that the arbitrary independence of a marvelous event, in terms of the official canon, was undermined, on the one hand, by a *rhythmic patterning* and on the other, by a *universalization*, both processes clearly modeled on the world of electronics and television, and that they in turn led to an *impersonalization* also typical of the media. Furthermore, the leadership itself had involuntarily encouraged the *media-ization* of the apparitions by maintaining that *what was seen* was something objective and separate from the subjectivity of the *seer*. I shall shortly return to this point.

One of the results of these processes was the *banalization* of the perceptual contact with the Madonna. When, in the experiences of collective seeing, for example, an effect of light and shadow is "named" as a Marian sign, the fact that in many cases it does not subsequently disappear becomes a practical problem. After a little while, the emotional tension winds down, people decide to walk away to the little plaza, to the bar, to rejoin their friends, and so on. Later, they go back to see if the Madonna is still there, then go away again, then go back to look once more, with progressively declining interest. The world reshaped in the form of celestial signs becomes an obvious one, however circumscribed in time and space, to which one becomes accustomed. Some believers rebel against this state of things, denying precisely for this reason that the things "named" in these circumstances are indeed celestial signs. But many others show every sign of being happily ensconced in this banalization of the prodigy.

Finally, the relaxation of emotional tension that arose in the first moving personal experiences of hermeneutic vision brought also changes of ethos that more than once left room for joking exchanges.

{25}

(1) fv:	I don't see anything.
(2) fv1:	But what about that cloud above everything?
(3) fv2:	She must not see the cloud.
(4) fv3:	I don't even see the cloud [*laughter*].
(5) fv1:	There you can see a bit of cloud like that . . .
(6) fv4:	What can you see?
(7) fv1:	It's that cloud which is beginning to move.
(8) fv3:	Oh—you see the cloud? [*laughter*].
(9) fv:	Do you see the cloud?
(10) fv4:	Some see a cloud—some see one thing—some see another. {April 18, 1986}

In short, the celestial vision is incorporated in the mode of spectator entertainment: *now* you can see *something* at *that point*. The almost obsessive insistence of the leadership, after a certain point, on nonstop prayer, seeks to head off just this kind of passivity on the part of spectators and instead eventually seeks to reflect collectively what is going on beyond the screen and open up an active relation with the sacred. But the rhythm of *strong* visions, of possessions, of people fainting, of screams, of *weak* visions, of people telling what they see, of petitions, of comments, of jokes, of departures and of arrivals, often interrupt the thread of prayer or work against it, imposing an immense theatralization of the events, a pageant of heaven come to earth.

Contemporary supernatural visions themselves explicitly refer to the visual model of television. *Electronic vision* is one of the metaphors most used by seers and others to explain the nature of *heavenly vision*. Vicka told of having seen the deceased mother of Ivanka, "once, momentarily at that—as though on TV" (Bubalo 1987, 104); another time, she saw "like a movie" the parish priest, who had been put in jail for "subversive activity" (Laurentin and Rupčić 1984a, 53). She described how the symbols, crosses, hearts, and suns, which the Madonna sometimes showed them when she appeared, disappeared "like pictures on television" (Laurentin and Rupčić 1984b, 165). Mantero is explicit: "When sometimes she shows to the youths scenes or pictures in addition to herself, they pass before their eyes like clips of a film of mysterious origin" (Mantero 1987, 54).

And that is what occurred when the Madonna appeared for "eight minutes" and showed Mirjana, who broke out crying, an imminent chastisement that would strike one region of the world (Ibid., 92), something repeated a few days later, always "as in a movie" (Ibid., 95). At Oliveto as well, some seers witnessed previews of chastisements: the disaster of the dike of Val di Fiemme on July 19, 1985; the terrorist attack on Fiumicino airport of December 27, 1985 (Carione and Serrone 1986, 23).

We already saw how the Madonna decided to tell her life to Vicka. Rastrelli maintains that the result was the 635 pages to be published after Mary gave her permission (Rastrelli 1987, 68); but Vicka said something different in an interview.

"How did you learn the life of the Madonna?"

"She showed it to me like a photo in a movie, then she explained it to me and said a few words to me. So I see it like a picture in the movies and the Madonna explains to me the meaning of the pictures." (Kraljević and Maggioni 1988, 256)

Here we are close to the sequences of a serial, with appointments, deadlines, and visits; the technique is that of an audiovisual with slides and commentary, but there is also the dimension of seeing it "as in a movie."

So film and television are metaphors for the *seen*. But one episode tells us something else. In the following quotation, Jelena is speaking.

A few days before Christmas a movie, *Ben Hur*, was playing in Čitluk. They said that Jesus was mentioned in it, how he was born and how he suffered. The movie was starting at 7 p.m. Marijana and myself were going to church every evening because Our Lady had asked this of us, and the Rosary and prayers were after Mass. Because of that my Dad said to me that I couldn't see the movie. I was sad for that reason. Then Our Lady said to me: "Do not be sad. On Christmas I'll show you how Jesus was born." (Those Christmas days an angel was appearing to me as in the previous year.) This was how the vision went: I see an angel. Then he disappears and I see darkness. In that darkness I see St. Joseph. He holds a staff in his hands. In that place there is some grass, stones on the road, and a few houses around. Mary is on a mule. It looks like she is crying but she is not. She is sad. She says, "I would be glad if someone would take us in for tonight, because I am tired." Joseph says, "Here are the houses; we will ask." And they knock at doors. Mary stands in front of the house. Joseph knocks on the door. People open the door, and when they see Joseph and Mary they close it. That is repeated two or three times. When they start towards the other houses the lights begin disappearing in them. They are sad. Joseph says, "There, there is an old house; surely no one sleeps in it. Surely it's abandoned." And they go there. Inside there is one mule. They put their own mule alongside the manger. Joseph gathers some pieces of wood and they make a fire. He also puts some hay in it but the fire consumes it immediately. So Mary is warmed more by the mule. Mary cries and is very sad. Joseph feeds the fire. *Suddenly* I see Jesus in front of Mary. He smiles as if he were one year old. He is joyful, and it seems as if he is speaking. He waves his hands. Joseph comes to Mary and Mary says, " Joseph, this day of joy has come, but it would be better to pray, because there are people who do not allow Jesus to be born." So they pray. *Suddenly* I see a little house only. It is lighted up a little bit. And *then suddenly* it becomes completely lighted up as in daytime, and the stars are in the skies. *I see* two angels above the stall. They hold a big banner, and written on it is: "We glorify you, Lord!" Above it there is like a big choir of angels. They sing and glorify God. *Then* I see the shepherds. They are weary, tired, and some are already sleeping. Some walk. The sheep and the lambs are with them. One angel approaches them and says, "Shepherds, hear the good news! God is born! You will find him sleeping in a manger in the stall. Know that I am telling you the truth." *Suddenly* a large choir of angels joins them singing.

Tomislav: "Did you look at this as in a movie?"

Jelena: "It looked real. I looked at that as I look at Our Lady." (Rooney and Faricy 1988, 97–98, my italics)

Hence, *instead* of the movie *Ben Hur*, which the seer wanted to go to see in order to see how Jesus was born and died, the Madonna proposed that she see something "like a film [It. *filmato*]" entirely dedicated to the birth of Jesus. One may note how the description is constructed like a veritable film script: the brief phrases that set the scenes, the wide and close-up fields of images, the heavily rhythmic scansion, and the "suddenly's" and "then's" that indicate a change of scene and thus eliminate the continuity of a real true-to-life scene. Yet the picture of the event, significantly set up as a film, is accepted as real, even hyper-real. The referent for the version of the birth of Christ was the film *Ben Hur*, which was replaced by a celestial version of the birth of Christ, which "seemed true," like the Madonna. The celestial vision here appears the exact replicate of the media vision, on which its form and imagery are based.

But at this point a new question arises. First of all, one recalls the visionary experiences I have defined as "trips" earlier in this book. What is the difference between those experiences and this vision of the birth of Jesus? Only what is derived from the explicit model of film from which this is drawn or that *Ben Hur* refers to? But were not there also clear, though not explicit, references to film imagery in the accounts of "trips"? If there is some relation, it must apply as well to the trips in which the seer interacts with the vision, whether in combat with vision figures or as a participant in the Passion, or otherwise.

There is a new question about the *experience* that the seer has of the vision-object. The reciprocal sense of removedness between the two parts of a television viewing—spectator and spectacle—seems useful in understanding the analogous sense of removedness in the *weak* visions and the consequent relative emotional indifference of the seers toward what they are seeing; but now that correlation seems less useful. In the "trips," the screen is broken through, that is, the other world becomes the seer's down-to-earth reality. Television, with its impenetrable fixed screen, no longer seems to be the model for visions. Yet one should not underestimate television's potential.

> Dear Maurizio, I thank you for the good you have done for me. I watched your show on Monday with Costanzo and I profited from it. May God forever bless your hands that do so much good to those who suffer. Let me say that due to a fall from a ladder I suffer so much in my back, in the lowest vertebrae, they hurt me so much and I cannot bend over or get up, and I suffer a lot. I did as you said, I got in front of the television with faith. After that I slept all night without the least pain and the next morning to me great joy I could bend down and get up perfectly, and a week later, I am well, Maurizio, I do everything without pain and without strain in my back [. . .] A friend [female] from near Lucca. (*Dopo Acquario. Lettere a Maurizio Arena* [Milan: Sugarco, 1979], 83)

This is a typical letter referring to one of the best-known instances of television healing, one connected to an appearance of Maurizio Arena, a popular star of postwar cinema, who was confirmed as a healer during *Acquario*, the television show hosted by Maurizio Costanzo, on February 19, 1979.

From that point on there was an increasing use of television for healing purposes, with transmissions during which magicians performed healing of various kinds (Apolito 1980, 128–97; Gallini 1990b). Here we are in the presence of complex interactions with "an image nevertheless conceived of as 'real'" (Gallini 1990b, 3). With them we move to a different terrain for analysis, one in which images in the media take on the possibility of miraclelike or healing actions typical of the direct intervention of heavenly figures or their images.

In this terrain, there is a definitive bridging of any gap between electronic image and reality, sign and referent. Here the general idea of "television cures" of magicians takes the specific form of "media-visionary" cures, such as that of Sister Nazarena Zoni, who got rid of her eye problems "while watching an audiovisual on Medjugorje" (Laurentin 1986a, 148). Hence, the level of miraculous cure once more confirms the contiguity of *appeared* images with *electronic* images.

At first, I took it for granted that spectators did not feel their reality coincided with that on the other side of the screen. But television healers have belied that assumption. These unusual uses of television help us understand more normal ones. As Morin said about cinema: "They are extreme phenomena of auto-cinematographic vision, of the photographic and cinematographic occult, of the mythology of total cinema, that throw light on the undifferentiated complexity of ordinary phenomena" (Morin 1956, 60).

Let us ask ourselves about the "anthropologically strange" obviousness of the normal use of television. This "normal use" is governed by an implicit *norm*, like a kind of instruction, about how to look at television and film, the two assimilated from the point of view of the "reality effect" of the image. This norm imposes a separation between what is beyond and what is in front of the screen. Such a separation is not "natural," even it is obvious, because it is learned behavior, born of aesthetic awarenesses (and behind that technological awarenesses) that are part of the *medium*.

Perception of film takes place in the context of an awareness that the image is not practical life; the mechanisms of objective perception are in motion, but they are not grafted on the tree of transmission. They spin wildly, but not in a vacuum, and transform their energy in emotional heat. *That is what, in the last analysis, prevents objective truth from getting integrated in the seriousness of practice and aesthetic conscious- ness.* (Ibid., 156, italics in original)

We can better understand the implicit norm for watching film or TV by seeing when it is violated or ignored. Examples of confusion between reality and image are present at the beginnings of cinema, outside of Western culture (Ibid., 52), and in the reactions of children as yet untrained in the distinction. The norm of ordinary use would have it that the screen is a *barrier*. When this norm is not observed, the screen can be used as a *bridge*. Such is the case of the television magicians for whom the screen is an obvious and unquestionable connection between magician and patient. The *reality* of the magical operation cancels out completely the value of the separation of the screen, substituting the total presence of the action taking place on it.

But in the visions as well there is a norm for behavior imposed by the leadership, implicit in what I call "the process of objectification of the apparition." The effect is to separate the event of the apparition from the subjectivity of its protagonists. The reasons for this process were given in *"It Is Said They Have Seen the Madonna."*

> The distinction in terms of credibility between protagonists and events is the particular position of the parish priest. The events are attributed an objectivity that is independent of the protagonists. The latter with their uncontrollable subjectivity might damage the validation of the events. So separating one from the other permits a protective circumscription of the events and the marginalization, to the point of concealment, of the seers. Speaking of the protagonists in relation to the events may compromise the objectiveness of the events with the un-circumscribable subjectivity of the protagonists. On the contrary, once the isolation, identification, and the consequent validation of the events has occurred, it becomes possible to distinguish the true from the false, seeing from fraud or suggestion, for no one person will be considered the author of the events, however deeply what happened "touched" them. (Apolito 1990, 121)

Based on this kind of objectification, the apparition has become regulated in regard to the experience that a seer could (was authorized to) have in such a way as to *separate* the experience of the vision and the object of the vision. One thinks of the sign "Seers subject to fainting cannot go back to the gate," or of the woman who felt called to the Madonna's gate and waited until the end of the prayer to answer the call. The effectiveness of this norm of separation was neither automatic nor immediate because it required a certain amount of training. If totally successful, it might result in the disappearance of the visions altogether.

Paradoxically, in the long run this kind of norm worked best with the kind of seer for whom it was not designed, the *weak* seer. The *strong* seers generally found it hard not to feel that what was happening beyond the screen was happening to *them, too.* One could even say that the distinction between *weak* and *strong* seers rested precisely in the adherence of the *weak* seers to the norms of objectification of *what was seen* and the insubordination of the *strong* seers. Moreover, the greater sensitivity of the *weak* seers to the norms set by the leadership was related to habits of consumption of electronic images, observing the norm that separated the two sides of the screen.

The official norm for celestial visions, imposed in particular by the parish priest, contrasted with a different, older, implicit norm, that legitimated the vision experience of *strong* seers. This older norm derived from the devotional tradition that the image coincides with the saint it represents (Galasso 1982, 69), and allows for the possibility that an icon can become transformed into a person. Apparitions are closely related to this possibility.

> Frequently, examples involve a saint who works a miracle, as with the widespread model of Saint Nicolas, who, in order to put an end to the famine in a town of which he was the patron, goes to buy grain from merchants, often pawning a ring. The merchants go to the town and give the grain to the inhabitants; when they enter the church they discover there the statue of the saint who made the purchase, while the inhabitants recognize the ring as the same one that used to be on the statue. Other saints and Madonnas show themselves to shepherds, woodcutters, etc., and ask them to call together the inhabitants of a town. When the inhabitants arrive they find the image of the saint or Madonna whom the messenger encountered. (Apolito 1982, 21)

In turn, these sacred images who can come alive are related to the entire field of folkloric images that may become dangerous, get out of hand, or escape from control from the building in which the formative power of culture wants to enclose them. They become *restless*, move about, directly demand the presence of the absent beings they represent: the dead, above all, but also persons far away, as well as saints and the divinity (Faeta 1989). Hence, we have three equivalent experiences: "break-through" healing television; interactive visions of *strong* seers; and *restless* images; and in contraposition, respectively: the television of the screen/barrier; objectified visions; and images that are only images.

All of this leads us to the need for a more comprehensive consideration of images in various contexts, which it is not possible to outline here. In terms of the media images, we are, as I said, just at the beginning of an anthropological analysis. But what we do know already reveals strong parallels between television and visions.

In short, if television spectators in general do not feel that their experiences of seeing coincide with what they are watching, it is because their experiences depend on a use of images based on implicit everyday norms. But healing television, which shows the medium capable of producing experiences in the spectator that coincide with what is beyond the screen, reveals and expresses a different norm of usage. In the same way, the experience of the *weak* seers who do not feel themselves involved in what they see beyond the screen of their visions depends on the most common kind of heavenly vision—and also of electronic viewing—the kind that everyone waits for "normally" to have: "What time are things seen?," "Where are things seen?," "How are things seen?," and so on. But the *strong* seers apply a different norm of seeing, common in a cultural area in which archaic images move and modern television heals.

In a world that expresses itself by way of television, the television way of life is accepted, adopted, and used by the Madonna herself. The supporters of the apparitions explain the long duration of the apparitions referring to the nature of the "message" on television: "We are in a repetitive world. There is television every day. What is not repeated is submerged. This renders the prolonged repetition of the message quite useful" (Laurentin and Rupčić 1984a, 105). In a TV world, therefore, the celestial message must be TV-like. And television is indeed a vehicle for news about Medjugorje. The pilgrimages, the visions, and the messages encounter a very power vehicle for propagation in the thousands of copies of videos that circulate among the believers. This use of television is all the more interesting because it is implicit and unwitting. Indeed, "officially" the Madonna and the Devil are in agreement that television and cinema are the Devil's anteroom.

But even this condemnation of television is spread by television itself. The Madonna calls for the avoidance of television because it inhibits prayer (Bianchi and Dogo 1985, 63). She suggested to a prayer group that formed around Jelena that they should avoid "disorderly passions and desires," including television (Laurentin 1986a, 158). On another occasion she said, "Turn off your televisions and radios and do God's programs" (*Medjugorje*, circular of the prayer group Regina Pacis of Turin, no. 4 [1985]). At Medjugorje, the Devil threatens the seers that he will put "films" in their heads (Sala and Mantero 1986, 101) or promises in more detail, "I will pay money to people who work in TV to put bad films on television to turn the young people away from prayer, I will put those films in the heads of the young people to turn them away from mass" (Ibid., 148).

The connection between film or televised images and the Devil was implicit in Benedetta's depiction of the Devil. She saw him dressed all in black, jumping on rooftops "like Zorro"; another encounter with the Devil seemed like it was clipped from the film *Entity*.

In spite of these experiences and messages, which explicitly warn against the use of television and cinema, the TV way of life is profoundly a part of the apparitions; it could even be held that the condemnation of television is a proof of its pervasiveness.

Identity, Time, Millennium

One day, a girl from the Rue Basse, of Lourdes, named Marie [Cazenave] who was well-known for her piety came back from the Grotto saying that she had heard inside the rocky cave of Massabielle a mysterious concert of celestial voices that worked a kind of narcotic intoxication on her senses. In her good faith, she said and believed that only angels were capable of producing such harmonies. The next day, the same girl went back to the Grotto intending to recite the Rosary there, but also with the secret hope of hearing once more the marvelous harmonies of the day before. Sure enough, hardly had she begun to pray, when ineffable notes, notes pure and smooth like those heard from seraphic voices, let themselves be heard by her rapt ears. She followed, without daring to breathe, the melodious and seductive chords, when little by little, but *in crescendo*, strange dissonances, false and strident tones began to cause a tumult and confusion in the musical poem. Soon the enchanting rhythms had become a great tumultuous disorder, and indescribable cacophony. Then all of a sudden, silence. A few seconds later a sinister din, like that of a struggle between horrible beasts, broke out in the depths of the caves. There were suffocating grunts, savage screams, the thud of falling combatants. Without waiting for the combat to conclude, the girl took flight and for many weeks did not dare return to the Grotto. (Estrade 1934, 192–93)

For Bernadette, Lourdes was *not* a dramatic apparition. Only once did the Devil come on the scene. The Madonna had "lifted an eyebrow and thrown a terrible glance" and the Devil disappeared (Ibid., 191). Only after the Marian apparitions ended did the diabolical ones begin.

The way the subsequent diabolical apparitions began is interesting. As with Marie Cazenave, figures emerged disguised as others in a travesty of identity. At Lourdes, many of the later seers, not recognized by the authorities, said they saw saints in the sky: Joseph, Paul, Peter, the evangelists, and all the other well-known saints. But the "the fictitious personages who came on stage in these different parodies, although adorned with a certain artificial beauty, were restless, agitated, and given to involuntary convulsions that rendered them repellent" (Ibid., 195). Whereas the construction of Bernadette's events clearly separated the apparitions of the Madonna from those of the Devil, in the dramatic apparitions that followed at Lourdes this separation was no longer possible. Bernadette wondered whether the being that was appearing was a soul in Purgatory, not the Devil. But at Fatima, the prototype for dramatic apparitions, the doubt, although it was rejected, was whether the Madonna might be the Devil himself (Da Fonseca 1987, 38).

Let us return to the first moments of a dramatic apparition. Is what one sees friend or enemy? Much is at stake in the doubt about what *frame* one is dealing with, diabolical or Marian. Does what is happening now come from our permanent protection or our permanent threat? From the being who provides the security of sacred history or the being who insinuates chance into human history? Once the Marian *frame* is established, one has a guarantee of protection from the unforseeable in history: whatever is going on is now under the sign of the Madonna.

All this follows as long as one stays on the level of cosmic drama: doubt is set aside and the certainty of the Madonna never fades. But when the cosmic drama slips into history, then there begins to occur cases of disguised identity. In these cases, even when the setting, the Marian *frame*, is established, the danger of the *eventual*, what might happen, does not disappear. It is expressed by the continual, disquieting alternation of Marian and diabolic apparitions, and often with confusion even as to the clothes of the protagonists. At Medjugorje, Mirjana saw Satan dressed in the Madonna's robes (Juarez 1987, 43). At Oliveto, this kind of disguise was even more common than in Yugoslavia.

What does this confusion of identity signify? The certitude of identity in apparitions is the result of certitude of victory in the cosmic struggle. Disguises of identity, in contrast, express the historical contingency of the struggle. A cosmic struggle is depicted, a historical struggle is experienced. The setting of the cosmic drama reassures believers, offering them a firm and definite articulation of protagonists and events. There cannot be confusion between Good and Evil because the fundamental clash has already occurred, the risks have been run, the results achieved. But when the cosmic drama becomes historic, it takes on all the riskiness of the contingent. Then nothing more seems sure, whether being or event.

In an apparition the images that appear are alive and not merely graphic, and the invariance of their profiles and the unchangeability of their identities cannot be effectively guaranteed by the official canon of iconography, rigid as to the expression of crystallized tradition and cosmological stereotype. What works better to counteract the *aliveness* of the images that may produce travesty of identity is their immersion in collective narrative.

By *collective narrative* of the apparitions I mean not only the official story or the coherent thread of events legitimated by the authorities, which the believers repeat to one another, but also the total set of fabulations that take the apparitions as a center of reference. This is a narrative stream much broader and less channeled than the coherent official line. It includes, in addition to the principal public events, individuals' own personal experiences at the apparition site, those of others, as well as the constitutive comments and interpretations transmitted by word-of-mouth.

But the power of this narrative is, above all, that it provides a *new context of description* of the individual and collective experiences of human actors, which become incorporated in the collective fabulation *centered* on the apparitions. It is a powerful context of description, capable of eclipsing those normally available to the collective networks for making sense of what is happening. Collective and individual experiences are not amorphous and unreflective. They are already symbolic formations, mediations between existence and cultural traditions of meaning. Putting it somewhat crudely and without getting into complex questions of phenomenology, one could say that what happens to me is not what I *feel* happens to me. Only this second level, what I feel to have happened, forms part of my deep experience. What I feel happened to me is not necessarily what I *say* (to myself and to you) happened to me. On this third level, in addition to the deep psychic reflexes of the preceding level, cultural models will intervene that will provide me with the descriptive contexts with which I can construct the narrative of what happened to me.

But what is the power of these models? They are multiple and contradictory. Is what is the meaning for me here and now the same as what it was there and yesterday? And what is it for someone else? And for both of us together? I say that this happened to me, but who can guarantee that I *catch* it correctly, that I translate it well in narration? And how do I combine what I am saying now with the rest, how do I get away from the story fragment, from the particularity of experience, from the precariousness of meaning? And when I am no longer alone, but find myself with others, what assures me that the processes of meaning that they have will be just and appropriate? Merely the fact that we are together? And why is it that when I am with other, different people, things seem different to me than they so evidently seemed with the first ones? And how can I begin to answer the doubts that come to me as soon as I am alone? Why is one never able to give a single structure to events and their narrations? Why is everything always in pieces? Why is what is here never anywhere else?

But here a new collective narrative, that of the apparitions, gives me, gives us, a *steady* plane of meaning, *strongly* collective, *decisively* plausible and evident within a story that is no longer just mine but everyone's, a story organic, certain, and guaranteed by its connection to absolute power. The traditional meaning of things, now from a higher perspective, appears clearly different. On the plane of the apparitions, experiences have applied to them new interpretive codes, of a different order. The collective narrative that takes shape maps experiences onto the frame of the cosmic drama and fixes them in the meaning derived from the drama.

Hence, what the collective narrative ultimately guarantees is the identity of the seers. Their identities are remade on the basis of the new event, are furnished by the narrative of the apparitions: mildness, goodness, piety, simplicity, harmony, and so on. Often in my field observations, I saw how the apparition facilitated the reshaping of personal identity into a clear, certain, positive contour, one backed by the Madonna herself. To begin with, simply being considered a seer provided a new, privileged, identity, that assumed a person's familiarity with the transcendent.

Furthermore, the Madonna entered into the individual lives in particular ways, with different visions, messages, times, styles, and tones, building new roles and statuses. The Madonna promised the seers individual protection, and that contributed to confirm a new protected identity. This identity brought sense and coherence to lives often experienced as precarious and fragmented. Nello, for example, had been in serious conflict with his father, who did not like Nello's casual way of dressing, his haircut, his friends, his disinterest in working in the factory with his brothers, and so on. Perhaps Nello's father also feared a sexual "difference" in his son, whom he criticized for cross-dressing in carnival. The conflict was so serious that the youth usually slept in his aunt's house, where he felt better "understood." When Nello saw the Madonna, his relations with his father became more serene. His father became his staunch supporter, and from then on Nello's choices were, all felt, guided by the Madonna. Nello slept at his aunt's house because the Madonna wanted him to. He was not to work because he was busy with his mission spreading the Marian messages. But Nello himself revised some of his choices when the Madonna requested some of the same things his father had: shorter hair, more respectable clothes. When carnival came and he wanted to dress as a woman, his aunt talked him out of it, because "now it is not right."

The leaders and the believers also participated in this reconfiguration of personal identity, albeit in ways on the whole less clear than the *strong* seers, by taking a part in the development of a narrative of the events as protagonists or narrators. What often comes to be called a "conversion" is precisely the experience of establishing a new, protected identity, in which one can perceive a strong element of psychological self-reassurance. The most evident aspect of this conversion is that fragmented experience is assembled in a coherent collective narrative; meaningless contingency becomes foreseeable, and historical chance becomes a catalogue of examples in which good overcomes evil.

This reconfiguration of identity is obviously easy when the drama is kept on the cosmic level, that is, when the apparition does not last long. The narration of the events becomes sacred history, and as such in it one can find a stability of identity and roles in both the figures that appear and the seers who see them. Each has the other. The retirement of Bernadette after the apparitions to a convent sanctioned definitive identities both for her and for the Madonna that appeared to her, identities set once and for all in the moment of the apparitions.

But even when the seer changes lifestyle and identity, the critical initial relation between the divine figure and the seer remains unchanged. The incongruous behavior of Maximin and Mélanie of La Salette after the apparition did not affect the credibility of the events, that is, the identity of the figure of the apparition, because the Madonna appeared only once and what the seers did later was held to be the result of "human limitations" (Masson 1988, 5). The Madonna no longer ensured the identity of the seers, because the relation was over. Analogously, the change in identity of the seers did not threaten the Marian identity because what established it was their previous identities and their roles at the moment of the apparition.

The risks are greater when the apparitions last longer. Indeed, a prolonged apparition enters into history and the chronicle of the daily lives of the seers.

The outcome of the drama is then no longer guaranteed in its cosmic dimension, but it begins to play out in the detailed daily experiences of the individual seers. The epic greatness of infinite figures is frittered away in the everyday limitations of finite individuals. In this situation, the Virgin's withering glance is no longer enough to make the Devil back off. The Devil waits in the path of the human protagonists, and there is no screen to protect them from getting involved with him. Hence, identities in the apparitions overlap, get mixed up, are superimposed because the experiences of the human protagonists, in their daily contacts, often escape the narrative and its symbolic protection.

In these cases, the continuity of the apparitions and the community that nourishes them depends on the continuity of the narrative. When the narrative is able to keep to the fore the cosmic scene (which, in any case, the believers perceive to be at the root of human history) and get believers to follow this scene closely, apparitions and identities are affirmed, confirmed, and firmed up. But when the narrative lets itself be re-articulated by human history, when it is forced to bring into the scene made up of immobile cosmic figures the capricious flux of human agents, then the narrative breaks down into a multitude of digressions that seek to follow in infinite complexity the daily drift of the various protagonists and the various communities of believers.

If the story depends on just one or a few seers in a limited geographical area who are well held to a narrative by the leadership, it is easier to ensure the rounded unity that people expect: everything holds together because the center of the narrative is under control. But when, as at Oliveto, the story gets lost in ramifications sustained by a number of seers, groups, and leaders in a number of towns, the effort to maintain coherence, unity, boundaries, and "dignity" in the narrative has to be much greater. In this case, the assault by human history on the continuity of the narrative within its original cosmic coordinates is continuous. The power of the narrative rests in its immobility as sacred history in the making. If instead it reflects too closely the individual gesture, the individual rhythms, and the course of daily affairs, it returns to the very fragmentation of collective and individual experience out of which, with the luminosity of new, powerful, collective meaning, it originally emerged. The ultimate danger is that the very community of the apparitions could break up.

At Oliveto, strategies were devised to avoid this risk. Because the risk derived from the *length* of the apparitions, procedures were devised to control time in order to neutralize the destructive tendencies of the real world and the effects of the intrusion of fragmented experience on the coherence of the vision narrative.

In the Marian messages, there are explicit and repeated attempts to control time. The Madonna foresees, promises, and reassures. In the daily development of contacts with the seers, the Madonna often foresees events that will occur in the next few days. It is as if one lived protected from the risks of the imponderable because, a little at a time, the future can be known; one has worry lifted when one constantly can see three or four days, a month, or a year ahead. The Madonna promised a female seer from Frattamaggiore to bless all families and satisfy all their requests for grace *next Tuesday* (AC, January 28, 1986). On another occasion, the same seer was promised that all the chastisements *for the next year* would be lifted thanks to prayer (AC, June 12, 1986).

Faced with the imponderable future, symbolically structured as the menace of divine chastisement, the message offers the instrument of control that consists in prayer. From time to time the seers let it be known that the prayer has worked, the chastisement has been canceled. The Madonna then assured people at Oliveto that many would see her, above all children and in different ways and, at Medjugorje, that she would not abandon them. In other words, she promised to remain visible in the future as a reassuring presence.

Other ways of controlling time are the revelation of future secrets about the future, like the ten secrets of Medjugorje, and the promise of a "sign." Obviously, a sign above all would be a way to verify the apparition, but implicitly it would also ensure the experience of an ordered structure of time along the lines of sacred history. A similar role is played by the messages that ensure the continued protection of individual seers or believers— Ubaldo, when he drove, always saw a light in front of his car, which he attributed to the Madonna (Faricy 1986, 39)—or the promise to grant everything that is requested in prayer (B, r, 44).

The same messages that give warning of attacks by the Devil have an implicit element of reassurance related to the foreseeability and possibility of control, that is, the elimination of the unforeseeable that the Devil in essence incarnates. In a message through a male seer, the Madonna asked for prayer "especially these days because the Devil tries to keep people away from this place, and tonight he has even tempted some people to avoid the prayer" (B 7, 26). Tommaso wrote down the message: "From now on

Satan will pursue you during every moment of your life" (AC, May 15, 1986).

Prophecy contributes to the sense that the Madonna controls time. What happened to Ada's father in the first months is a good example. Ada reported that the Madonna predicted Ada would suffer from the opposition of her father for a little while longer, and a little girl reported a message in which the Madonna said that Ada should not worry "because her father will change and she will be able to come when she wants" (AC, October 26, 1985). Armida even foresaw Ada's father's death. The subsequent death demonstrated clearly to everyone that history was in the hands of the Madonna as the Mother of God.

But when there emerged accounts in which the Madonna seemed to ignore what was happening in the present (Where was Ada? Where was Fulvio? Where was Jakov?) and what would happen in the future (What will you be when you grow up?), the result was a disquieting unease. In these accounts, signs of the Madonna's impotence produced a disturbing rush of historicity.

Another kind of control over time, understood as a "dehistoricization" (a term De Martino [1961] uses in his analysis of magic in Lucania), is the structuring of human experience on the model of mythical experience. The Passion-journey of Nello is a particularly clear example, but so too are the sufferings of seers as expiation for the sins of the world (Aurelia and others), the call to a special mission for particular seers as a way to participate in Mary's earthly mission, and the stigmatizations promised or experienced. Again, Nello was at the forefront, but there were others as well, including a male seer from Catania (Faricy 1986, 75) and a female seer reported in the *Bollettino* (15, 24). For Fulvio, Remo announced stigmata and the pains of the Passion; in spite of some doubts, Fulvio waited in anguish, and, as it turned out, in vain. The Madonna appeared to a male seer who felt very sad.

My Mother, why do I feel so sad and why is my desire to weep so strong even now when I am before you?

My son, your sadness is because of the evil that is invading the world. This evening I have given you a drop of my sorrow to taste. (B, r, 28–29)

But from the point of view of the control over time, the apparitions conceal an unresolvable contradiction, which derives from the attempt to control time by time itself, contingency by contingency On the one hand, apparitions present themselves as ways to control future human history by means of the protection of figures from the other world; on the other hand, the very way they occur shows up their own historical dependency—they occur in a contingent context in which the transcendent figures themselves succumb to the whim of chance. The peril is thus doubled because contingency occurs in a dramatic setting (or rather this setting serves to configure—but only partially—history in mythic form) in which the seer is involved. How can one be sure that the seer will come out victorious?

This kind of uncontrollability is addressed by a procedure that seeks to eliminate the contingency of history itself from the Marian apparition: its own historical production. Significantly, this procedure, which came from the leadership, did not involve narrative but rather the canon of images. It had to do with the conventionalization of images that the seers reported a few months after the first apparitions, and was the result of a process of correction and control of the seers' accounts by the Committee. Indeed, the Committee also functioned to filter out the dangerous *singularity* of the various contingent apparitions at Oliveto through the canon of traditional Marian iconography. The Immaculate Conception, the Madonna of Consolation, the Sorrowing Mary, and the Crucifix are all kinds of traditional graphic representations that forestall the risk of counterfeits of a *true* presence of the Madonna by possibly doubtful identities.

Conventionalization employs the traditional images of other famous apparitions such as Lourdes and Fatima, whose evocative power eliminate possible innovations in identity. Even the multiple visions referred to respond to this mechanism of conventionalization. They bring into play traditional iconographies that mark off the limits of possible visions: the Madonna who weeps, the Madonna who laughs, the Madonna who crushes the serpent's head, the Madonna kneeling on a little cloud, Jesus on the cross, the Child Jesus. Doubtless the multiple visions were often the result of hermeneutic deciphering. For example, Nunzia saw the Madonna holding the baby, then the Madonna with her hands joined, then the former, again, and then the latter (AC, January 1, 1986). But the hermeneutic that is *possible* develops in a context that renders these transformations coherent.

Similarly, the risky alternation of Madonna and Devil or, even worse, the presentation of the Devil rigged out as the Madonna or an angel, are "cooled down" by rhetorical warnings about the danger with vivid examples. The *Bollettino* reported a testimony of Ubaldo:

> When I went out to the gate I saw the Devil to had taken on the appearance of the Madonna and he said to me: "Follow my paths

because I will do big things for you. I was the most beautiful of God's angels and if you do not follow me watch what I'll do to your brothers." At that moment I saw my four brothers under his feet. Then I saw the Madonna who reassured me, saying: "Have no fear of the Devil, what he told you are only lies; your family is under my protection." (B, r, 19)

The fearsome travesty of identity here becomes the rhetorical mask for a scene that presents identities that are *certain* and lays out the power relations that are *true*. The feared mistake is resolved in a definite and conclusive presentation.

The conventionalization of images is reinforced to capture the entire range of visible possibilities and, hence, after rejecting all the low forms of weak visions, explains and legitimates other possibilities, including visions of crowns in heaven {April 12, 1986}, birds that fly in the shape of crowns, angels that form a crown with the words "The gates of Paradise are open for you" (AC, January 28, 1986), and writings like, "Venite," "Pax," "Ave," "V. M.," "A. V. M." and "YWX."

The vision location is similarly conventionalized to avoid loss of control and inscrutability of possible sites. In addition to the area in front of the gate, the Madonna was seen in church next to the priest officiating mass (B, r, 46). She also appeared in church beside a large monstrance, which held a host on which people saw the face of Jesus (B, r, 10). And next to the priest, she blessed the congregation (B 13, 29) with a luminous scepter (B, r, 63).

But the most effective way to block off the *contingency* of the apparitions, the source of the dangerous creativity around the Marian presence, is to limit drastically the kinds of collective construction of the narrative, preventing the incorporation of collective and individual accounts of seers' and believers' experiences in the official narrative. In this manner, time was brought back under the Committee's control and the Madonna returned to her traditions. This was the Committee's interest in shucking off singular details to get at the general message; this was the operation to manipulate the visions and the words. From another perspective, it was a way to objectify the apparitions, which separated the event of the apparition from the point of view of its protagonists. This process rescued the apparition from the effects of its own *long duration*, from the contingencies that ate away at the sacred history and changed cosmic drama into human theater.

Of course, this effort, rather than eliminating individual and collective experiences simply excluded them, leaving in the public arena residual material that was impossible to change or explain. But the believers themselves supported the strategy, which was effected by ritualizing the apparitions. Only those who agreed to have their personal identities reconfigured into a profile undefined in real world terms (but one in which the Madonna played a central role) could become part of the narrative.

The leadership applied this policy carefully to the most important seers, and proposed it daily to the believers. One drawback of the policy was, as I have already noted, that the leaders had to use individuals to control who belonged to the group to be controlled. And the individuals, the seers, did not completely share the authorities' interests. The Committee rewarded and promoted only those seers who agreed to follow its directives. But even so, into the accounts of these recognized seers there slipped disquieting testimony of individual experiences, expressed symbolically in images that interrupted the smooth surface of the hegemonic symbolic construction. Lives protected by the narrative of apparitions, prodigies, and signs of the absolute could not always be preserved from the menace of the experiences.

Nello was often taken by the Devil then released after recourse to his spiritual director. Many other seers, including important ones, alternated Marian and demonic visions and reports. In these cases, believers were fascinated by the accounts of heaven but disturbed by those about the Devil. But even the latter served as a last defense against the dangers of human history to the extent that they are incorporated into the collective narrative and inserted into the setting of the drama. With them, the life stories become more vital, dynamic, but in the last analysis are still protected in the context of the cosmic drama in which the church authority assures a final victory.

From time to time, however, seers turn up whose stories incorporate the dangers of human history, stories that represent their own and others' existential experiences and break the special symbolic nexus (*experience-narrative*) legitimated by the leadership. When this happens the danger is enormous, for then the life story is no longer protected and incorporated in the possible narrative of the drama, or the drama has an uncertain ending, or even worse, has a negative ending.

Such was the case primarily with nonconforming seers who produced images that could not be configured in the dynamic of the control of history expressed by Committee policy, but who nevertheless were endowed with cultural significance and symbolic recognition. These seers, when they left Oliveto, would go back to their hometowns to organize collective cultural life in completely new and dangerous symbolic ways, a subject worthy of another study. The seers excluded by the Committee would leave the Oliveto apparition community in search of new followers or other ways to control the world.

The hermeneutic visions themselves—prohibited, suppressed, excluded—result in a disquieting production of images that cannot be configured by those in control. Although over time they became commonplace on television, at the start, in the first experiences, they could come close to evoking darkness, the horrid, chaos.

Believers or seers did not intend to subvert the coherence of the collective narrative. The cosmic drama is protective, its human-historical "degeneration" perilous and aggravating. But the very *duration* of the apparitions inevitably enriched cosmic news with the daily problems of the human protagonists, their networks, and the interactions through which the development of the events was constructed. Human history, using cosmic language, eventually came to dominate it.

Hence it was the believers and seers themselves who supplied the last recourse for eliminating contingency from the apparitions, a recourse that the leadership was opposed to and that it ignored or combated, a recourse that valued the code of collective narrative more than that of images, horizontal speech more than the stereotyped vision. In this sense, this recourse was a response to the leadership's attempt to reorganize oral behavior to serve the canon of images. With speech it is possible for the believers to bring their own experience under the protection of the collective narrative; the canonical image that the leadership proposes is reduced to its own stereotypical form.

What rouses the suspicions of researchers at Oliveto is evidence of the ultimate recourse of the *elimination of duration in the duration*: the exclusion of the dead. The dead are rarely present in the prodigious events. It will be recalled that at the beginning some thought that the apparition might be a dead soul from the castle; the interpretation of Fulvio and others of Aurelia's knight is in terms of a soul in Purgatory. But when the Oliveto phenomenon took on its definitive cultural meaning, only for minority groups of believers did the dead and the souls in Purgatory have particular relevance. Despite the visions of Purgatory of a number of seers, the Madonna very rarely asked for prayers for souls in Purgatory (for example in B 7, 7), something inexplicable from the point of view of the archaic culture of Campania in which the cult of souls in Purgatory is so deeply rooted (cf. Ciambelli 1980).

In the *Bollettino*, only rarely did such requests appear, though not because of Don Giovanni's skepticism on the subject, for he himself shared the idea that the knight who appeared to Aurelia the first days was a soul in Purgatory. Nello's father told me once that his son interceded with the Madonna for a dead relative {August 5, 1988}; a female seer asked the Madonna about the fate of her dead mother (B 7, 24); and a male seer asked about a dead friend (AC, December 25, 1985).

But these cases seem more to be worries resulting from affective family or friendly relations than signs of the collective attitude toward relations between the living and the dead. The dead occasionally returned, but only as new sources of messages and mediation with the Madonna or as souls who came down in earthly bodies to prophesy, heal, and participate in the cosmic drama in which the Madonna was the main figure, as in the case of young Armando, who died tragically and returned in spirit among his friends in Salerno, according to a leaflet handed out in Oliveto.

This exclusion of the dead seems to mean that people are attributing *very little importance to the past* in their organization of time. In other words, there is a reversal of the traditional perception of time as the ordered development from a past, represented by the dead who remember and return, to a future ensured by the protective dead, while the present is ensured by the protective circularity of the mythic figures themselves.

What appears to be replacing the traditional sequence is an acceleration of time, an anticipation of the future that crowds in on the present; in short, a millenarian climate of the end of the world, in which there is a rupture with the past (Lanternari 1981, 328) and the archaic circularity of time is reduced to a single point, a pure instant that explodes. It is as though in order to control time one has to prefigure it and get close to its end. The power of the Devil—human history—appears to overcome the possibilities of control both in the traditional conceptions of time and in the symbolic resources that the leadership makes available. Its power, which sometimes even the Madonna herself cannot check, continuously threatens. Faced with this danger, the only thing that seems possible is the acceleration of the end of time, to arrive quickly at the final victory of the cosmic drama, which has always been assured, when the forces of good will win. It is the certainty of an ultimate palingenisis that generates the images of a time coming to its end. With these images, since evil is produced by history, it is history itself that must be cut short, brought to a close, eliminated. Historicity is totally identified with *evil*: "The world is nothing but sin," reads the message of a male seer on July 13, 1986 (B, r, 66).

The elimination of evil requires the elimination of the world. The Marian messages of Oliveto have a consistent theme—one present in other contemporary apparitions as well and even in the doctrines of the Jehovah's Witnesses—that creates a grim daily mood of the end of the world. Already in the first winter of the apparitions seers began to release catastrophic messages. "The world is on the brink of the abyss," reported Benedetta on November 2, 1985 (B, r, 6); "The time left before the catastrophe is very short," echoed Tommaso six weeks later (AC, December 15, 1985).

A steady series of messages about the end of the world followed. On January 10, 1986, Benedetta, especially prolific in this theme, provided another: "Peace is about to come to an end on earth [. . .] I will fight the final battle with Satan which will end with the triumph of my Immaculate Heart and the coming of the Reign of God in the world" [leaflet]. On March 9, 1986, Giuseppe reported, "These things will happen soon and when they do it will be the end of the endings. Then my Son will come down to earth and with the power of His Arm will make judgment" (B, r, 19). Again on April 11, 1986, from Benedetta: "My children, times run out to the end" (B, r, 25); and four days later from Ubaldo: "Time is short" (B, r, 28), and Benedetta, "The world is on the brink of the abyss" (leaflet). On June 24, 1986, Gerardina reported, "The world is at war and the sky is about to split in two" (B, r, 58), and on July 13, from Vincenzo: "The world is now in ruins" (B, r, 66).

The mood was maintained through the following years: "This short time that you have left" (January 1987) (B, r, 7, 23); "The world is moving toward the abyss" (September 1987) (B, r, 11, 12); "The days are short" (November 1987) (B, r, 12, 2); "The day draws near" (January 1988) (B 18); "Before very long there will occur profound signs that will define our destiny" (February 1988) (B 21); "The reign of God is near" (May 1988) (B 13, 28); "The times are close" (December 1988) (B 15, 18).

In addition to these messages published by the Committee, messages and reports of all kinds from a variety of sources sharpened the perception of the end of time. From Medjugorje, similar messages arrived. A nun who is a friend of Mirjana reported that the seer wept a lot after the apparition of May 2, 1991. "She says that there is no more time left now: people must convert at once" (*Medjugorje*, periodical published by the Associazione "Comitato Medjugorje," no. 53 [Milan, 1991], 320). Small bands of devout persons arrived in Oliveto and handed out messages about the end of the world; even the dead were enlisted and came in dreams to announce it. The prophecy of three days of darkness at the end of March frightened many believers who flocked to Oliveto over the following weeks. When pilgrims asked Benedetta to tell them the long Marian message she received a few days earlier, she suggested that they read it at the Committee headquarters and summarized it for them:

{26}

The world is in peril. {March 15, 1986}

On the same day, another visionary, Ubaldo, saw the Madonna. When he came down from the gate, the believers asked him what she told him and he replied,

{27}

The usual things—the entire world is in peril.

One afternoon in April 1986, as I reached the little plaza I was surprised to see children and girls sobbing and a woman with her eyes red who was trying to calm them down. I was told that a male seer in a state of *trance* had written down a message from the Madonna that more or less said, "Pray for your earthquake." What did the Madonna mean? That there would be another earthquake? The memory of the recent terrible earthquake of 1980 threw the entire plaza into an unbridled panic. The parish priest had to intervene, asking through a megaphone that seers not release messages, but instead bring them to him so he could verify whether they came from the Madonna or Satan.

Don Giovanni attempted to keep fear from spreading among the believers present, but in so doing, in addition to having a direct effect, he had an indirect effect as well. By leaving open the possibility that the message about the end of the world was an evil proposition from the Devil, perhaps involuntarily, the parish priest undermined the millenarian expectations. If the prophecies were diabolical, then it was possible that the millenarian hope for control over human history was unfounded. The parish priest and the Committee tried to attenuate—but they neither wished to nor were able to totally eliminate—the dark mood of the end of the world by impeding the spread of terrifying messages, moderating the tone of those that were recognized and giving them a religious meaning, and suggesting prayer as a personal defensive weapon against the impending dangers.

We saw how the word "catastrophe" in Tommaso's message was replaced by "chastisement." This change is a good example of the Committee's rejection of the climate of panic about the end of the world. Instead, they preferred the safer traditional view of evil as divine punishment for the sins of the world. The attribution to God of negative miracles, in the form of chastisements of sinners, God's enemies, arose in the Middle Ages (Miccoli 1974, 509) and continues in our time. The Committee adopted this traditional conception of the relations of God and the world and emphasized the messages in which the Madonna complained that she could no longer "restrain the avenging arm of Jesus."

Two views of cosmic drama are in conflict here: one is millenarian, horizontal, fatalistic; the other is based on hierarchical control, pastoral action, and good deeds. Rather than prophecies about the imminent end of the world, the Committee preferred the threat of chastisement, *unless* one prays, *unless* we redeem ourselves—a call for conversion and prayer rather than a wait for the end. The call for prayer was hammered home in numerous messages to counter and mimic the millenarian elements in the cultural attitudes of many believers. But even in these cases, panic might have taken hold, and then there came messages in which people were told not to be afraid. Hence Tommaso, the day after reporting a message of menace, reported another in which the Madonna asked "not to be afraid of the messages" because those who believed in Jesus should not "fear anything" (AC, January 12, 1986).

Often this reassurance was nevertheless delivered in millenarian terms. For example, Tommaso had reassured believers in another way by an eloquent message: "The Madonna told me: 'If the Lord had not seen (*sic*) at least 2/4 of the population of the world praying, he would have destroyed the wilted part of the earth and multiplied the good part'" (AC, December 17, 1985). Not by chance, this message was not published in the *Bollettino*. Neither (even less likely) was that of Serena of January 10, 1986, in which the Madonna and Jesus, in a vein of social utopia, said, "I am the Virgin Mary and I am Christ the Lord, we will heal the sick, protect the Christians, and send the rich away empty-handed. The rich will perish and the weak will rejoice" (AC).

The *Bollettino* did publish the message reported by Vincenzo on December 1, 1986, "Pray, I will separate the good fruits from the bad ones. Pray, my heart throbs with mercy" (B 7, 16). The parish priest's preference for the pastoral work of conversion by way of the menace of chastisements rather than the feeling of the coming end was expressed in a idea published several times in the *Bollettino*. If the Madonna "announces catastrophes and chastisements, it is only in order to call us from the path of sin and death." Fear was countered by hope. "The messages of the Madonna about chastisements from God to a humanity astray, burdened with grave individual and social sins, fundamentally can be considered messages of hope, because the catastrophes, earthquakes, famines, disasters, can be eliminated if people pray and do penance" (B, r, 10). The way of life proposed here does not involve a passive waiting for "what is about to happen any day now" but rather an intense activity of prayer.

Rather than expectations of a cataclysmic denouement based on a rejection of time and implicit expectations of the end of human history, the parish priest preferred the control over time, a domesticated diachronic. From this point of view, prophecies with a short, specified, timeline were more useful, ones whose truth could be verified, thereby demonstrating the power of the Madonna and the opportunity of conversion.

When in the spring of 1986 radioactive contamination was spreading from the Chernobyl disaster, someone related it to a message of the Madonna the previous July that there would come a time when people would see rivers of milk that could not be drunk {June 14, 1986}. A later message, of May 24, 1986, reframed the disaster in a dynamic of sin and punishment: "The ugly period of a toxic cloud has passed, but there are other perils that threaten to explode in the world" (B, r, 43). The parish priest then took up the matter and after recalling Fatima and the "prophecies" that came true in regard to World War II, suggested that Chernobyl "is giving us a taste these days of what unfortunately might occur!" (B, r, 22–23).

Many seers fell in line with the parish priest's objectives and reported messages that alternated threats of demonstrations of power and hope for the just, assisting in a dramatic configuration of the events. On December 16, 1986, Lucia said that the Madonna "can not longer hold back her son's hand"; four days later Tommaso reported, "the arm of her son has stopped moving" and added, "but remember that just as the Lord put you on the earth so can he can get rid of you (pray)" (AC). The back-and-forth between threat and hope was the best tactic employed by the parish priest for control over temporality in the frame of cosmic drama.

So, on the one hand, grim and punitive images of the imminent end of the world, in which the just, in a climate of predestination, will be saved and the evil will perish; on the other hand, instructive models that promote prayer and penance as a way to avoid chastisements in a time that has not yet ended. These dark moods prevailed; rarely were there messages with an alternative, *happy*, end to the world for all humankind. Perhaps it was not by chance that they came from children, Mauro and Serena (who shortly thereafter, nonetheless, adapted and delivered prophecies about the absolute darkness of the world).

There will come a time in which they will see me everywhere in the world and all will be happy {November 18, 1985}.

One day there will be peace and men will rebuild the faith {January 9, 1986}.

EPILOGUE

OFTEN IN THE OLIVETO EVENINGS, when the "Neapolitans" predominated, a group of people would suddenly become animated in the street. There would be cries, invocations, excitement, and then three or four men would emerge from the group, carrying on their shoulders a shouting or immobile companion. People knew that this meant there had been an encounter with the transcendent.

The youngest members of the Committee, diligent and alert, would quickly go to the group, supplying the help that they were used to giving: clearing the way to the Committee headquarters, getting the curious to stand back, and inquiring where the seer came from and what was the cause of his state. Some in the crowd would pass a crucifix or rosary over the body of the seer, while other shrank back in fear.

Once the seer recounted his experience, doubts about the seer's state would be resolved by the Committee. But for the pilgrims out in the plaza, curious and ignored, a new hermeneutic field had opened. Who, what, how, why had the indisposition been provoked? Probably it was an emotional response to a vision of the Madonna, but it might also be something ugly and terrible, a suffering spirit, a damned soul, the Devil.

The succession of crises on some afternoons, a sudden spread to nearby persons who fell down or in some way showed signs of indisposition, demonstrated that *the battle* was going badly, that this was an evening for drama. Then prayers would increase in volume and intensity, worried eyes would scan the sky, the accredited seers would emerge from the crowd in order either to reassure people or increase their fear with statements and Marian messages. The instructions of the parish priest and the calls for prayer as a Marian viaticum went unheeded. The pilgrims sensed that on that evening the Devil had come back to fight fiercely. One could hear the frightening descriptions of the visions spread by unorthodox seers. There was an effervescence of images in which the Madonna herself was unable to keep her identity sure. Images of evil seemed to invade everything.

These body-states, these seers, these persons possessed by the Devil, and this crowd that watched in fear and looked for signs that would clarify the current state of the battle, hardly ever occur at Oliveto now. The strategy of downplaying visionary behavior has had its intended effect.

One might direct anthropological curiosity toward understanding just where these passions and collective tensions have gone and how people still express these fears of the future—the future that is the imminent end and the future of the everyday. For a few months, Oliveto had been a stage on which thousands of pilgrims constructed a collectively symbolic configuration of cosmic-historical drama, a stage for human anguish over existential dangers perceived individually and configured collectively.

Now that the legitimate signs are once more just the official ones, this collective emotional magma has been broken up and dispersed to other places where people have a daily opportunity of providing possible, common forms for collective passions to express themselves; to other places where the feeling of evil is restrained—to the extent that this is possible—in its terrifying capacity for destruction.

But Oliveto was not just the place where collective passions could be expressed. Situations such as that at Oliveto precipitated the experiences of suffering of individuals and small groups and spread them in a mood of collective panic that *produced* a choral dimension of drama. Individual anguish expressed in the same arena was more than the sum of its parts: it produced a *new* collective anguish. Daily social contact found thousands of ways to mediate and absorb painless individual suffering, but when it became collective it invaded all possible symbolic space and affected the entire cultural experience, finally creating a collective passion organized along pre-established symbolic lines. It then became the norm to dwell in this collective passion, to speak, think, and act in accord with it. In other words, Oliveto expressed the scenario of the collective drama to which Oliveto itself gave form and content.

Already some years ago a message went forth from Medjugorje: this is Satan's century. Oliveto and other places confirmed it. Visionary Catholicism calls its followers together to join combat with the Devil in the assault that, according to some of them, marks the beginning of the end and that involves even the physical bodies of the believers.

In this grim and pessimistic religious view, it is life itself, as a conjunction of open events, that is evil. Through a system of symbolic referents, life is transformed in a *closed form*, protected metahistorically, that can permit a foreordained array of good. Life's *open form* must be exorcised and is embodied by the Devil, so as to allow the positive embodiment of its closed form (the victory of the Madonna). The great spread of Marian apparitions, with its corresponding diabolical apparitions, can be considered an enormous symbolic operation that reorganizes life and history in ordinary terms, but one that is closed and narrow, controllable on a plane of "dehistorification" that is both mythic and ritualistic.

But this symbolization is not necessarily able to impose itself as supreme or, more powerful yet, as total in the lives of the pilgrims. It is just one of the symbolic forms in their multifaceted lives. The planes of organization and expression in these lives are plural and have polycentric referents. They coexist in ways more or less knowingly accepted, shared, and public, forming a structure of multiple levels of identity that cannot be expressed in a single schema, not even in the myth and ritual of the cosmic drama.

But that is a another story.

Bibliography

Apolito, P. 1990. *"Dice che hanno visto la Madonna": Un caso di apparizioni in Campania.* Bologna: Il Mulino.

———. 1983. "La Vecchia e il Bambino del terremoto." *La ricerca folklorica* 7, "Cultura popolare e cultura di massa," ed. A. Signorelli, pp. 123–27.

———. 1982. "'Bello cum'a te ma re carn'e ossa cum'a me': L'immagine nella cultura popolare meridionale." *Campo: Rivista trimestrale di cultura del Mezzogiorno* 2, nos. 11–12: 18–33.

———. 1980. *Lettere al mago.* Naples: Liguori.

Aubert, R. 1967. "Fatima." In *Dictionnaire d'histoire et de géographie ecclésiastiques*, t. XVI, pp. 679–82. Paris: Letouzey et Ané.

Balducci, C. 1988. *Il diavolo ". . . esiste e lo si può riconoscere."* Casale Monferrato: Piemme.

———. 1974. *La possessione diabolica.* Rome: Edizioni Mediterranee.

Balthasar, H. U. von. 1986. *Teodrammatica.* 4 vols. Milan: Jaca Book.

Bateson, G. 1958. *Naven.* Stanford, Calif.: Board of Trustees of the Leland Stanford Junior University. Ital. trans., abridged in *Uomo e mito nelle società primitive*, ed. C. Leslie (Firenze: Sansoni, 1965), pp. 285–324. Now complete, *Naven* (Turin: Einaudi, 1988).

Bax, M. 1990. "The Madonna of Medjugorje: Religious Rivalry and the Formation of a Devotional Movement in Yugoslavia." *Anthropological Quarterly* 63, no. 2 (April): 63–75.

Benjamin, W. 1955. *Das Kunstwerk im Zeitalter seiner technischen Reproduzierbarkeit.* Frankfurt am Main: Suhrkamp Verlag. Ital. trans., *L'opera d'arte nell'epoca della sua riproducibilità tecnica* (Turin: Einaudi, 1966).

Bertani, A. 1986. "Alla Chiesa la prudenza, ai fedeli l'obbedienza." *Jesus* 8 no. 5 (May): 21–23.

Bettelheim, B. 1976. *The Uses of Enchantment: The Meaning and Importance of Fairy Tales.* New York: Alfred A. Knopf. Ital. trans., *Il mondo incantato: Uso, importanza e significati psicanalitici delle fiabe* (Milan: Feltrinelli, 1977).

Bianchi, L., and L. Dogo. 1985. *Medjugorje (Testimonianze 1981–85).* Gera Lario.

Billet, B., and R. Laurentin et al. 1973. *Vraies et fausses apparitions dans l'église.* Paris: Edition P. Lethielleux.

Blandino, G. 1982. "Miracolo e leggi di natura." *La Civiltà Cattolica* 133, no. 3159: 224–38.

Bogatirev, P., and R. Jakobson. 1929. "Die Folklore als eine besondere Form des Schaffens." *Donum Natalicium Schrijnen*, Nijmegen-Utrecht, pp. 900–913. Ital. trans., "Il folclore come forma di creazione autonoma," *Strumenti critici* 1 (1967): 223–40.

Boissaire, P. G. 1891. *Lourdes: Histoire médicale.* Lourdes.

Bonin, L., and E. Rensetti. 1979. *La questione mistica e altri saggi.* Rome: Editrice Gruppo Operativo.

Bonora, G. 1987. *Dio solo parla all'anima: Armida Passaro racconta le visioni e i colloqui avuti negli anni cinquanta con la Madonna.* Salerno: De Luca.

Bosco, T. 1986. *Lucia Francesco Giacinta / Le apparazioni di Beauraing*. Turin: ElleDiCi Leumann.

Bourguignon, E. 1979. *Psychological Anthropology: An Introduction to Human Nature and Cultural Differences*. New York: Holt, Rinehart and Winston. Ital. trans., *Antropologia psicologica* (Laterza: Bari, 1983).

Brunvand, J. A. 1986. *The Mexican Pet*. New York: W. W. Norton and Company. Ital. trans., *Leggende metropolitane* (Genoa: Costa and Nolan, 1988).

Bubalo, J. 1987. *A Thousand Encounters with the Blessed Virgin Mary in Medjugorje; The Seer Vicka Speaks of Her Experiences*. Chicago: Friends of Medjugorje.

———. 1985. *Mille incontri con la Madonna*. Padua: Edizioni Messaggero.

Burke, P. 1978. *Popular Culture in Early Modern Europe*. London. Ital. trans., *Cultura popolare nell'Europa moderna* (Milan: Mondadori, 1980).

Cambria, A. 1985. "Non foss'altro, la Madonna li ha strappati alla Tv." *Il Giorno*, 11 November.

Cantinat, J. 1987. *Marie dans la Bible*. Lyon: Editions Xavier Mappus. Ital. trans., *La Madonna nella Bibbia* (Cinisello Balsamo: Edizioni Paoline, 1987).

Carione, G., and L. Serrone. 1986. *Rapporto sui fenomeni anomali, ritenuti soprannaturali . . . verificatisi ad Oliveto Citra (SA) con evidenti manifestazioni spesso ricorrenti nella fenomenologia ufologica*. Centro Ufologico Nazionale, rapporto curato dalla sede CUN di Salerno.

Caro Baroja, J. 1965. *El carnaval (análisis histórico-cultural)*. Madrid: Taurus.

Carroll, M. P. 1985. "The Virgin Mary at La Salette and Lourdes: Whom Did the Children See?" *Journal for the Scientific Study of Religion* 24, no. 1: 56–74.

———. 1983. "Visions of the Virgin Mary: The Effect of Family Structures on Marian Apparitions." *Journal for the Scientific Study of Religion* 22, no. 3: 205–21.

Cassirer, E. 1933. "Le langage et la construction du monde des objets." *Journal de psychologie normale et pathologique* 30: 18–44.

Cazzamalli, F. 1951. *La Madonna di Bonate: Apparizioni o visioni?* Milan: Fratelli Bocca.

Ceresa, P., and D. Marcucci. 1986. "Ricorso alle apparizioni per scongiurare l'Apocalisse." *Jesus* 8 (March): 23–25.

Christian, W. A., Jr. 1987. "Tapping and Defining New Power: The First Month of Visions at Ezquioga, July 1931." *American Ethnologist* 14, no. 1: 140–66.

———. 1981. *Apparitions in Late Medieval and Renaissance Spain*. Princeton: Princeton University Press.

Ciambelli, P. 1980. *Quelle figlie quelle spose: Il culto delle Anime Purganti a Napoli*. Rome: De Luca Editore.

Cipriani, R., ed. 1979. *Sociologia della cultura popolare in Italia*. Naples: Liguori.

Comuzzi, A. 1989a. "Il ragazzo pulito di Belpasso." *Jesus* 11 (May): 66–70.

———. 1989b. "A Oliveto Citra con proprio rischio spirituale." *Jesus* 11 (July): 48–53.

———. 1987. "Sugli altari due veggenti di Fatima." *Jesus* 9 (December): 82–83.

Da Fonseca, L. G. 1987. *Le meraviglie di Fatima*. Rome: Edizioni Paoline. Revised and updated by G. Alonso.

Dal Lago, A., and P. P. Giglioli. 1983. "L'etnometodologia e i nuovi stili sociologici." In *Etnometodologia*, ed. A. Dal Lago and P. P. Giglioli, 9–54. Bologna: Il Mulino.

De Martino, E. 1973 [1948]. *Il mondo magico.* Turin: Boringhieri.

———. 1961. *Sud e magia.* Milan: Feltrinelli.

De Simone, D. 1986. "E Satana fuggì dal corpo di una ragazza." *Il Mattino* 12.11.

Di Nola, A. M. 1987. *Il diavolo.* Rome: Newton Compton.

Eco, U. 1981. "Simbolo." *Enciclopedia Einaudi,* 12: 877–915. Turin: Einaudi.

Estrade, J. B. 1934. *Les apparitions de Lourdes: Souvenirs intimes d'un témoin.* Lourdes: Imprimerie de la Grotte. Ital. trans., *Le apparizioni de Lourdes narrate da Bernadette a Jean-Baptiste Estrade* (Cinisello Balsamo: Edizioni Paoline, 1986).

Faeta, F. 1989. *Le figure inquiete: Tre saggi sull'immaginario folklorico.* Milan: Angeli.

Faricy, R. 1986. *Maria in mezzo a noi: Le apparizioni a Oliveto Citra.* Padua: Edizioni Messaggero.

Faricy, R., and L. Pecoraio. 1989. *Mary Among Us: The Apparitions at Oliveto Citra.* Steubenville, Ohio: Franciscan University Press (an abridged translation of the 1987 Italian original).

———. 1987. *Maria in mezzo a noi: Le apparizioni a Oliveto Citra.* Padua: Edizioni Messaggero (revised edition of Faricy 1986).

Frigerio, L., L. Bianchi, and G. Mattalia. 1986. *Dossier scientifico su Medjugorje.* Milan. Copyright © Frigerio, Bianchi, and Mattalia.

Galasso, G. 1982. *L'altra Europa: Per un'antropologia storica del Mezzogiorno d'Italia.* Milan: Mondadori.

Gallini, Clara. 1990a. "Le folle di Lourdes." In *Il terzo Zola: Emile Zola dopo i "Rougon-Macquart,"* ed. G. C. Menichelli. Studi e ricerche di letteratura e linguistica francese, vol. 3. Naples: Dipart. Studi Letterari e Linguistici dell'Occidente, Istituto Universitario Orientale.

———. 1990b. "I media e la loro efficacia simbolica." Paper delivered to the conference *Riti d'oggi: Le pratiche simboliche nella società contemporanea.* Naples, April 26–27, 1990, unpublished manuscript, 12 pp.

———. 1988. "Immagini da cerimonia: Album e videocassette da matrimonio." *Belfagor* 43, no. 6: 675–91.

———. 1983a. *La sonnambula meravigliosa. Magnetismo e ipnotismo nell'Ottocento italiano.* Milan: Feltrinelli.

———. 1983b. "Fotografie di fantasmi." *Campo: Rivista trimestrale di cultura del Mezzogiorno* 4, nos. 14–15: 30–32.

Galot, J. 1985. "Le apparizioni private nella vita della Chiesa." *La Civiltà Cattolica* 136, no. 3235: 19–33.

———. 1981. "Sofferenza dell'uomo e parola di Dio." *La Civiltà Cattolica* 132, no. 3155: 429–45.

Garfinkel, H. 1967. "What is Ethnomethodology?" In *Studies in Ethnomethodology.* Englewood Cliffs, N.J.: Prentice-Hall, pp. 19–33. Ital. trans., "Che cos'è l'etnometodologia," in *Etnometodologia,* ed. A. Dal Lago and P. P. Giglioli (Bologna: Il Mulino, 1983), pp. 55–87.

Geertz, C. 1973. *The Interpretation of Culture.* New York: Basic Books. Ital. trans., *Interpretazioni di culture* (Bologna: Il Mulino, 1987).

Gehlen, A. 1957. *Die Seele im technischen Zeitalter.* Hamburg: Rowohlt Taschenbuch Verlag GmbH. Ital. trans., *L'uomo nell'era della tecnica* (Milan: Sugarco Edizioni, 1984).

Giacomini, S. 1991. "Il miracolo di Medjugorje sconfessato dalla Chiesa." *Repubblica* 4.1, p. 21.

Givone, S. 1988. *Disincanto del mondo e pensiero tragico.* Milan: Il Saggiatore.

Goffman, E. 1981. *Forms of Talk.* Philadelphia: University of Pennsylvania Press. Ital. trans., *Forme del parlare* (Bologna: Il Mulino, 1987).

Graham, R. A. 1981. "Profezie di guerra: Fatima e la Russia nella propaganda dei belligeranti dopo il 1942." *Civiltà Cattolica* 132: 15–26.

Gramaglia, P. A. 1983. *Verso un "rilancio" mariano? Voci d'oltre terra.* Turin: Claudiana.

Guitton, J. 1976. *Rue du Bac ou la superstition dépassée.* Paris: SOS. Ital. trans., *La Vergine a Rue du Bac* (Catania: Edizioni Paoline, 1976).

Hymes, D. 1974. *Foundations in Sociolinguistics: An Ethnographic Approach.* Philadelphia: University of Pennsylvania Press.

Juarez, K. 1987. *La Madonna di Medjugorje. Perché è vera, perché appare.* Milan: Editoriale Albero.

Kapferer, J. 1987. *Rumeurs.* Paris: Seuil. Ital. trans., *Le voci che corrono* (Milan: Longanesi, 1988).

Knotzinger, K. 1987. *Antwort auf Medjugorje.* Graz: Verlag Styria. Ital. trans., *Risposta a Medjugorje* (Casale Monferrato: Piemme, 1987).

Kraljević, S., and C. Maggioni. 1988. *Incontri a Medjugorje: Storia e testimonianze.* Milan: Mursia.

Kurtz, D. V. 1982. "The Virgin of Gualalupe and the Politics of Becoming Human." *Journal of Anthropological Research* 38: 192–210.

Lafaye, J. 1976. *Quetzalcoatl and Guadalupe: The Formation of Mexican National Consciousness.* Chicago: University of Chicago Press.

Lanternari, V. 1981. "Sogno/Visione." *Enciclopedia Einaudi.* Turin: Einaudi, 13: 94–126.

Laurentin, R. 1991. *The Apparitions of the Blessed Virgin Mary Today.* 2d ed. Dublin: Veritas.

———. 1988a. *Multiplication des apparitions de la Vierge aujourd'hui: Est-ce elle? Que veut-elle dire?* (Paris: Editions Fayard. Ital. trans., *Le apparizioni della Vergine si moltiplicano: È lei? Cosa vuol dirci?* (Casale Monferrato: Piemme, 1989).

———. 1988b. *Sept années d'apparitions: Le temps de la moisson? Dernières nouvelles de Medjugorje* n. 7. Paris: OEIL. Ital. trans., *Settimo anno delle apparizioni di Medjugorje: Giugno 1988. Il tempo del raccolto?* (Brescia: Editrice Queriniana, 1988).

———. 1988c. *Seven Years of Apparitions: Latest News from Medjugorje*, no. 7 (Fall 1988), trans. Juan Gonzalez Jr. Milford, Ohio: The Riehle Foundation.

———. 1988d. *Learning from Medjugorje: What is the Truth?*, trans. Francis Martin. Gaithersburg, Md.: Word Among Us Press.

———. 1987. *Apparitions de Marie à Medjugorje: Où est la vérité?* Paris: Editions du Berger. Ital. trans., *Breve storia delle apparizioni di Maria a Medjugorje: Dov'è la verità?* (Brescia: Queriniana, 1988).

———. 1986a. *Medjugorje: Récit et message des apparitions.* Paris: OEIL.

———. 1986b. "La Chiesa in difficoltà di fronte alle apparizioni." *Jesus* 8, no. 4 (April): 23–25.

————. 1961–64. *Lourdes: Histoire authentique des apparitions.* 6 vols. Paris: Lethielleux.

————. 1957–61. *Lourdes: Dossier des documents authentiques.* 6 vols. Paris: Lethielleux.

Laurentin, R., and R. Lejeune. 1988a. *Messages and Teachings of Mary at Medjugorje: Chronological Corpus of the Messages,* trans. Juan Gonzalez Jr. Milford, Ohio: Faith Publishing Company.

————. 1988b. *Message et pédagogie de Marie à Medjugorje.* Paris: OEIL. Ital. trans., *Messaggio e pedagogia di Maria a Medjugorje* (Brescia: Queriniana, 1988).

Laurentin, R., and L. Rupčić. 1984a. *Is the Virgin Mary Appearing at Medjugorje? An Urgent Message for the World Given in a Marxist Country,* trans. Francis Martin. Washington, D.C.: Word Among Us Press.

————. 1984b. *La Vierge apparaît-elle à Medjugorje? Un message urgent donné au monde dans un pays marxiste.* Paris: OEIL. Ital. trans., *La Vergine appare a Medjugorje: Un messaggio urgente dato al mondo in un paese marxista* (Brescia: Queriniana, 1984).

Lévi-Strauss, C. 1950. "Introduzione all'opera di Marcel Mauss." In *Sociologie et anthropologie,* ed. M. Mauss. Paris: Presses Universitaires de France. Ital. trans., *Teoria generale della magia e altri saggi* (Torino: Einaudi, 1965).

Locatelli, A. 1979. *Il riconoscimento dei miracoli di Lourdes.* Milan: Nuove Edizioni Duomo.

Loewenich, W. von. 1956. *Der moderne Katholizismus.* Witten/Ruhr: Luther-Verlag. Ital. trans., *Il cattolicesimo moderno* (Milan: Feltrinelli, 1962).

Lombardi Satriani, L. M., and M. Meligrana. 1982. *Il ponte di san Giacomo: L'ideologia della morte nella società contadina del Sud.* Milan: Rizzoli.

Lucia (suor). 1973. *Memórias e cartas de irmá Lúcia.* Porto: Nossa Senhora de Fátima, L.E. Ital. trans., *Lucia racconta Fatima: Memorie, lettere e documenti* (Brescia: Queriniana, 1977).

Maindron, G. 1984. *Des apparitions à Kibeho. Annonce de Marie au coeur de l'Afrique.* Paris: OEIL. Ital. trans., *Apparizioni a Kibeho. Annuncio di Maria nel cuore dell'Africa* (Brescia: Queriniana, 1985).

Malanga, C., and R. Pinotti. 1990. *I fenomeni B.V.M.: Le manifestazioni mariane in una nuova luce.* Milan: Mondadori.

Mantero, P. 1987. *La Madonna di Medjugorje.* Milan: Sugarco.

Mantero, P., and G. Chersola. 1989. "Oliveto Citra: terra di veggenti." *Il Segno del Soprannaturale* 2, no. 12 (April): 15–17.

Margnelli, M., and G. Gagliardi. 1987a. "Indagini scientifiche, mediche, pscologiche, psicofisiologiche, transculturali sulla 'Epifania mariale' di Oliveto Citra (SA) durante gli anni 1985–1986."

————. 1987b. "Le apparizioni della Madonna da Lourdes a Medjugorje." *Riza Scienze* 16 (July).

Marnham, P. 1981. *Lourdes: A Modern Pilgrimage.* New York: Coward, McCann and Geoghegan.

Marotta, R. 1990. *Apparizioni ad Oliveto Citra: bilancio.* Tesi di laurea, Università di Salerno, c.so laurea Sociologia.

Mascitelli, E. 1990. "In luogo delle icone perdute: A proposito di un libro di Sergio Givone." *Fenomenologia e società* 13, no. 2: 143–48.

Masson, R. 1988. *La Salette, 19 settembre 1846: La Madonna vestita di primavera.* Rome: Editrice Rogate.

Mauss, M. 1950. *Sociologie et anthropologie.* Paris: Presses Universitaires de France. Ital. trans., *Teoria generale della magia e altri saggi* (Turin: Einaudi, 1965).

Menarini, R., and V. Padiglione. 1978. "Il miracolo della Vergine delle tre fontane." In *Questione meridionale, religione e classi subalterne,* ed. F. Saija. Naples: Guida.

Meo, S. M. 1986. "Fame di soprannaturale." *Jesus* 8 (March): 25.

Messori, V., and J. Ratzinger. 1984. *Rapporto sulla fede.* Cinisello Balsamo: Edizioni Pauline.

Miccoli, G. 1974. "La storia religiosa." In *Storia d'Italia,* vol. 2: *Dalla caduta dell'Impero romano al secolo XVIII,* pp. 431–1079. Turin: Einaudi.

Morin, E. 1956. *Le cinéma ou l'homme imaginaire: Essai d'anthropologie sociologique.* Paris: Edition de Minuit. Ital. trans., *Il cinema o l'uomo immaginario* (Milan: Feltrinelli, 1982).

Mucci, G. 1989. "Le apparizioni: Teologia e discernimento." *La Civiltà Cattolica* 140, no. 3347: 424–33.

Niccoli, O. 1985. "Visioni e racconti di visioni nell'Italia del primo cinquecento." *Società e storia* 7, no. 28 (April–June).

———. 1982. "I re dei morti sul campo di Agnadello." *Quaderni storici* 51, XVII, 3 (December).

Preston, J., ed. 1982. *Mother Worship.* Chapel Hill: University of North Carolina Press.

Rastrelli, P. 1987. *La Madonna di Medjugorje.* Naples: Dehoniane.

Ronzoni, E., and N. Sanvito. 1986. "Si ricomincia da Maria." *Il Sabato* 25: 7–9.

Rooney, L., and R. Faricy. 1988. *Medjugorje Journal: Mary Speaks to the World.* Chicago: Franciscan Herald Press (first published in 1987 by McCrimmon Publishing Co. Ltd., Great Wakering, Essex, England). Ital. trans., *Cronache di Medjugorje* (Padua: Messaggero).

———. 1986. *Medjugorje Up Close: Mary Speaks to the World.* Chicago: Franciscan Herald Press.

———. 1984. *Mary, Queen of Peace: Is the Mother of God Appearing in Medjugorje?* New York: Alba House.

Rossi, A. 1976. *Un caso di magia tra I monti Picentini.* Salerno: Università degli studi.

———. 1969. *Le feste dei poveri.* Bari: Laterza. New ed., Palermo: Sellerio, 1986.

Rossi, A., and R. De Simone. 1974. *Immagini della Madonna dell'Arco.* Rome: De Luca.

Rossi, F. 1985. *La Donna che diede il volto a Dio.* Rome: Edic.

Rossi, P. 1981. "L'analisi sociologia delle "religioni universali."" In P. Rossi, ed., *Max Weber e l'analisi del mondo moderno.* Turin: Einaudi.

Rouget, G. 1980. *La musique et la trance.* Paris: Gallimard. Ital. trans., *Musica e trance* (Turin: Einaudi, 1986).

Rupčić, L. 1983. *Gospina Ukazanja U Medjugorju.* Ital. trans., *Apparizioni della Madonna a Medjugorje* (Milan: Editrice Ancora, 1985).

Sahlins, M. 1985. *Islands of History.* Chicago: University of Chicago Press. Ital. trans., *Isole di storia* (Turin: Einaudi, 1986).

Sala, E., and P. Mantero. 1986. *Il miracolo di Medjugorje.* Roma: Edizioni Mediterranee.

Sanga, G. 1979. *Il peso della carne: Il culto millenaristico del profeta Domenico Masselli di Stornarella.* Brescia: Grafo Edizioni.

Sheen, F. J. 1957. *La Madonna.* Catania: Edizioni Paoline.

Spaziante, G. 1988. "Guarigioni straordinarie. Problematiche e casistica clinica in rapporto con la vicenda di Medjugorje." In *Incontri a Medjugorje: Storia e testimonianze,* ed. S. Kraljevic and C. Maggioni. Milan: Mursia.

Tentori, T. 1979. "Cultura popolare e ideologia: Religiosità popolare in Campania." In *Sociologia della cultura popolare in Italia,* ed. R. Cipriani. Naples: Liguori.

Thompson, S. 1932–36. *Motif-Index of Folk Literature.* 6 vols. Bloomington: Indiana University Press.

Thurston, H. 1933. "Lourdes and La Salette: A Contrast." *The Month* (December): 526–37.

———. 1927. "The False Visionaries of Lourdes." *The Month* (October): 289–301.

Turner, E., and V. Turner. 1982. "Postindustrial Marian Pilgrimage." In *Mother Worship,* ed. J. Preston, pp. 145–73. Chapel Hill: University of North Carolina Press.

———. 1978. *Image and Pilgrimage in Christian Culture: Anthropological Perspectives.* New York: Columbia University Press.

Turner, V. 1982. *From Ritual to Theatre: The Human Seriousness of Play.* New York: Performing Arts Journal Publications. Ital. trans., *Dal rito al teatro* (Bologna: Il Mulino, 1986).

———. 1969. *The Ritual Process: Structure and Anti-Structure* (1966). Chicago: Aldine. Ital. trans., *Il processo rituale* (Brescia: Morcelliana, 1972).

Villani, L. 1887. *Florilegio storico della Ven. effigie di Maria SS. del Carmelo vulgo—delle Galline—in Pagani.* Angri: Tipografia Angelis.

Walker, D. P. 1981. *Unclean Spirits: Possession and Exorcism in France and England in the Late Sixteenth and Early Seventeenth Centuries.* London: Scholar Press. Ital. trans., *Possessione ed esorcismo: Francia e Inghilterra fra Cinque e Seicento* (Turin: Einaudi, 1984).

Walsh, W. J. 1906. *The Apparitions and Shrines of Heaven's Bright Queen.* 3 vols. New York: Cary-Stafford Company.

Weber, M. 1922. *Wirtschaft und Gesellschaft.* Tübingen: Mohr. Ital. trans., *Economia e società,* 2 vols. (Milan: Edizioni di Comunità, 1974).

Wolf, E. 1958. "The Virgin of Guadalupe: A Mexican National Symbol." *Journal of American Folklore* 71: 34–39.

Wolf, M. 1979. *Sociologie della vita quotidiana.* Espresso Strumenti, Editoriale "L'Espresso."

Zimmerman, D. H., and M. Pollner. 1970. "The Everyday World as a Phenomenon." In *Understanding Everyday Life,* ed. J. D. Douglas, pp. 80–103. London: Routledge and Kegan. Ital. trans., "Il mondo quotidiano come fenomeno," in *Etnometodologia,* ed. A. Dal Lago and P. P. Giglioli (Bologna: Il Mulino, 1983).

Index